HOT
PROSPECTS

HOT PROSPECTS

ROGER LANDRY

WARNER BOOKS

A Warner Communications Company

Copyright © 1990 by Angel Entertainment/MIB

Warner Books, Inc., 666 Fifth Avenue, New York, NY 10103
W A Warner Communications Company
Printed in the United States Of America

First printing: March, 1990

10 9 8 7 6 5 4 3 2 1

Cover design by Martha Sedgewick

Library of Congress Cataloging-in-Publication Data

Landry, Roger.
    Hot prospects / by Roger Landry.
        p.   cm.
    ISBN 0-446-39129-8 :
    1. Baseball players—United States—Biography. 2. Baseball
  players—United States—Statistics. I. Title.
GV865.A1L36   1990
796.357'092'2—dc20   89-24946
[B]   CIP

HOT
PROSPECTS

CONTENTS

AMERICAN LEAGUE EAST

Baltimore Orioles

Boston Red Sox

Detroit Tigers

New York Yankees

AMERICAN LEAGUE WEST

California Angels

Oakland Athletics

Seattle Mariners

NATIONAL LEAGUE EAST

NATIONAL LEAGUE WEST

THE TOP PROSPECTS

INTRODUCTION

Baseball's Hot Prospects is a book designed to look into the future of the major leagues. At one point in time, every great player was just a prospect waiting for a chance. Don Mattingly played over four seasons in the Yankee farm system before displacing Ken Griffey at first base in New York, and Wade Boggs toiled for six years in the minors before cracking the Boston lineup. In this book, you will be introduced to 260 of the brightest stars in the minor leagues. Many of them will be in the major leagues this year and some will certainly be the superstars of tomorrow.

For the most part, this book is organized by team. Each of the twenty-six major league organizations has a system of affiliates, called the farm system, designed to groom young talent for future years. There is some information common to every farm system overview, which begins the discussion of every club. Each has a list of the organization's affiliates, which leagues or classifications they represent, their 1989 won-loss records and a combined record for the system as a whole.

One word of caution. Just because an organization posts an outstanding record in the minor leagues, there is no guarantee that major league talent is being developed, or vice versa. The Boston Red Sox support perennial losers in their farm system, yet the organization has continually turned out some of the finest rookies in the game.

In recent years, there has been an increased emphasis placed on winning at the Triple A level. Teams are competing

Introduction

for fans, and fans like to see winners. So many clubs are signing former big league players on their way out in order to attract people and field a stronger squad. The average age on several Class AAA rosters last year was older than some major league squads.

The organization's record of developing talent, their future prospects on the rise, their commitment to scouting and coaching, and their areas of strength and weakness make up the rest of the farm system discussion. For example, if you were to read the section for the New York Mets, the development of pitching would be noted as an area of strength. The Mets' success in the major leagues is largely attributable to selecting, and cultivating, strong, young arms.

After the analysis of a team's farm system comes the meat of this work—the player profiles. These profiles deal mainly with a player's strong points and shortcomings on the field, but there is also some discussion of the player's background— i.e. awards, injuries or trades—development and likely role in team plans. San Diego catcher Sandy Alomar, for example, is solid in nearly every facet of the game. His power production was up last year and should continue to improve as he fills out his 6'5" frame and gains confidence at the plate. However, he plays in an organization with, arguably, the best young catcher in baseball—Benito Santiago. So, the chances are good that Alomar will be traded.

Of interest to many fans will be the photographs, personal data and complete professional statistics which accompany each player's profile.

Prospects are ranked within each organization in the order of their expected big league impact. The number-one prospect for an organization will not necessarily be the player

Introduction

likely to reach the major league squad first.

While the method of ranking these prospects is greatly influenced by statistics, numbers cannot be the sole measuring device for minor leaguers. There is a far wider variety of playing conditions outside the major leagues. The International and Eastern circuits, for example, have traditionally been dominated by pitchers. The cooler weather and frequent rain in the northeast cuts down on the length a ball will carry—a home run in New Britain is truly a major accomplishment. In the Pacific Coast League, however, balls fly out of the stadiums in Colorado Springs and Albuquerque on a regular basis. There are consistently higher power figures and batting averages in the PCL than in any other minor league.

A summary and brief analysis of an organization's 1989 June draft follows the player profiles. The club's choices from the top ten rounds are listed along with their positions and former schools. Then, the professional debuts of the top picks are highlighted, along with the number of players taken in the draft and a breakdown by position. Some teams were able to secure the services of one or more highly touted players, while several organizations may have jumped the gun on suspect talent. And the number of college versus high school players selected by each team is of particular interest. But, it is not always the case that teams in need take the more developed players from major college programs. In fact, of the twelve organizations with losing records at the major league level last year, nine took high school seniors in the first round.

The final section of **Baseball's Hot Prospects** looks at the absolute best hopes at each position. The top three prospects at all eight positions plus three areas of pitching—right-handed starters, left-handed starters and relievers—are

Introduction

compared and analyzed, while those just a cut below are also discussed. If you're looking for a quick overview of last year's impact rookies, this is the place to go.

If you're already a fan of minor league baseball, or if you follow your team's prospects through the system, I hope you find this book useful. If minor league baseball and the players who perform herein are new to you, I hope you'll find **Baseball's Hot Prospects** interesting. The game of professional baseball is not limited to twenty-six major league teams. There are 159 clubs operating to support the foundations of the great American pastime.

* NOTE: September, 1989 has been used as the cutoff date for all player trading.

TORONTO BLUE JAYS

1989 Farm System Record
332-383 (.464)

Syracuse	IL	AAA	83	62	.572
Knoxville	SL	AA	67	76	.469
Dunedin	FSL	A	69	71	.493
Myrtle Beach	SAL	A	59	83	.415
St. Catherines	NYP	A	31	45	.408
Medicine Hat	PIO	Rookie	23	46	.333

Toronto is noted for their success in signing the top Dominican baseball talent. The organization's stronghold in that area has come at the expense of U.S. scouting, but it has also stocked the system with young, talented players at a nominal cost. Over the past several years, the Blue Jay farm system has been rated one of the best in baseball. If the number of minor league players lost to winter meeting drafts is any indication, this rating is deserved; Toronto had seventeen players taken away in 1989.

This organization believes in the best available athlete theory and, as a result, the typical Blue Jay prospect is a player with excellent speed and offensive capabilities. However, Toronto has had a problem advancing prospects to the major leagues. Rob Ducey, Sil Campusano and Glenallen Hill are just a few of the "can't miss" players drifting around in the club's minor league system. A change in this trend may be near. Last summer Junior Felix broke through, and several other young prospects showed signs of maturing. If even half of Toronto's top youngsters live up to their billings, the Blue Jays could be the team of the '90s.

The Blue Jays' top prospects are:

Alex Sanchez	Derek Bell
Luis Sojo	Francisco Cabrera
Mark Whiten	Dennis Jones
Jimmy Rogers	Steve Cummings
Denis Boucher	Juan Guzman

Alex Sanchez
Pitcher

An All-American pitcher in his senior year at UCLA in 1986, Sanchez was Toronto's 1987 first round draft choice. He debuted as a professional in 1987 with an 8-3 record at St. Catherine's of the New York-Penn League. That season, Alex led the league in games started (17) and strikeouts (116), and won the Robert Stedler Award as the circuit's top prospect.

In his two subsequent campaigns, the young right-hander continued to excel. In 1988, Sanchez was named to the Southern League All-Star team when he posted a 12-5 record and threw a league-high 166 strikeouts before being promoted to Class AAA Syracuse. In 1989, 14 solid starts and a 2.72 ERA at Syracuse earned him a spot on the major league staff in July.

Sanchez is the Blue Jays top pitching prospect. He has a powerful throwing arm, excellent mechanics, durability and command of four pitches: a 90 mph fastball, hard slider, change- up and an outstanding breaking ball. In addition to his raw ability, Alex knows how to pitch. He gets ahead of hitters well and makes few mistakes. Toronto fans can expect to see him in the big leagues again this season.

height	weight	bats	throws				birthplace				birthdate			
6'3"	186	R	R				Concord, CA				4/8/66			

year	team	league	g	ip	h	so	bb	gs	cg	sho	sv	w	l	era
1987	St. Catherines	NYP	17	95	72	116	38	17	0	0	0	8	3	2.64
1987	Myrtle Beach	SAL	1	3	2	4	0	0	0	0	1	0	0	3.00
1988	Knoxville	SL	24	149	100	166	74	24	2	0	0	12	5	2.53
1988	Syracuse	IL	10	58	47	57	43	10	1	0	0	4	3	3.59
1989	Syracuse	IL	28	169	125	141	74	27	1	1	0	13	7	3.13
1989	Toronto	AL	4	12	16	4	14	3	0	0	0	0	1	10.03

Derek Bell
Outfielder

Selected by the Blue Jays in the second round of the June 1987 free agent draft, Derek has the perfect blend of talents to become a star. He can hit for average and power, run like a deer and has a strong, accurate arm from the outfield. In 1988, before being promoted to Class AA Knoxville, he virtually owned SAL pitching—winning the batting title by more than 30 points.

Offensively, Bell reminds some scouts of Eric Davis. He stands very erect at the plate and can turn on the inside pitch with his quick-wristed stroke. His line-drive power and speed have combined to turn more than 35% of his hits into extra bases. On the base paths, Derek relies more on speed than savvy to steal bases. Additional work on his technique could produce 25-30 steals per year in the major leagues.

In the outfield, Bell has good instincts and an excellent throwing arm. If there has been any problem with his game, it would be a lack of concentration in the field. Derek occasionally gets a late start on fly balls and needs to hit his cutoff man more consistently. Give him one more year in the farm system before he debuts in Toronto.

height	weight	bats	throws				birthplace				birthdate			
6'2"	195	R	R				Tampa, FL				12/11/68			

year	team	league	g	ab	r	h	2b	3b	hr	rbi	sb	bb	so	avg.
1987	St. Catherines	NYP	74	273	46	72	11	3	10	42	12	18	60	.264
1988	Myrtle Beach	SAL	91	352	55	121	29	5	12	60	18	15	67	.344
1988	Knoxville	SL	14	52	5	13	3	1	0	4	2	1	14	.250
1989	Knoxville	SL	136	513	72	124	22	6	16	75	15	26	92	.242

Luis Sojo
Shortstop

Acquired by Toronto as a non-drafted free agent on January 3, 1986, Sojo's solid campaign at Class A Myrtle Beach in 1988 earned him the R. Howard Webster Award as the team's MVP as well as a spot on the South Atlantic League All-Star squad. In 1989, he jumped to Class AAA and provided the spark for the International League East champion Syracuse Chiefs.

Luis does a solid job offensively, but will not dazzle the crowds. At the plate, he is a contact hitter and a tough man to strike out. Some scouts feel he may develop some power as he matures. However, with only 20% of his hits going for extra bases, Sojo has yet to display that potential. Although not blessed with great speed, he is a fine base runner, and is capable of stealing some bases.

In the field, Luis exhibits good range and a strong arm. He was rated as the top defensive shortstop in the SAL by league managers in 1988. Unfortunately for Sojo, he plays in an organization with, perhaps, the finest shortstop in baseball—Tony Fernandez. In order to reach the big leagues with Toronto, Luis may have to work on his play at another infield position.

height	weight	bats	throws	birthplace	birthdate
5'11"	174	R	R	Barquismeto, Venezuela	3/1/66

year	team	league	g	ab	r	h	2b	3b	hr	rbi	sb	bb	so	avg
1987	Myrtle Beach	SAL	72	223	23	47	5	4	2	15	5	17	18	.211
1988	Myrtle Beach	SAL	135	536	83	155	22	5	5	56	14	35	35	.289
1989	Syracuse	IL	121	482	54	133	20	5	3	54	9	21	42	.276

Francisco Cabrera
Catcher

A product of the Blue Jays' extensive Latin scouting effort, Cabrera was signed as a non-drafted free agent on September 17, 1985. In his four years of minor league service, Francisco has excelled both at, and behind, the plate and has been selected to two All-Star teams—1988 Southern League and in the 1989 International League.

Offensively, Cabrera is an aggressive hitter with some power. He has a quick-wristed swing that produces line drives and a good deal of extra-base hits. His 21 homers led all Blue Jay farmhands in 1988. Francisco's speed is not his greatest asset, but he runs well for a catcher.

Selected as the best defensive catcher in the SAL by league managers in 1988, Cabrera sets a good target for his pitchers and calls a solid game, yet he still needs some polish in the field. His size and agility provide an excellent base to work from, but Francisco needs to work on his blocking technique in order to cut down on past balls. He has a strong, major league quality arm and is capable of throwing out runners. At twenty-three years old, he could be Toronto's starting catcher in 1990.

height	weight	bats	throws	birthplace	birthdate
6'4"	195	R	R	Santo Domingo, Dom. Rep.	10/30/66

year	team	league	g	ab	r	h	2b	3b	hr	rbi	sb	bb	so	avg
1986	Ventura	CAL	6	12	2	2	1	0	0	3	1	0	4	.167
1986	St Catherines	NYP	68	246	31	73	13	2	6	35	7	16	48	.297
1987	Myrtle Beach	SAL	129	449	61	124	27	1	14	72	4	40	82	.276
1988	Dunedin	FSL	9	35	2	14	4	0	1	9	0	1	2	.400
1988	Knoxville	SL	119	429	59	122	19	1	20	54	4	26	75	.284
1989	Syracuse	IL	113	428	59	128	30	5	9	71	4	20	72	.299
1989	Toronto	AL	3	12	1	2	1	0	0	0	0	1	3	.167
1989	Richmond	IL	3	6	0	2	1	0	0	1	0	0	0	.333
1989	Atlanta	NL	4	14	0	3	2	0	0	0	0	0	0	.214

Mark Whiten
Outfield

Mark was selected by the Blue Jays in the fifth round of the January 1986 free agent draft for his outstanding athletic ability. Mark has received numerous accolades with the Toronto organization. He was Medicine Hat's MVP in 1986, a South Atlantic League All-Star in 1987 and winner of the 1987 Howe News Bureau's SAL Star of Stars Award for statistical excellence.

Defensively, Mark may be ready for the big leagues now. Although he has the speed and ability to play center field, Whiten will most likely play right field for one good reason—he has a cannon. Some scouts who saw him lead the SAL in 1987 with 18 assists and 4 double plays from his outfield position say his may be the best arm in baseball.

Offensively, Whiten has the speed and power to be an impact player. He is patient at the plate and not averse to taking a walk. However, he strikes out too much for a player who can steal bases successfully 75% of the time. Mark's long swing packs 20-25 home runs a season potential, but he has trouble covering the strike zone and handling breaking pitches. Blue Jay fans can expect Whiten to work on his swing in Syracuse this season before debuting in the Sky Dome.

height	weight	bats	throws	birthplace	birthdate
6'3"	210	R	R	Pensacola, FL	11/25/66

year	team	league	g	ab	r	h	2b	3b	hr	rbi	sb	bb	so	avg
1986	Medicine Hat	PIO	70	270	53	81	16	3	10	44	22	29	56	.300
1987	Myrtle Beach	SAL	139	494	90	125	22	5	15	64	49	76	149	.253
1988	Dunedin	FSL	99	385	61	97	8	5	7	37	17	41	69	.252
1988	Knoxville	SL	28	108	20	28	3	1	2	9	6	12	20	.259
1989	Knoxville	SL	129	423	75	109	13	6	12	47	11	60	114	.258

Dennis Jones
Pitcher

Dennis is a tall, hard-throwing left-hander drafted out of Gadsden State Junior College in the eighth round of the January 1985 free agent draft. In his first year as a professional, Jones was moved from the bull pen to a starting role for the Blue Jay's Gulf Coast League rookie squad. His first start produced a victory over the Pirates when he recorded 9 strikeouts in 5 innings pitched. Although Jones' won-loss records have not been impressive, his potential remains high.

Dennis throws an above-average fastball with good movement, an overhand curve and a change-up. When he gets the ball over the plate, he can be overpowering. In his first three professional seasons, Jones struck out 238 batters in 208 innings. Control has been Dennis' problem, though. In the same 208 innings, he has given up 162 bases-on-balls.

Toronto can afford to take their time with Jones. With solid starters at the major league level, and several other blue-chip prospects in the system, Dennis can work out his control difficulties in the minor leagues. Young, hard-throwing left-handed starters are worth the wait.

height	weight	bats	throws	birthplace	birthdate
6'4"	177	L	L	Gadsden, AL	7/26/66

year	team	league	g	ip	h	so	bb	gs	cg	sho	sv	w	l	era
1985	Bradenton		15	58	45	77	41	9	0	0	0	2	6	3.41
1986	Florence	SAL	17	55	45	62	49	14	0	0	0	0	5	5.86
1987	Myrtle Beach	SAL	29	69	51	78	50	15	0	0	0	6	5	2.75
1988	Knoxville	SL	18	84	54	98	63	17	0	0	0	8	4	2.58
1989	Knoxville	SL	26	79	66	83	90	12	0	0	0	1	6	5.47

Jimmy Rogers
Pitcher

A fine raw athlete, Jimmy was an All-State performer at Daniel Webster High School in Tulsa, Oklahoma in both baseball and football. However, it was his performance as a pitcher at Seminole Junior College that caught the attention of major league scouts. In his one year as a starter with Seminole, Rogers won 17 of 20 regular season decisions and two games in the JUCO World Series. He was selected by Toronto in the sixteenth round of the June 1986 free agent draft.

In a poll of league managers taken by Baseball America in 1988, Jimmy was named the top pitching prospect in the South Atlantic League, when he led the circuit with 18 victories (the highest total in all of the minor leagues) and 198 strikeouts. He has a live, strong arm and shows good movement with his pitches. But Rogers has some difficulty on the mound with his control. Used primarily as a shortstop in high school, Jimmy is still learning to pitch and needs to work on his mechanics. Blue Jay fans shouldn't expect to see him in the Sky Dome for two to three years.

height	weight	bats	throws	birthplace	birthdate
6'2"	185	R	R	Tulsa, OK	1/3/67

year	team	league	g	ip	h	so	bb	gs	cg	sho	sv	w	l	era
1987	St. Catherines	NYP	13	56	44	57	24	12	0	0	0	2	4	3.36
1988	Myrtle Beach	SAL	33	188	145	198	95	32	2	0	0	18	4	3.35
1989	Knoxville	SL	32	158	136	120	132	30	1	0	0	12	10	4.56

Steve Cummings
Pitcher

Steve has been at, or near, the top of his leagues in victories, ERAs, games started and innings pitched in each of his four years as a professional. Drafted by the Blue Jays in the second round of the June 1986 free agent draft, Cummings followed an excellent rookie campaign at St. Catherines with an 18-8 season at Dunedin in 1987. That year he won his last nine decisions to earn the R. Howard Webster Award as the team's MVP. Before being drafted, Steve earned an associate's degree in science at the University of Houston.

A real competitor on the mound, Steve shows good movement and control over his 85+ mph fastball, tight-breaking curve and straight change. He rarely gives in to hitters and issues less than 3 walks per 9 innings. Cummings is advanced in his approach to the game for a young pitcher, and knows what it takes to win.

It is possible that Steve could pitch in the major leagues this season. He has occasionally worked in long relief and could fill that role for Toronto before taking on a starting role.

height	weight	bats	throws	birthplace	birthdate
6'2"	205	B	R	Houston, TX	7/15/64

year	team	league	g	ip	h	so	bb	gs	cg	sho	sv	w	l	era
1986	St. Catherines	NYP	18	110	80	86	34	18	2	0	0	9	5	2.04
1987	Dunedin	FSL	32	187	189	111	60	29	2	2	0	18	8	2.94
1988	Knoxville	SL	35	213	206	131	64	33	3	1	0	14	11	2.75
1989	Syracuse	IL	19	106	97	60	41	17	3	1	0	7	5	3.14
1989	Toronto	AL	5	21	18	8	11	2	0	0	0	2	0	3.00

Denis Boucher
Pitcher

When Boucher signed with Toronto as a free agent in 1987, it caused a commotion in the Canadian sports community for two reasons. First of all, it made Denis ineligible to pitch for the 1988 Olympic team—he had been a starter for the 1987 Pan American team. Secondly, he left the Montreal Expos without a chance to draft the native Quebec pitcher they so desperately wanted.

The interest in Denis Boucher the pitcher is well-founded. He has three quality pitches in his fastball, curveball and change-up, and knows how to use them. Boucher reminds some scouts of Toronto starter Jimmy Key in the way he changes speeds and moves his pitches around. He has excellent instincts for the game and shows a great deal of poise.

Denis made his professional debut in the South Atlantic League with Myrtle Beach in 1988 and remained in Class A for the 1989 season with Dunedin in the Florida State League. Although his won-loss records have not been dazzling, his pitching has been solid, as evidenced by his hits-to-innings-pitched ratio and ERAs. The Blue Jays can afford to be patient with Boucher, who is only twenty-one years old. Don't expect to see him north of the border until 1992.

height	weight	bats	throws	birthplace	birthdate
6'1"	190	R	L	Lachine, Quebec	3/7/68

year	team	league	g	ip	h	so	bb	gs	cg	sho	sv	w	l	era
1988	Myrtle Beach	SAL	33	197	161	169	63	32	1	1	0	13	12	2.84
1989	Dunedin	FSL	33	164	142	117	58	28	1	1	0	10	10	3.06

Juan Guzman
Pitcher

Acquired by the Blue Jays from the Dodgers in exchange for infielder Mike Sharperson in September, 1987, Juan has one of the best raw arms in the organization. He was used exclusively as a starter in the Los Angeles farm system and posted a 15-15 record in his two seasons with Vero Beach and Bakersfield. In 1988, Toronto assigned Guzman to Class AA Knoxville and moved him to the bull pen after only two starts. Juan went on to post a 4-5 record with a 2.36 ERA, to notch 6 saves and to strike out 91 batters in only 84 innings of work.

Guzman didn't start playing baseball until he was sixteen years old. His lack of experience and early training show in his mechanics and sporadic control. However, when Juan gets the ball over the plate, he dominates hitters. With a live arm that produces a 95 mph fastball, complimented by a fine change-up, this young right-hander has the two quality pitches necessary to make a fine reliever. With one or two more years work in the minors, Juan Guzman should be a solid addition to the Toronto bull pen.

height	weight	bats	throws	birthplace	birthdate
5'11"	182	R	R	Santo Domingo, Dom. Rep.	10/28/66

year	team	league	g	ip	h	so	bb	gs	cg	sho	sv	w	l	era
1986	Vero Beach	FSL	26	131	114	96	90	24	3	2	0	10	9	3.49
1987	Bakersfield	CAL	22	110	106	111	83	21	0	0	0	5	6	4.75
1988	Knoxville	SL	46	84	52	91	60	2	0	0	6	4	5	2.36
1989	Knoxville	SL	22	47	34	50	60	8	0	0	0	1	4	6.23
1989	Syracuse	IL	14	20	13	28	30	0	0	0	0	1	1	3.98

Draft Analysis

Top Ten Picks:

1. Eddie Zosky, Shortstop (Fresno State University)
2a. Michael Moore, Outfield
    (Beverly Hills High School, Beverly Hills, CA)
2b. Brent Blowers, Outfield
    (St. Laurence High School, Burbank, IL)
3. John Olerud, First Base/Left-hand Pitcher
    (Washington State University)
4. Troy Bradford, Right-hand Pitcher
    (Cochise County Community College)
5. Ricky Steed, Right-hand Pitcher
    (Covina High School, Covina, CA)
6. Mark Loeb, Catcher (San Bernardino Valley Junior College)
7. Jeff Irish, Catcher (Milford High School, Highland, MI)
8. Lonell Roberts, Outfield (Bloomington High School,
    Bloomington, CA)
9. Jeff Hammonds, Outfield (Scotch Plains-Fanwood High School,
    Scotch Plains, NJ)
10. Shawn Haltzclaw, Outfield (Auburn University)

Toronto is recognized as one of the finest organizations in baseball, and the 1989 draft should do nothing but help that rating. In addition to securing the services of Eddie Zosky—the finest middle infielder in the draft—the Blue Jays surprised everyone by selecting college standout John Olerud. It was widely known that Olerud intended to return to Washington State for his senior season; but Toronto bought him away from the Cougars with a substantial six-figure bonus. The organization is so high on their third round choice that Cito Gaston had him pinch-hitting and filling in defensively during last year's pennant race.

The other striking factor of Toronto's draft was the number of players they selected—seventy-six. Only Houston took more athletes. This could signal a new commitment to scouting in the U.S. for an organization which already owns the Latin talent base.

If there was one blemish on the Toronto record last June, it was the failure to sign top pitching selection Troy Bradford. However, with two of the top young talents already inked to contracts and thirty-four more pitching draftees to evaluate, the Blue Jays must be pleased.

MILWAUKEE BREWERS

1989 Farm System Record
361-320 (.530)

Denver	AA	AAA	69	77	.473
El Paso	TL	AA	63	73	.463
Stockton	CAL	A	89	53	.627
Beloit	MWL	A	62	72	.463
Helena	PIO	Rookie	38	30	.559
Peoria	ARIZ	Rookie	40	15	.727

The biggest disappointment to baseball fans in Wisconsin last summer was the performance of Gary Sheffield. The nephew of Dwight Gooden was considered the top candidate for Rookie of the Year in the American League when teams broke spring training, but was back in the minors by early August. This was a rare setback for an organization which may have been the most solid in all of baseball over the past five years. The Brewers' minor league affiliates haven't only won, they've also produced plenty of major league talent.

Priorities in the Brewer farm system include replenishment of young pitching talent and the development of another catcher. Milwaukee gambled and lost when 1988 first-round pick Alex Fernandez opted to pitch for the University of Miami; and the organization has played top catching prospect Tim McIntosh more frequently in the outfield to preserve his knees.

There is good speed and defense in the system. Outfielder Ramon Sambo stole 47 bases to go with a .322 batting average at Class AA El Paso last summer, while six other minor leaguers recorded 20 or more thefts. If the past is any indication of the future, Milwaukee should shore up their shortcomings within two years.

The Brewers' top prospects are:

Greg Vaughn	Bill Spiers
Ramser Correa	LaVell Freeman
Randy Veres	Narciso Elvira
Leonardo Perez	George Canale
Matias Carrillo	Doug Henry

Greg Vaughn
Outfield

Greg Vaughn has simply dominated minor league pitchers since signing with the Brewers as a number-one draft pick out of the Univ. of Miami in June of 1986. Greg led his league in home runs and was selected to an All-Star team four times each, hit .300 or better two times and topped the 100 RBI mark twice. Over that period, more than 45% of Vaughn's hits have gone for extra bases. With those kinds of numbers, it's no wonder he earned a call to the major leagues last August.

Offensively, Greg has put in some hard work with weights and has increased the bat speed in his big, quick swing to the point that he hits as hard as anyone in the game. To go with this tremendous power, Greg has good speed and base-running instincts. In 1987 he was the only player in all minor league baseball to reach the 30 home runs/30 stolen bases plateau.

In the field, Greg is average at best. Scouts say that his arm will probably dictate a future in left field. Despite his questionable defensive ability and the presence of right-handed power hitters Rob Deer and Joey Meyer in the Brewer lineup, Vaughn's potential with the bat should make him a Milwaukee regular in 1990.

height	weight	bats	throws	birthplace	birthdate
6'0"	195	R	R	Sacramento, CA	7/3/65

year	team	league	g	ab	r	h	2b	3b	hr	rbi	sb	bb	so	avg
1986	Helena	PIO	66	258	64	75	13	2	16	54	23	30	69	.291
1987	Beloit	WML	139	492	102	150	31	6	33	105	36	102	115	.305
1988	El Paso	TL	131	505	104	152	39	2	28	105	22	63	120	.301
1989	Denver	AAA	110	387	74	107	17	5	26	92	20	62	94	.276
1989	Milwaukee	AL	38	113	18	30	3	0	5	23	4	13	23	.265

Bill Spiers
Shotstop/Third Base/ Outfield

The Brewers' first-round selection in the June 1987 free agent draft, Bill made his major league debut ahead of schedule when Gary Sheffield ran into problems in 1989. To many Milwaukee observers, it was just a matter of time before Spiers made the shortstop position his own. A versatile athlete, Bill earned 11 varsity letters in high school and played on the 1986 ACC and Gator Bowl Champion Clemson football team.

At twenty-three, Spiers has excellent range and quickness, a strong arm and good center-of-the-diamond awareness. Bill was named the top defensive shortstop in the California League in 1988 before earning a promotion to El Paso. The question with this young glove man will be his bat. He drives the ball to all fields when he maintains a short stroke, but tends to get long and loose at times. When Spiers reaches base, however, he is a threat. Although not blessed with outstanding speed, his quickness and technique should produce 15-20 steals per season in the big leagues.

Overall, Bill is a clutch, all-out performer on the field and should be a fixture in Milwaukee for many years to come. When Gary Sheffield returns to the major leagues, it could be at third base.

height	weight	bats	throws	birthplace	birthdate
6'3"	190	L	R	Orangeburg, SC	6/5/66

year	team	league	g	ab	r	h	2b	3b	hr	rbi	sb	bb	so	avg
1987	Helena	PIO	6	22	4	9	1	0	0	3	2	3	3	.409
1987	Beloit	WML	64	258	43	77	10	1	3	26	11	15	38	.298
1988	Stockton	CAL	84	353	68	95	16	3	5	52	27	42	41	.263
1988	El Paso	TL	47	168	22	47	5	2	3	21	4	15	20	.280
1989	Denver	AAA	14	47	9	17	2	1	2	8	1	5	6	.362
1989	Milwaukee	AL	114	345	44	88	9	3	4	33	10	21	63	.255

Ramser Correa
Pitcher

Signed by the Brewers as a non-drafted free agent in May of 1987, the younger brother of Edwin Correa of the Texas Rangers netted the largest contract ever given a first-year player out of Puerto Rico. However, Ramser has yet to live up to his billing. Tendonitis in his elbow and shoulder have limited Correa to little or no work in his three professional seasons. And when he has taken the mound, the young right-hander has been inconsistent. But, Ramser is a top prospect because of his age and potential.

At 6'5" and 200 pounds, he has the prototype body for a pitcher. The mechanics of his loose, easy delivery are excellent. Scouts project that Correa will have three above-average pitches—fastball, slider and curve. Ramser's fastball reaches 87-89 mph and shows outstanding movement. To this point, however, the hop on his pitches has caused some control problems. With Correa's questionable health and ability to throw strikes, Brewer fans shouldn't expect to see him for several years. When he does arrive, though, he could be something special.

height	weight	bats	throws	birthplace	birthdate
6'5"	200	R	R	Carolina, Dom. Rep.	11/13/70

year	team	league	g	ip	h	so	bb	gs	cg	sho	sv	w	l	era
1987	Helena	PIO	3	6	10	0	8	2	0	0	0	0	1	0.00
1988	Helena	PIO	13	43	38	34	24	7	0	0	0	2	2	3.95
1989	Helena	PIO	2	3	3	2	2	1	0	0	0	0	0	0.00

LaVell Freeman
Outfield

Although LaVell will be a twenty-seven-year-old rookie in 1990, his major league future still looks bright. Selected in the first round of the January 1983 free agent draft, Freeman has proven his worth as a hitter in the Brewers' farm system. In seven seasons as a professional, he topped the .300 mark five times, including a dazzling .395 to lead the Texas League in 1987. His many accolades include two batting titles, one MVP Award and three All-Star selections.

Freeman is a sound all-around player. He has decent speed both in the field and on the base paths, a solid throwing arm and an excellent work ethic. He has worked hard on his defense and it's shown great improvement over the past two seasons. However, if Freeman is to stay in the big leagues, it will be due to his bat. He has a solid, level stroke and makes frequent contact. Although not a power hitter, LaVell collects quite a few extra-base hits with line drives into the gaps. If the Brewers don't find a place for him this season, look for Freeman to be traded. He's ready for the major leagues.

height	weight	bats	throws	birthplace	birthdate
5'9"	170	L	L	Sacramento, CA	2/18/63

year	team	league	g	ab	r	h	2b	3b	hr	rbi	sb	bb	so	avg
1983	Paintsville	APP	71	264	64	81	17	0	7	50	13	42	47	.307
1984	Stockton	CAL	80	290	41	68	10	4	0	22	15	44	81	.234
1984	Beloit	WML	49	170	29	50	14	1	2	33	7	23	37	.294
1985	Stockton	CAL	137	544	89	171	25	2	7	92	38	53	74	.314
1986	El Paso	TL	128	515	101	166	31	5	14	91	15	59	89	.322
1987	El Paso	TL	129	526	117	208	42	4	24	96	13	70	95	.395
1988	Denver	AA	111	384	54	122	26	7	5	59	10	44	71	.318
1989	Denver	AA	46	135	19	30	6	1	2	17	3	15	27	.222
1989	Milwaukee	AL	2	3	1	0	0	0	0	0	0	0	2	.000
1989	Oklahoma City	AA	52	167	13	42	8	2	1	10	4	9	37	.251

Randy Veres
Pitcher

Selected by Milwaukee in the secondary phase of the first round of the January 1985 free agent draft, Randy has spent time at each level of the Brewer farm system on his way to the majors. Although he has not been statistically impressive in his five professional campaigns, Veres has shown the potential that makes him a solid prospect as a right-handed starter.

Randy is a power pitcher with an 88-90 mph fastball that explodes into the strike zone. When he has problems, it's been due to a fascination with breaking pitches and a difficulty in getting them over the plate. For 1989, Veres dropped his curve ball, and used a slider and change-up to go with the fastball instead. Once he realizes that he can control a game with his hard stuff, Randy will be much more effective.

Milwaukee has been patient with Veres so far and his improved repertoire and control could pay dividends in the major leagues sometime this season. Brewer fans, however, can expect Randy to begin the year at Denver.

height	weight	bats	throws	birthplace	birthdate
6'3"	190	R	R	Sacramento, CA	11/25/65

year	team	league	g	ip	h	so	bb	gs	cg	sho	sv	w	l	era
1986	Beloit	MWL	23	113	132	87	52	22	3	1	0	4	12	3.89
1987	Beloit	MWL	21	127	131	98	52	21	6	0	0	10	6	3.12
1988	Stockton	CAL	20	110	94	96	77	19	1	1	0	8	4	3.35
1988	El Paso	TL	6	39	35	31	12	6	0	0	0	3	2	3.66
1989	El Paso	TL	8	43	43	41	25	8	0	0	0	2	3	4.78
1989	Denver	AA	17	107	108	80	38	17	2	1	0	6	7	3.95
1989	Milwaukee	AL	3	8	9	8	4	1	0	0	0	0	1	4.32

Narciso Elvira
Pitcher

Only twenty-two years old, Elvira is already a veteran of four professional campaigns. He was signed by the Brewers as a free agent during the 1987 season out of Leon in the Mexican League. What Narciso brought north with him were three solid pitches and a propensity for the strikeout. In his two-and-a-half seasons in the Milwaukee farm system, the young left-hander has fanned an average of 10.15 batters per 9 innings and has reached 14 in a game twice.

On the mound, Elvira reminds some scouts of Milwaukee ace Ted Higuera. He has a similar build and is extremely competitive. Occasional control problems have kept Narciso in Class A ball for the past two seasons, but, with maturity and a developing change-up, he should progress rapidly through the system. He has a good moving fastball that reaches the high 80s and a late-breaking curve that was voted the best in the California League in 1987.

As with many of their young pitchers, the Brewers are willing to wait an extra year or two in developing the finished product. Milwaukee fans may not see Narciso in Count Stadium until 1992, but he should be worth the wait.

height	weight	bats	throws	birthplace	birthdate
5'10"	175	L	L	Veracruz, Mexico	10/29/67

year	team	league	g	ip	h	so	bb	gs	cg	sho	sv	w	l	era
1987	Beloit	MWL	4	27	15	29	12	4	1	1	0	3	0	1.33
1988	Stockton	CAL	25	135	87	161	79	23	0	0	0	7	6	2.93
1989	Stockton	CAL	17	115	92	135	43	17	6	2	0	8	5	3.04
1989	El Paso	TL	7	33	48	18	23	7	0	0	0	2	2	7.64

Leonardo Perez
Pitcher

A teammate of fellow pitching prospect Narciso Elvira at Leon in the Mexican League, Perez was also signed by the Brewers as a non-drafted free agent in the summer of 1987. In his first full season in the Milwaukee organization in 1987, Leonardo notched 10 victories for Beloit of the Midwest League while averaging better than one strikeout per inning.

At twenty-three, this right-hander shows good form in the art of pitching. He throws an excellent moving fastball that pushes 90 mph, a fine straight change and a late-breaking curve that keeps hitters off balance. Perez wastes little time on the mound and is not afraid to challenge batters.

If there's been any question about Leonardo, it's been his problem with throwing the breaking ball for strikes. To compensate, he tends to rely too heavily on his fastball. The Brewers like his live arm and project him in the major leagues within three years, but they'll give Perez time to develop confidence and control with his curve before giving him the call.

height	weight	bats	throws	birthplace	birthdate
6'0"	180	R	R	Los Medina, Nayarit, Mexico	8/8/66

year	team	league	g	ip	h	so	bb	gs	cg	sho	sv	w	l	era
1987	Stockton	CAL	2	4	2	5	6	0	0	0	1	0	0	8.31
1988	Beloit	MWL	22	123	96	124	31	17	5	1	0	10	8	2.05
1988	Stockton	CAL	1	7	7	5	3	1	0	0	0	0	0	2.57
1989	Stockton	CAL	5	22	18	18	5	5	0	0	0	0	0	4.09

George Canale
First Base

Selected in the sixth round of the June 1986 free agent draft, George may well be the Brewers' starting first baseman within two years. In four professional seasons, he has shown excellent potential both at the plate and in the field, as well as an outstanding work ethic. Canale was an All-State performer at Cave Spring High School in Roanoke, Virginia before moving on to Virginia Tech where he earned two All-Metro distinctions and one All-American selection.

At first base, George has few peers. Voted by opposing managers as the top defensive first baseman in the California League in 1987, his quick reflexes and soft hands produce many sparkling plays and allow for few errors. On offense, Canale shows excellent power potential and enough speed to leg-out quite a few doubles. His problem thus far has been a reluctance to go with the pitch. He wants to pull everything; as a result, he hits too many weak ground balls.

With Greg Brock at first base, Milwaukee can wait at least one more season before pushing Canale into the lineup. When they do, however, this young player will open some eyes around the league.

height	weight	bats	throws	birthplace	birthdate
6'1"	195	L	R	Memphis, TN	8/11/65

year	team	league	g	ab	r	h	2b	3b	hr	rbi	sb	bb	so	avg
1986	Helena	PIO	65	221	48	72	19	0	9	49	6	54	65	.326
1987	Stockton	CAL	66	246	42	69	15	1	7	48	5	38	59	.280
1987	El Paso	TL	65	253	38	65	10	2	7	36	3	20	69	.257
1988	El Paso	TL	132	496	77	120	23	2	23	93	9	59	15	.242
1989	Denver	AA	144	503	80	140	33	9	18	71	5	71	134	.278
1989	Milwaukee	AL	13	26	5	5	1	0	1	3	0	2	3	.192

Matias Carrillo
Outfield

Although Matias turned twenty-five in February, his production in the minor leagues over the past two seasons suggests that he may be ready for a big league assignment now. Selected in the December 1987 National Association Draft from the Pirate organization, Carrillo is yet another example of the Brewers' emphasis on Mexican talent. He is a fine athlete with good speed and a strong throwing arm. Capable of playing either right or left field, Matias will probably be a fill-in or role-type player for Milwaukee in 1990.

At the plate, Carrillo is a line-drive hitter with some power. His compact stroke and quick wrists let him handle fastballs and breaking balls with equal effectiveness. Early in his career, Matias had a tendency to chase pitches out of the strike zone. While his eye and discipline have improved considerably, he still strikes out a bit too much.

In the field and on the base paths, Carrillo is above-average. Along with his physical skills, Matias has good technique and a head for the game. While he won't steal bases in bunches or outrun fly balls into the gap, Carrillo should be a steady major league performer.

height	weight	bats	throws	birthplace	birthdate
5'11"	185	L	L	Los Mochis, Sinaloa, Mexico	2/24/64

year	team	league	g	ab	r	h	2b	3b	hr	rbi	sb	bb	so	avg
1986	Nashua	EL	15	52	3	8	1	0	0	0	2	4	13	.154
1987	Salem	CAR	90	284	42	77	11	3	8	37	15	19	41	.271
1988	El Paso	TL	106	396	76	118	17	2	12	55	11	26	79	.298
1989	Denver	AA	125	400	46	104	14	4	10	43	22	24	90	.260

Doug Henry
Pitcher

Selected by the Brewers in the eighth round of the June 1985 free agent draft, Doug emerged as the organization's top relief pitching prospect in 1988 when he finally regained the velocity on his fastball. After starring at one of the premier college programs in the country—Arizona State—the former Pan American team member suffered through two mediocre campaigns as a starter in the Midwest League before moving to the bull pen with Stockton. In a combined season at Class A and AA in 1988, Henry posted an 11-1 mark with seven saves and a 1.98 ERA.

To complement his 89 mph heater, Doug throws an effective forkball and hard slider. His pitches all show good movement and he can throw them for strikes. Although there are still some in the Brewer organization that would like to see Henry in a starting role, his personality seems to be perfect for the bull pen. A quick worker, he likes to challenge hitters and get ahead in the count early. A successful spring training in 1990 could land this young right-hander in Milwaukee for the upcoming season.

height	weight	bats	throws	birthplace	birthdate
5'11"	182	R	R	Sacramento, CA	12/10/63

year	team	league	g	ip	h	so	bb	gs	cg	sho	sv	w	l	era
1986	Beloit	MWL	27	143	153	115	56	24	4	1	1	7	8	4.65
1987	Beloit	MWL	31	132	145	106	51	15	1	0	2	8	9	4.88
1988	Stockton	CAL	23	70	46	71	31	0	0	0	7	7	1	1.78
1988	El Paso	TL	14	45	33	50	19	1	1	1	0	4	0	3.15
1989	Stockton	CAL	4	11	9	9	3	3	0	0	0	0	1	0.00
1989	El Paso	TL	1	2	3	2	3	1	0	0	0	0	0	13.50

Draft Analysis

Top Ten Picks:

1a. Cal Eldred, Right-hand Pitcher (University of Iowa)
1b. Gordon Powell, Third Base (Hughs High School, Cincinnati, OH)
2. Rusty Rugg, Left-hand Pitcher (Downsville High School, Downsville, LA)
3a. Bryan Dodson, First Base (Christian Brothers High School, Sacramento, CA)
3b. John Byington, Third Base (Texas A&M University)
4. Bill Brakeley, Left-hand Pitcher (University of Delaware)
5. Jason Zimbauer, Right-hand Pitcher (Andrew High School, Orland Hills, IL)
6. Tony Diggs, Second Base (University of North Florida)
7. Daniel Perez, Outfield (Hanks High School, El Paso, TX)
8. Brant McCreadie, Right-hand Pitcher (Kaiser High School, Honolulu, HI)
9. Eric Patton, Right-hand Pitcher (Saddleback Community College)
10. John Finn, Third Base (Arizona State University)

The Brewers moved to fill their need for young pitching talent with solid picks in the first and second rounds. Iowa product Cal Eldred showed good poise in a brief stint in the Midwest League (2-1, 2.30 ERA and 32 Ks in 31 innings). He should advance quickly. Left-hander Rusty Rugg may be more of a project, but has the dominating quality to make it time well spent. As a high school senior, Rugg punched out 132 batters in only 60 innings of work. His pro debut in the Pioneer League produced a 4-0 mark and an average of nearly 12 strikeouts per game.

On the offensive front, Milwaukee used five picks in the first ten rounds to replenish their stock of young infielders. Third round selection Gordon Powell batted .302 in 54 games at the rookie level and first baseman Bryan Dodson showed good power and hitting technique at Helena (.310, 6 HRs and 42 RBIs in 65 games).

Overall, the Brewers took forty-nine players in the draft—eighteen pitchers, fifteen infielders, twelve outfielders and four catchers. Thirty-one of them came from college programs and only one of their top ten choices failed to sign—Daniel Perez. It was another solid performance for a strong organization.

CLEVELAND INDIANS

1989 Farm System Record
294-264 (.527)

Colorado Springs	PCL	AAA	78	64	.549
Canton	EL	AA	70	69	.504
Kinston	CAR	A	34	35	.493
Watertown	NYP	A	47	30	.610
Burlington	APPY	Rookie	31	37	.456
Sarasota	GCL	Rookie	34	29	.540

Cleveland's winning percentage has been in the top ten for each of the past two seasons. In general, this is a club on the rise, with plenty of young talent in the system. Former General Manager Joe Klein and Farm Director Jeff Scott built a solid talent base through the draft with their many high-round picks—four first round selections in 1988. Indian affiliates are deep in pitching and sport several outstanding middle infield prospects. The future development of these players, and the course of the system, is now in the hands of former Baltimore administrators Hank Peters and Tom Giordano.

In addition to Cleveland's top prospects, Indian fans should watch the progress of two young outfielders as well. First, there's Beau Allred. He hit a combined .301 at Canton-Akron and Colorado Springs with 15 home runs and 79 RBIs. Beau also knows defense and could reach the big leagues later this year. Second, there's Troy Neel. This young man hit .292 with 21 home runs and 73 RBIs in Class AA. He should move into the top prospect class this summer as well.

The Indians' top prospects are:

Joey Belle	Mark Lewis
Mike Walker	Kevin Wickander
Jeff Shaw	Jeff Mutis
Luis Medina	Carl Keliipuleole
Charles Nagy	Tom Lampkin

Joey Belle
Outfield

Throughout Joey's stellar college career at LSU and his first two seasons as a professional, the knock on this young player was that he had a bad attitude. Belle's short temper led to suspensions from the College World Series and his 1988 Waterloo club, a release from a Mexican League team and a walkout six weeks into the season with Class A Kinston. To Joey's credit, he approached the 1989 season with a workmanlike attitude and became a steady producer at Class AA Canton. By late July, he already had 20 doubles, 20 home runs and 66 RBIs. His numbers and improved disposition earned Joey a promotion to the major leagues.

Drafted in the second round by Cleveland in 1987, Belle's potential on the field is unlimited. At the plate, Joey can hit for both average and power. He handles breaking balls and fastballs equally well and could hit .280 or better with 20 home runs per season in the majors. As a fielder, Belle uses his speed and excellent throwing arm to play a fine right field. His emergence as an everyday player may mean the return of Cory Snyder to third base.

height	weight	bats	throws	birthplace	birthdate
6'2"	200	R	R	Shreveport, LA	8/25/66

year	team	league	g	ab	r	h	2b	3b	hr	rbi	sb	bb	so	avg
1987	Kinston	CAR	10	37	5	12	2	0	3	9	0	8	16	.324
1988	Kinston	CAR	41	153	21	46	16	0	8	39	2	18	45	.301
1988	Waterloo	MWL	9	28	2	7	1	0	1	2	0	1	9	.250
1989	Canton	EL	89	312	48	88	20	0	20	69	8	32	82	.282
1989	Cleveland	AL	62	218	22	49	8	4	7	37	2	12	55	.225

Mark Lewis
Shortstop

A two-time All-State selection at Hamilton High School in Ohio, and the 1988 Gatorade Circle of Champions High School Player of the Year, Mark set national records in RBIs (212) and hits (222), while batting .545 with 42 home runs and a 1.025 slugging percentage in his four-year high school career. Lewis was the second player chosen in the June 1988 free agent draft and he signed with Cleveland for a $188,000 bonus. In his first professional season with the Burlington Indians of the Appalachian League (Rookie classification), Mark earned recognition as the circuit's top prospect as well as an All-Star selection.

Mark is a well-rounded player on the field. He shows excellent technique and concentration at the plate, and his quick-wristed stroke produces plenty of extra-base hits. He projects as a .280-.300 hitter on the major league level. On defense, Lewis is a slick-fielding shortstop with sure hands, a quick release and a powerful, accurate throwing arm. His ability to make plays in the hole and turn the double play could make Mark a big league regular by 1991.

height	weight	bats	throws	birthplace	birthdate
6'1"	170	R	R	Hamilton, OH	11/30/69

year	team	league	g	ab	r	h	2b	3b	hr	rbi	sb	bb	so	avg
1988	Burlington	APP	61	227	39	60	13	1	7	43	14	25	44	.264
1989	Kinston	CAR	93	349	50	94	16	3	1	32	17	34	50	.269
1989	Canton	EL	7	25	4	5	1	0	0	1	0	1	3	.200

Mike Walker
Pitcher

Selected by Cleveland in the second round of the January 1986 free agent draft, Mike begins his fifth professional season in 1990. He has progressed steadily through the Tribe's farm system, posting winning campaigns at Waterloo in the Midwest League, Kinston in the Carolina League and Williamsport in the Eastern League, while pacing his circuit one time each in strikeouts, victories, innings pitched and complete games. His 15-7 mark at Class AA Williamsport in 1988 represented the best record of any pitcher in the Indian organization that summer.

On the mound, Walker wastes little time and challenges hitters with an excellent forkball and a 90 mph fastball. Although his breaking pitches have yet to develop, the movement on Mike's other pitches are his prime asset. Scouts report that his fastball shows outstanding hop into the strike zone and that his forkball breaks sharply and late. If there has been a problem with Walker's pitching, it has been control. From 1986-88, he issued 210 bases on balls in 409 innings pitched—an average of 4.62 per 9 innings. Undoubtably, the harnessing of his control will dictate Mike's progression to the major leagues.

height	weight	bats	throws		birthplace				birthdate			
6'1"	175	R	R		Chicago, IL				10/4/66			

year	team	league	g	ip	h	so	bb	gs	cg	sho	sv	w	l	era
1986	Burlington	APP	14	70	73	42	44	13	1	0	0	4	6	5.89
1987	Waterloo	MWL	23	145	133	144	68	23	8	0	0	11	7	3.59
1987	Kinston	CAR	3	21	17	19	14	3	0	0	0	3	0	2.61
1988	Williamsport	EL	28	164	162	145	74	27	3	0	0	15	7	3.72
1988	Cleveland	AL	3	9	8	7	10	1	0	0	0	0	1	7.27
1989	Colo. Springs	PCL	28	168	193	97	93	28	4	0	0	6	15	5.79

Kevin Wickander
Pitcher

The top relief pitching prospect for Cleveland, Kevin was originally drafted as a starter out of Grand Canyon College in Phoenix, Arizona in the second round of the June 1986 free agent draft. After beginning his professional career with a 9-10 record over two seasons, Wickander was shifted to the stopper's role at Class AA Williamsport in 1988. He responded by dominating Eastern League hitters, posting 16 saves and a stellar 0.63 ERA in 24 games. Although his performance suffered after being promoted to Colorado Springs, the Indians hope the drop-off was due to irregular work rather than a lack of ability.

Kevin's best pitch is his cut fastball. Interestingly enough, the pitch developed after Wickander injured the tendon in his left index finger in a brawl with the Prince William Yankees in 1987. The increased pressure of his middle finger on the ball began to produce excellent movement. In addition, the left-hander throws a regular fastball in the mid-80 mph range that shows outstanding movement into the strike zone.

Wickander seems well-suited to short relief. He throws strikes, has a deceptive move to the plate and his arm bounces back well after a short rest. Tribe fans can expect to see Kevin in Cleveland this season.

height	weight	bats	throws		birthplace				birthdate			
6'2"	202	L	L		Fort Dodge, IA				1/5/65			

year	team	league	g	ip	h	so	bb	gs	cg	sho	sv	w	l	era
1986	Batavia	NYP	11	46	30	63	27	9	0	0	0	3	4	2.91
1987	Kinston	CAR	25	147	128	118	75	25	2	0	0	9	6	3.42
1988	Williamsport	EL	24	29	14	33	9	0	0	0	16	1	0	0.63
1988	Colo. Springs	PCL	19	33	44	22	27	0	0	0	0	0	2	7.16
1989	Colo. Springs	PCL	45	42	40	41	27	0	0	0	11	1	3	2.95
1989	Cleveland	AL	2	3	6	0	2	0	0	0	0	0	0	3.38

Jeff Shaw
Pitcher

The first player selected in the January 1986 free agent draft, Jeff Shaw is looking to reach his star potential in 1990. After putting together two solid seasons with Batavia and Waterloo to open his professional career, Jeff suffered through a less than spectacular 1988 campaign at Class AA Williamsport. Although Shaw was 5-2 with a 1.72 ERA on May 21, he failed to post another victory and finished the season with 17 straight losses. If there is a positive side to Jeff's '88, it's that he did not pitch poorly. He posted a respectable 3.63 ERA and gave up less than 4 earned runs in 12 of his setbacks.

The young right-hander relies mainly on two pitches. He has a big-league fastball—upper 80 mph range—which moves well into the strike zone, and an excellent change-up that consistently gets over the plate. Shaw's progression to the major leagues will depend on how well he can harness some minor control problems, and on the development of a third pitch. Tribe fans can expect Jeff to work in the farm system for at least one more season before he reaches Cleveland.

height	weight	bats	throws	birthplace	birthdate
6'2"	185	R	R	Washington Courthouse, OH	7/7/66

year	team	league	g	ip	h	so	bb	gs	cg	sho	sv	w	l	era
1986	Batavia	NYP	14	88	79	71	35	12	3	1	0	8	4	2.54
1987	Waterloo	MWL	28	184	192	117	56	28	6	4	0	11	11	3.52
1988	Williamsport	EL	27	163	173	61	75	27	6	1	0	5	19	3.63
1989	Canton	EL	30	154	134	95	67	22	6	3	0	7	10	3.62

Jeff Mutis
Pitcher

Chosen by the Indians with their third first round draft pick in the June 1988 free agent draft, Jeff has the tools to become a solid big-league starter. The young left-hander was an All-American selection in his freshman year at Lafayette College in Easton, Pennsylvania, and All-East Coast Conference as a freshman and junior. Although slight tendonitis allowed him to appear in only four games in his first professional season, Mutis posted victories in each of his starts and gave up only 14 hits in 28 innings pitched while striking out 23 batters. He followed his debut with a fine campaign at Class A Kinston in 1989 and could make the jump to Triple A this year.

With a fastball clocked in the upper 80 mph range, and two solid breaking pitches—slider and curve—Jeff can dominate hitters. His ball shows excellent movement and he throws strikes. Hard-throwing left-handed pitchers are at a premium in baseball, but Tribe fans can expect Mutis to be given several more years to develop on the farm. However, by 1992 Jeff could be a key member of a solid young staff in Cleveland.

height	weight	bats	throws	birthplace	birthdate
6'2"	185	L	L	Allentown, PA	1/20/66

year	team	league	g	ip	h	so	bb	gs	cg	sho	sv	w	l	era
1988	Burlington	APP	3	22	8	20	6	3	0	0	0	3	0	0.41
1988	Kinston	CAR	1	6	6	3	2	1	0	0	0	1	0	1.59
1989	Kinston	CAR	16	99	87	68	20	15	5	2	0	7	3	2.62

With 6 home runs in his first 16 games in the major leagues, Luis made a big splash with the Indians in September, 1988. However, high expectations for the power-hitting youngster went unfulfilled in 1989 due to a rash of strikeouts that sent Medina back to Colorado Springs.

Drafted seven times before he finally signed with Cleveland as a ninth round pick in June 1985, Luis has been a productive farmhand since leaving Arizona State. Twice he has led the league in home runs—35 in 1986 for Waterloo of the Midwest League in 1986 and 28 in 1988 for Colorado Springs of the Pacific Coast League—and has paced his circuit in hits and RBIs once.

Luis Medina
Outfield/First Base

With a long, powerful stroke, Medina collects plenty of doubles as well as home runs. His problem areas have been a lack of discipline at the plate and an inability to handle the breaking pitch consistently. If Luis is able to cut down on his strikeouts, his future with Cleveland will most likely be as a Designated Hitter. He is only average at first base or left field; and his speed, agility and throwing arm preclude other positions.

height	weight	bats	throws	birthplace	birthdate
6'3"	195	R	L	Santa Monica, CA	3/26/63

year	team	league	g	ab	r	h	2b	3b	hr	rbi	sb	bb	so	avg
1985	Batavia	NYP	76	290	43	77	16	0	12	43	7	32	72	.266
1986	Waterloo	MWL	136	505	107	160	25	5	35	110	6	75	109	.317
1987	Williamsport	EL	96	341	61	109	15	6	16	68	10	48	75	.320
1988	Colo. Springs	PC	111	406	81	126	28	6	28	81	1	42	107	.310
1988	Cleveland	AL	16	51	10	13	0	0	6	8	0	2	18	.255
1989	Colo. Springs	PCL	51	166	17	29	8	0	3	19	0	19	50	.175
1989	Cleveland	AL	30	83	8	17	1	0	4	8	0	6	35	.205

Keliipuleole was drafted by Cleveland in the fourth round of the June 1987 free agent draft out of Brigham Young University. He was used as a reliever in college and retained that role in his first two seasons of professional baseball. He recorded 21 saves, a 2.56 ERA and better than one strikeout per inning pitched in stints with Waterloo, Kinston and Williamsport. In 1989, the Indians chose to use Carl both in relief and as a spot starter at Williamsport. But, without a well-defined role on the staff, his numbers fell off slightly.

Carl has the make up and training to be a fine bull pen pitcher. His arm is resilient enough to pitch every day and he has two quality pitches. Keliipuleole's fastball has major league velocity, pushing 90 mph on

Carl Keliipuleole
Pitcher

occasion. His number-one pitch, however, is an impressive forkball which breaks late and quickly. But, without a third pitch, Carl is not yet ready for a starting assignment. The Tribe would be well-advised to let the young right-hander develop as a stopper. With Doug Jones pushing thirty-four this season, Cleveland may soon need help from the farm system.

height	weight	bats	throws	birthplace	birthdate
5'11"	198	R	R	Guam	1/7/66

year	team	league	g	ip	h	so	bb	gs	cg	sho	sv	w	l	era
1986	Waterloo	MWL	29	59	38	50	22	0	0	0	6	3	3	2.43
1987	Kinston	CAR	31	46	39	63	28	0	0	0	7	1	4	2.72
1988	Williamsport	EL	28	32	35	28	17	0	0	0	8	1	4	2.56
1989	Canton	EL	27	89	90	64	35	10	1	1	2	5	5	3.94

A member of the Gold Medal U.S. Olympic team in Seoul and the Indians' first round draft pick in the June 1988 free agent draft, Nagy is a University of Connecticut product and two-time All Big East Pitcher of the Year. A fine athlete and accomplished pitcher at the age of twenty-three, Charles is just as comfortable coming out of the bull pen as he is starting. His first professional assignment in 1989 at Class AA Canton saw the Indians use him in both roles in a steady, if unspectacular, season.

Nagy is not just a hurler on the mound. He has good command of a fastball that he throws four different ways and has shown a good slider and curve as well. Moreover, Charles will not beat himself. He is a fine fielder, will challenge hitters and keeps his head in the game at all times. The only question remaining about Nagy's big league future is how he'll be used in Cleveland. With bull pen prospects like Wickander and Keliipuleole on the way up, the Tribe may opt to make Charles a starter. In any case, this young right-hander should be on the fast track to Cleveland.

Charles Nagy
Pitcher

height	weight	bats	throws	birthplace	birthdate
6'4"	200	L	R	Fairfield, CT	1/5/67

year	team	league	g	ip	h	so	bb	gs	cg	sho	sv	w	l	era
1989	Kinston	CAR	13	95	69	99	24	13	6	4	0	8	4	1.51
1989	Canton	EL	15	94	102	65	32	14	2	0	0	4	5	3.35

A two-time All PAC-10 performer at the University of Portland in Oregon, and the Tribe's eleventh selection in the 1986 June free agent draft, Lampkin's value at the major league level will be confined to a backup role for at least the next few years. But he hits from the left side, a rare commodity for a catcher—a trait that should find Tom in the big leagues throughout the 1990s.

Offensively, Lampkin showed vast improvement at Class AAA Colorado Springs in 1989. Although the Pacific Coast League is renowned as a hitter's circuit, Tom's average and extra base hit totals gave Cleveland new interest in the young backstop.

Behind the plate, Tom is an accomplished receiver. His strong, accurate arm along with his aptitude for blocking balls in the dirt and calling a solid game earned him the rating of top defensive catcher in the Eastern League in 1988. Now twenty-six, Lampkin has the tools to start for many teams in the major leagues. It remains to be seen whether his name will come up in trade talks, or if he'll play part-time in Cleveland this year.

Tom Lampkin
Catcher

height	weight	bats	throws	birthplace	birthdate
5'11"	185	L	R	Cincinnati, OH	3/4/64

year	team	league	g	ab	r	h	2b	3b	hr	rbi	sb	bb	so	avg
1986	Batavia	NYP	63	190	24	49	5	1	1	20	4	31	14	.257
1987	Waterloo	MWL	118	397	49	106	19	2	7	55	5	34	41	.266
1988	Williamsport	EL	80	263	38	71	10	0	3	23	1	25	20	.270
1988	Colo. Springs	PCL	34	107	14	30	5	0	0	7	0	9	12	.280
1989	Colo. Springs	PCL	63	209	26	67	10	3	4	32	4	10	18	.321

Draft Analysis

Top Ten Picks:
1. Calvin Murray, Third Base/Outfield (W.T. White High School, Dallas, TX)
2. No Selection (Choice to Dodgers as compensation for Class 'B' free agent Jesse Orosco)
3. Jerry DiPoto, Left-hand Pitcher (Virginia Commonwealth University)
4. Jessie Levis, Catcher (University of North Carolina)
5. Alan Embree, Left-hand Pitcher (Prairie High School, Vancouver, WA)
6. Mark Charbonnet, Outfield (Gahr High School, Cerritos, CA)
7. John Martinez, Catcher (Juana Diaz, P.R.)
8. Curtis Leskanic, Right-hand Pitcher (Louisiana State University)
9. Chad Allen, Right-hand Pitcher (Gonzaga University)
10. John Cotton, Second Base (Angelina Junior College)

Cleveland recognized their organizational deficiencies in both offensive punch and speed prior to the last draft. Then, they set out to rectify the problems. Thirty-four of the last fifty-three selections were used to garner position players with good overall athletic ability. Foremost among them was high school phenom Calvin Murray, who batted .453 and stole 44 bases as a senior. Unfortunately, the Tribe did not heed the young outfielder's warning that he would not sign. After a frustrating summer of negotiations, Cleveland lost the rights to Murray when he attended his first class at the University of Texas. Calvin was one of three first round picks to opt for college instead of the pros.

The Indians' second pick (third round) was one of the first players to sign, however. Left-hander Jerry DiPoto went straight to the New York-Penn League and posted a 6-5 record and a 3.61 ERA. Most promising was his strikeout total of 98 in 87 innings of work. The other standout draftee was catcher Jessie Levis. In a 55-game performance covering three different leagues—Appalachian, Carolina and Pacific Coast—Levis hit .320 with 6 home runs and 27 RBIs.

Aside from the inability to sign their top pick, Cleveland's 1989 draft may well be remembered for the pitchers brought into the system. Of the twenty selected, seventeen came from college programs, and they could advance rapidly.

BALTIMORE ORIOLES

1989 Farm System Record
264-300 (.468)

Rochester	IL	AAA	72	73	.497
Hagerstown	EL	AA	67	72	.482
Frederick	CAR	A	73	65	.529
Erie	NYP	A	25	49	.338
Bluefield	APPY	Rookie	27	41	.397

Once considered the finest talent base in all of baseball, the Orioles' farm took much of the blame for Baltimore's 1987-1988 demise. The emphasis on pitching, defense and home grown talent was abandoned in favor of the free agent market and the "win now" mentality. The organization forfeited the rights to four high-round draft choices—two number-one, a number-two and a number-three pick—in 1985 and 1986 in favor of signing Fred Lynn, Don Aase, Juan Beniquez and Lee Lacy. None of those players are still with the team.

Thankfully, the arrival of General Manager Roland Hemond brought a reverse in tactics. Baltimore unloaded several aging stars—Mike Boddiker and Eddie Murray among others—for talented young players—Juan Bell, Mike Deveraux, Curt Schilling, Chris Hoiles and Brady Anderson—and have stocked the system with some fine pitching prospects via the draft. In addition to the ten players detailed in this section, Oriole fans should keep their eyes on second baseman Luis Mercedes (.309 with 36 RBIs and 29 stolen bases at Frederick), third baseman Leo Gomez (.281 with 18 HRs and 78 RBIs at Hagerstown) and first baseman David Segui (.319 with 11 HRs and 76 RBIs at Frederick/Hagerstown). Each of these could advance quickly.

The Orioles' top prospects are:

Pete Harnisch	Steve Finley
Ben McDonald	Juan Bell
Chris Meyers	Chris Hoiles
Arthur Rhodes	Jose Mesa
Ricky Gutierrez	Stacy Jones

Though Harnisch did not impress the Orioles as a rookie starter in 1989, he has the potential to be a dominant big league hurler throughout the next decade. A two-time ECAC Player of the Year at Fordham University, Pete was selected by Baltimore in the first round of the June 1987 draft. His one full season in the minor leagues produced an 11-7 record, 4 shutouts, a 2.45 ERA, and 184 strikeouts in 190 innings of work. The organization is confident that the talent which produced these numbers will be evident in Harnisch's 1990 performance.

Pete's number-one pitch is an explosive, rising fastball that registers at 90+ mph on the radar gun. He complements it with a good slider and a tight curve. His problems last year stemmed from being too fine with his pitches and falling behind in the count early. It was the first time in Harnisch's career that he'd encountered control problems and he should regain success when he starts to challenge hitters again. Pete is a dogged competitor who pitches with a great deal of emotion, but in order to reach his potential, he must learn to channel his energies toward the batter. The Orioles' coaches will try to make sure that attitude takes root this year.

Pete Harnisch
Pitcher

height	weight	bats	throws		birthplace			birthdate			
6'1"	195	B	R		Commack, NY			9/23/66			

year	team	league	g	ip	h	so	bb	gs	cg	sho	sv	w	l	era
1987	Bluefield	APP	9	53	38	64	26	9	0	0	0	3	1	2.56
1987	Hagerstown	CAR	4	20	17	18	14	4	0	0	0	1	2	2.25
1988	Charlotte	SL	20	132	113	141	52	20	4	2	0	7	6	2.58
1988	Rochester	IL	7	58	44	43	14	7	3	2	0	4	1	2.16
1988	Baltimore	AL	2	13	13	10	9	2	0	0	0	0	2	5.54
1989	Rochester	IL	12	87	60	59	35	12	3	1	0	5	5	2.58
1989	Baltimore	AL	18	103	97	70	64	17	2	0	0	5	9	4.62

As a fundamentally sound player with good speed and great defense, Steve truly fits the mold of an Oriole outfielder. Just two years after being taken in the fourteenth round of the June 1987 draft, Finley filled a vital role as one of Manager Frank Robinson's young platoon players and showed the skills to warrant consideration for a full-time job this year.

There is no doubt that Finley knows how to handle a bat. In two minor league campaigns, Steve compiled a .312 average and won the 1988 Class AAA International League batting title. He has a quick, compact swing with line drive power to the alleys, can turn on the inside pitch for an occasional home run, and is the best bunter in the organization. Defensively, Finley may also be the Birds' best outfielder. He has excellent range, sure hands and a fine, accurate throwing arm. He rarely misses a cutoff man and always throws to the proper base.

Only twenty-five years old, Finley has a long major league career ahead of him. He is a steady, if unspectacular, performer who should hit .280 or better if he plays everyday.

Steve Finley
Outfield

height	weight	bats	throws		birthplace			birthdate			
6'2"	175	L	L		Union City, TN			5/12/65			

year	team	league	g	ab	r	h	2b	3b	hr	rbi	sb	bb	so	avg
1987	Newark	NYP	54	222	40	65	13	2	3	33	26	22	24	.293
1987	Hagerstown	CAR	15	65	9	22	3	2	1	5	7	1	6	.338
1988	Hagerstown	CAR	8	28	2	6	2	0	0	3	4	4	3	.214
1988	Charlotte	SL	10	40	7	12	4	2	1	6	2	4	3	.300
1988	Rochester	IL	120	456	61	143	19	7	5	54	20	28	55	.314
1989	Hagerstown	EL	11	48	11	20	3	1	0	7	4	4	3	.417
1989	Rochester	IL	7	25	2	4	0	0	0	2	3	1	5	.160
1989	Baltimore	AL	81	217	35	54	5	2	2	25	17	15	30	.249

Ben McDonald
Pitcher

Had McDonald signed with Baltimore when he was drafted in June, there is little doubt that he would have been the top prospect in the organization. As it was, however, Ben came on board late in August and made only two minor league starts before joining the major league club. Though his arm must have been tired after a full spring schedule, the college World Series and work in the Cape Cod League, he did show some promise in his brief professional stint.

The Orioles would have made Ben the first overall pick in the June draft. He was the most dominant hurler in the country at LSU and garnered nothing but praise from opposing players and managers. He can throw five different pitches for strikes and blow batters away with a 95 mph fastball. Doubly impressive is the fact that, at 6'7", McDonald has fine pitching mechanics and great offspeed stuff.

While his short career as a professional may keep Ben from earning a major league job this spring, any modicum of success at the minor league level could find him in Baltimore by mid-season. The Oriole staff is sorely in need of a power pitcher and Ben should fill that role for many years to come.

height	weight	bats	throws	birthplace	birthdate
6'7"	212	R	R	Denham Springs, LA	11/24/67

year	team	league	g	ip	h	so	bb	gs	cg	sho	sv	w	l	era
1989	Frederick	CAR	2	9	10	9	0	2	0	0	0	0	0	0.00
1989	Baltimore	AL	6	7	8	3	4	0	0	0	0	1	0	8.59

Juan Bell
Shortstop

The younger brother of Toronto outfielder George Bell, Juan was the key player acquired by Baltimore in the deal that sent Eddie Murray to the Los Angeles Dodgers last winter. He is expected to eventually take over the big league shortstop job from Cal Ripken, Jr. However, Craig Worthington's emergence as a third baseman may delay twenty-two-year-old Bell's arrival for another season. There is room for improvement in both his strikeout totals and on-base percentage from last year and he'll most likely begin the 1990 campaign back in Triple A.

A switch-hitter, Juan displays some power from the left side of the plate, but is basically a singles threat. He is a spray hitter with a good, quick stroke and the speed to take the extra base or beat out an infield chopper. If Juan can hit .250 in the major leagues, his glove work will earn him a job. Bell has outstanding range at shortstop and the acrobatic ability to make spectacular plays. With an amazingly strong arm for a player of his stature, Juan can throw out even the swiftest runners from the hole. If there is any knock at all on his defense, it would be consistency. He sometimes shows lapses on routine plays, something that management will be keeping a close eye on this summer.

height	weight	bats	throws	birthplace	birthdate
5'11"	160	B	R	San Pedro de Macoris, Dom. Rep.	3/29/68

year	team	league	g	ab	r	h	2b	3b	hr	rbi	sb	bb	so	av
1986	Dodgers	GCL	59	217	38	52	6	2	0	26	12	29	28	.240
1987	Bakersfield	CAL	134	473	54	116	15	3	4	58	20	43	91	:245
1988	SanAntonio	TL	61	215	37	60	4	2	5	21	11	16	37	.279
1988	Albuquerque	PCL	73	257	42	77	9	3	8	45	7	16	70	.300
1989	Rochester	IL	116	408	50	107	15	6	2	32	17	39	92	.262

Chris Meyers
Pitcher

Although Meyers had a losing record in a combined season at Frederick and Hagerstown, the 27 games he appeared in represented a huge success in Baltimore management's eyes. The Orioles' number-one pick in the June 1987 draft, Chris had his 1988 campaign cut short by shoulder problems and the status of his health was uncertain last spring. If fully recovered, this twenty-one-year-old lefty has the right ingredients to reach the major leagues very quickly.

In addition to an outstanding work ethic and a solid understanding of the art of pitching, Myers has a smooth, fluid delivery. He works with three pitches—an 88 mph fastball with last second movement, a sharp-breaking curve and a wonderful straight change-up. Chris can change speeds well with the fastball and hit locations with any of the three. While he does not overpower batters, Meyers' mound mastery accounted for 4 complete game victories in 6 starts at Class AA last fall and he should earn a spot on the Triple A roster for the upcoming campaign. In the years to come, he could be the Birds' ace on a staff of talented young pitchers.

height	weight	bats	throws	birthplace	birthdate
6'1"	180	R	L	Tampa, FL	4/14/69

year	team	league	g	ip	h	so	bb	gs	cg	sho	sv	w	l	era
1987	Bluefield	APP	10	50	36	60	28	10	0	0	0	3	2	2.32
1988	Hagerstown	EL	7	40	36	21	10	7	1	0	0	1	1	2.72
1989	Frederick	CAR	22	140	138	118	53	21	4	0	0	8	10	3.99
1989	Hagerstown	EL	6	45	41	25	12	6	4	2	0	4	2	2.56

Chris Hoiles
Catcher/First Base

Although the arrival of Mickey Tettleton arrested the O's urgent need for a catcher, Chris still looks like the most likely candidate to fill that spot into the late '90s. Acquired by Baltimore in the deal that sent Fred Lynn to the Tigers, Hoiles spent his first full season at the Triple A level in 1989 and put up some decent power numbers to go with a .245 average. In four years as a professional, Chris has earned All-Star honors in 1986 and 1987, tied for a batting title in 1986, and garnered the home run crown in 1987. Though Hoiles may not begin the 1990 season in Baltimore, he is next in line behind Tettleton and Bob Melvin, should an injury occur.

Like most catchers, Chris doesn't have much speed. However, his strong swing produces plenty of gap line drives that go for extra bases. If Hoiles can hit even .260-.270, his defense will keep him in the major leagues. Noted for calling a good game, this twenty-five-year-old is also very agile behind the plate and blocks the ball well. He has consistently ranked among his league's leaders in throwing out would-be base stealers with a near 40% success rate. A big plus in the eyes of Baltimore management is the fact that by the time Chris reaches the Orioles, he'll already have worked with many of the club's young pitchers.

height	weight	bats	throws	birthplace	birthdate
6'0"	195	R	R	Bowling Green, KY	3/20/65

year	team	league	g	ab	r	h	2b	3b	hr	rbi	sb	bb	so	avg
1986	Bristol	APP	68	253	42	81	19	2	13	57	10	30	20	.320
1987	Glens Falls	EL	108	380	47	105	12	0	13	53	1	35	37	.276
1988	Toledo	IL	22	69	4	11	1	0	2	6	1	2	12	.159
1988	Glens Falls	EL	103	360	67	102	21	3	17	73	4	50	57	.283
1989	Rochester	IL	96	322	41	79	19	1	10	51	1	31	58	.245

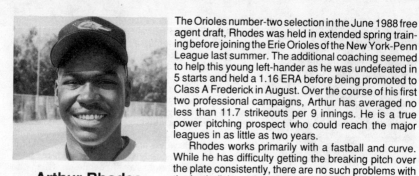

The Orioles number-two selection in the June 1988 free agent draft, Rhodes was held in extended spring training before joining the Erie Orioles of the New York-Penn League last summer. The additional coaching seemed to help this young left-hander as he was undefeated in 5 starts and held a 1.16 ERA before being promoted to Class A Frederick in August. Over the course of his first two professional campaigns, Arthur has averaged no less than 11.7 strikeouts per 9 innings. He is a true power pitching prospect who could reach the major leagues in as little as two years.

Rhodes works primarily with a fastball and curve. While he has difficulty getting the breaking pitch over the plate consistently, there are no such problems with the fastball. It reaches the plate at 92-94 mph and rides away from right-handed hitters. Arthur's two-pitch repertoire can be very tough on left-handed hitters—he's held them to a .170 average thus far. Until Rhodes reaches Triple A, or even the big leagues, Baltimore will not tamper with his live arm. He'll get by on velocity and ball movement in the minor leagues, but may need to add a change-up down the road. Oriole fans should expect to see Rhodes assigned to Frederick to begin the 1990 campaign.

Arthur Rhodes
Pitcher

height	weight	bats	throws	birthplace	birthdate
6'1"	173	L	L	Waco, TX	10/24/69

year	team	league	g	ip	h	so	bb	gs	cg	sho	sv	w	l	era
1988	Bluefield	APP	11	35	29	44	15	7	0	0	0	3	4	3.31
1989	Erie	NYP	5	31	13	45	10	5	1	0	0	2	0	1.16

A ninth-year pro out of the Dominican Republic, Jose was originally signed by Toronto as a free agent in 1981. He was acquired by Baltimore, along with Oswald Peraza, in the deal that sent Mike Flanagan to the Blue Jays on August 31, 1987, and he made his major league debut just 10 days later. Even though Mesa has missed much of the past two seasons with soreness in his elbow, the organization feels confident that their twenty-three-year-old right-hander can challenge for a spot on the major league staff this spring.

Jose's inconsistency as a starter prompted the club to try him out of the bull pen in Rochester last summer. He throws as hard as any pitcher in the organization and can complement his 95 mph fastball with a hard slider, a curve and a forkball. While Mesa does not lack the composure for a closer's role, he may lack the control. Over the course of his career, Jose has issued an average of nearly 5 walks per 9 innings pitched and has a tendency to get very wild at times. While the Orioles might want to look at Mesa in the minor leagues for part of the upcoming season, he may see action as Gregg Olson's setup man before the year is out.

Jose Mesa
Pitcher

height	weight	bats	throws	birthplace	birthdate
6'3"	170	R	R	Azua, Dom. Rep.	5/22/66

year	team	league	g	ip	h	so	bb	gs	cg	sho	sv	w	l	era
1985	Kinston	CAR	30	107	110	71	79	20	0	0	1	5	10	6.16
1986	Knoxville	SL	9	41	40	30	23	8	2	0	0	2	2	4.35
1986	Ventura	CAL	24	142	141	113	58	24	2	1	0	10	13	5.21
1987	Knoxville	SL	35	193	207	115	104	35	4	0	0	10	13	5.21
1987	Toronto	AL	6	31	38	17	15	5	0	0	0	1	3	6.03
1988	Rochester	IL	11	16	21	15	14	2	0	0	0	0	3	8.62
1989	Hagerstown	EL	3	13	9	12	4	3	0	0	0	0	0	0.00
1989	Rochester	IL	7	10	6	3	6	1	0	0	0	0	2	5.40

A first round bonus pick for the Orioles in the June 1988 free agent draft, Ricky will have a difficult time cracking the major league lineup anytime soon. With incumbent Cal Ripken in the major leagues and Juan Bell the heir apparent to the shortstop job, Gutierrez may have to switch positions somewhere in the system. However, this young man does show excellent potential with the bat, and he should only improve as his twenty-year-old body fills out.

Like many young hitters, Gutierrez has been somewhat overmatched in his first encounters with professional pitching. He is susceptible to inside fastballs and must learn to wait on the breaking pitch. Despite these drawbacks, Ricky does have a strong swing when he's not fooled, and he could develop into a 15 home run hitter in the big leagues. Defensively, Gutierrez uses his base stealing speed to flag down balls behind second base and in the hole. He is a very smooth glove man with an arm strong enough to play from third base. All in all, Ricky is a raw talent who could take four or five years to develop. However, the wait may be worthwhile.

Ricky Gutierrez
Shortstop

height	weight	bats	throws	birthplace	birthdate
6'1"	170	R	R	Miami, FL	5/23/70

year	team	league	g	ab	r	h	2b	3b	hr	rbi	sb	bb	so	avg
1988	Bluefield	APP	62	208	35	51	8	2	2	19	5	44	40	.245
1989	Frederick	CAR	127	456	48	106	16	2	3	41	15	39	86	.232

The Orioles thought enough of Jones' potential to make him their third round draft pick in 1988. He was a teammate and roommate of Gregg Olson at Auburn University, and he posted a 22-15 record in three years of collegiate play. Though Stacy does not have the overpowering repertoire of his good friend, he does know how to pitch and could advance in the farm system fast enough to reach the big leagues by 1992.

In two professional campaigns, Stacy has compiled an 11-10 mark with 121 strikeouts in 175 innings of work. He has good control for such a tall pitcher and should improve in most statistical categories as he further refines his smooth motion. Jones is not afraid to challenge hitters—though his lack of finesse has resulted in more than one hit per inning pitched—and works the inside portion of the plate effectively. 1990 should find Stacy at Class A Frederick to begin the season, but he could advance to Double A with a good start. He will be a solid number-three or -four starter in the majors.

Stacy Jones
Pitcher

height	weight	bats	throws	birthplace	birthdate
6'6"	225	R	R	Gadston, AL	5/26/67

year	team	league	g	ip	h	so	bb	gs	cg	sho	sv	w	l	era
1988	Hagerstown	EL	6	38	35	23	12	6	3	0	0	3	1	2.87
1988	Erie	NYP	7	54	51	40	15	7	3	0	0	3	3	1.33
1989	Frederick	CAR	15	822	93	58	35	15	3	1	0	5	6	4.90

Draft Analysis

Top Ten Picks:

1. Ben McDonald, Right-hand Pitcher (Louisiana State University)
2a. Keith Schmidt, Outfield (Burton High School, Burton, TX)
2b. Tommy Taylor, Right-hand Pitcher (Louisa County High School, Mineral, VA)
3. Eric Alexander, Right-hand Pitcher (University High School, Los Angeles, CA)
4. T.R. Lewis, Third Base (Sandalwood High School, Jacksonville, FL)
5. Matt Anderson, Left-hand Pitcher (Buena High School, Sanford, NC)
6. Allen Davis, Outfield (Lee County Senior High School, Ventura, CA)
7. Dan Melendez, First Base (St. Bernard High School, Mar Vista, CA)
8. Shawn Heiden, Right-hand Pitcher (Hillcrest High School, Sandy, UT)
9. Mike Lansing, Shortstop (Wichita State University)
10. Charles Mottola, Outfield (Aquinas High School, Ambroke Pines, FL)

With a talented young crop of major league outfielders and solid incumbents at each of the infield positions, the Orioles went for pitching in the 1989 draft. What they came up with was the nation's top pitching prospect in Ben McDonald and a host of good, live arms.

Although Baltimore's 1989 rotation of Jeff Ballard, Bob Milacki, Dave Johnson and Pete Harnisch was productive in terms of wins and losses, Nolan Ryan alone recorded more strikeouts than all of them combined. Help should be on the way in the form of power pitchers McDonald, Mike Quist and Matt Anderson—all of whom fanned more than one batter per inning in their first professional campaigns.

Among the position players selected by Baltimore in the June draft, fans should keep their eyes on high school phenom T.R. Lewis—a third baseman out of Sandlewood High School in Jacksonville, Florida—and catcher James Roso. Roso is a product of Linn-Breton Community College in Oregon, who hit better than .300 in Class A Erie.

BOSTON RED SOX

1989 Farm System Record
274-359 (.433)

Pawtucket	IL	AAA	62	84	.425
New Britain	EL	AA	60	76	.441
Lynchburg	CAR	A	70	66	.515
Winter Haven	FSL	A	52	87	.374
Elmira	NYP	A	30	46	.395

For the second year in a row, the Red Sox farm system had the worst record in baseball. In fact, Boston management shows little concern or interest in the records of its affiliates; instead, the emphasis is on the development of prospects. There is no team in the game with more home-grown players than Boston. Boggs, Clemens, Greenwell and Burks are just a few of the stars to work their way through the system and there are more good players on the way.

The dearth of wins in the system does point out a lack of depth, however. There are only two pitchers with ERAs under 3.00 (Mike Rochford's 2.37 and Tom Bolton's 2.89 at Pawtucket) and one .300 hitter (Phil Plantier at Lynchburg) on the five farm clubs. One reason may be that Boston has consistently drafted fewer players than any other team. In 1986, for example, the Red Sox selected only 23 times in comparison to a norm of about 35. Although the club's percentage in developing their players is good by baseball standards, it will need to expand the talent pool in years to come.

In addition to the top prospects, Boston fans should watch for the aforementioned Mr. Plantier (27 HRs and 105 RBIs to go with his .300 average) and Tim Naehring (.286 with 7 HRs and 68 RBIs at New Britain/ Pawtucket).

The Red Sox top prospects are:

Carlos Quintana	Scott Cooper
Mickey Pina	Eric Hetzel
Josias Manzanillo	Dan Gabriele
Todd Pratt	Reggie Harris
Tom Fischer	Bob Zupcic

1989 was to be the coming-out party for Carlos as a major league rookie. However, his brief early season stint in Boston was a rocky one and Quintana was sent back to Triple A Pawtucket for another year of seasoning. Still, the future looks bright for the twenty-four-year-old Bosox slugger. Signed as a free agent in November 1984, Carlos has put together five solid campaigns in the Boston farm system, piling up numerous accolades and leading his clubs in virtually every important offensive category.

Quintana has few shortcomings at the plate. With a short, powerful swing, Carlos can handle both fastballs and breaking pitches effectively. He has learned to go with the pitch rather than trying to pull everything, and has excellent power to left and right-center fields. On defense, the young Venezuelan can play either right or left field more than adequately. He gets a good jump on the ball and his arm is above-average in both strength and accuracy. While 1989 may not have been all Quintana hoped it would be, 1990 should find him in the Red Sox lineup on a regular basis.

Carlos Quintana
Outfield/First Base

height	weight	bats	throws	birthplace	birthdate
6'0"	170	R	R	Estado Miranda, Venezuela	8/26/65

year	team	league	g	ab	r	h	2b	3b	hr	rbi	sb	bb	so	avg
1986	Greensboro	SAL	126	443	97	144	19	4	11	81	26	90	54	.324
1987	New Britain	EL	56	206	31	64	11	3	2	31	3	24	33	.310
1988	Pawtucket	IL	131	471	67	134	25	3	16	66	3	38	72	.285
1988	Arkansas	TL	5	6	1	2	0	0	0	2	0	2	3	.333
1989	Pawtucket	IL	82	272	45	78	11	2	11	52	6	53	39	.287
1989	Boston	AL	34	77	6	16	5	0	0	6	0	7	12	.208

The tenuous status of Wade Boggs prior to the 1989 season turned much attention toward young Scott Cooper. The Red Sox third round pick in the June 1986 free agent draft, Cooper was being touted as Boston's next third baseman. Even though he cooled off somewhat in 1989, and Boggs signed a new long-term contract, Scott is still seen as a legitimate prospect by the organization. In his four seasons in the farm system, he has been a two-time All-Star selection, paced his team in home runs twice, and led the Carolina League in hits, doubles and total bases in 1988.

Offensively, Cooper could develop into a top-notch run-producer. Although he doesn't have great speed, his short, quick swing produces enough line drives so that nearly 40% of his hits go for extra bases. Scouts say that Scott should learn to pull the ball with experience and that home runs could follow in bunches. At the "Hot Corner," this young prospect has all the tools— excellent first-step reflexes and a strong arm. The only concern here is that his throws are sometimes erratic. If Scott isn't playing for Boston within two years, it's a safe bet that he'll be with another big league club.

Scott Cooper
Third Base

height	weight	bats	throws	birthplace	birthdate
6'3"	200	L	R	St. Louis, MO	10/13/67

year	team	league	g	ab	r	h	2b	3b	hr	rbi	sb	bb	so	avg
1986	Elmira	NYP	51	191	23	55	9	0	9	43	1	19	32	.287
1987	Greensboro	SAL	119	370	52	93	21	2	15	63	1	58	69	.250
1988	Lynchburg	CAR	130	497	90	148	45	7	9	73	0	58	74	.298
1989	New Britain	EL	124	421	50	104	24	2	7	39	1	55	84	.247

Signed by Boston as a free agent in June of 1987, Pina is cut in the mold of the typical Red Sox power-hitting outfielder. He has been a bright spot in the organization for both his attitude and production. Mickey won the annual Tony Latham Award in November 1987 as the player who showed the most enthusiasm in the Florida Instructional League; he followed that up by garnering the Carolina League MVP Award in 1988 when he topped the circuit in home runs, RBIs, game-winning RBIs, runs and assists from his outfield position (20).

Pina has all the tools necessary to excel on the field. He has a big, long swing that produces excellent home run power to all fields. Although scouts felt that as Mickey moved to higher levels, pitchers would find holes in his swing, Pina's average actually increased at Pawtucket in 1989 while his strikeout ratio dropped. Although he's not a base-stealing threat, Mickey's speed is sufficient to cover left field without difficulty, and though his arm is below-average in strength, Pina consistently throws out runners challenging him with outstanding accuracy. Red Sox fans can expect this young man from Massachusetts to reach the big leagues within two years.

Mickey Pina
Outfield

height	weight	bats	throws			birthplace				birthdate		
6'0"	195	R	R			Boston, MA				3/8/66		

year	team	league	g	ab	r	h	2b	3b	hr	rbi	sb	bb	so	avg
1987	Elmira	NYP	60	196	44	54	15	2	12	45	6	28	64	.276
1988	Lynchburg	CAR	136	472	91	129	31	4	21	10	11	84	118	.273
1989	New Britain	EL	46	154	22	40	10	0	2	26	4	26	47	.260
1989	Pawtucket	IL	71	260	32	74	15	0	14	45	2	22	68	.285

A product of Crowley, Louisiana and LSU, Hetzel was chosen by the Red Sox first in the secondary phase of the June 1985 draft.

After missing the entire 1986 season with a slipped disk in his back, Hetzel rebounded to finish second in the Florida State League in complete games (11) and innings pitched (193) and fifth in strikeouts (136). That season, he lost 7 starts in succession when Winter Haven scored only 5 total runs in his support over that span. 1988 saw Eric pace the PawSox in strikeouts (122) while losing 10 games when his team scored only 19 behind him.

Despite the hard luck, Hetzel remains a top prospect in the Boston organization. He throws a 90 mph fastball with a natural sinking motion and a split-finger fastball that earned the admiration of Mike Scott during a winter workout in 1988. Eric dominates hitters primarily with these two pitches. If there has been a problem with the young right-hander, it has been a lack of concentration. A little support from the bats in the Boston lineup could cure that problem quickly and make Hetzel a fixture in the big league rotation this season.

Eric Hetzel
Pitcher

height	weight	bats	throws			birthplace				birthdate		
6'3"	178	R	R			Crowley, LA				9/25/63		

year	team	league	g	ip	h	so	bb	gs	cg	sho	sv	w	l	era
1985	Greensboro	SAL	15	76	87	822	48	0	0	0	0	7	5	5.57
1986	Did Not Play													
1987	Winter Haven	FSL	26	193	186	136	87	26	11	0	0	10	12	3.55
1988	Pawtucket	IL	22	127	129	122	51	22	2	1	0	6	10	3.96
1989	Pawtucket	IL	12	80	65	79	32	12	4	1	0	4	4	2.48
1989	Boston	AL	12	50	61	33	28	11	0	0	0	2	3	6.26

Josias Manzanillo
Pitcher

When Josias has been healthy, he has shown outstanding potential as a right-handed starter. Josias missed most of the 1987 campaign and all of 1988 with a right shoulder injury after posting a fine 13-5 season with Winter Haven in 1986. Boston hopes that successful arthroscopic surgery last April will allow Manzanillo to continue his push toward the big league in 1990.

Signed at the tender age of fifteen by the Red Sox in January 1983, Josias is skilled in the art of pitching going into his seventh professional season. His combination of an 88-90 mph fastball, a solid major league curve and an improving change-up held opposing batters to a .217 average in 1986, and his control has been excellent. Although his solid season at New Britain in 1989 was a good start, Boston will give Josias at least one more year in the farm system before he appears in Fenway Park.

height	weight	bats	throws	birthplace	birthdate
6'0"	195	R	R	San Pedro de Macoris, Dom. Rep.	10/16/67

year	team	league	g	ip	h	so	bb	gs	cg	sho	sv	w	l	era
1983	Elmira	NYP	12	38	52	19	20	4	0	0	0	1	5	7.98
1984	Elmira	NYP	14	26	27	15	26	0	0	0	1	2	3	5.26
1985	Greensboro	SAL	7	12	12	10	18	0	0	0	0	1	1	9.75
1985	Elmira	NYP	19	40	36	43	36	4	0	0	1	2	4	3.86
1986	Winter Haven	FSL	23	143	110	102	81	21	3	0	0	13	5	2.27
1987	New Britain	EL	2	10	8	12	8	2	0	0	0	2	0	4.50
1988	Did Not Play													
1989	New Britain	EL	26	147	129	93	85	26	3	1	0	9	10	3.72

Dan Gabriele
Pitcher

The Red Sox' number-one draft pick in June 1985, Dan has been brought along slowly in the farm system thus far. After posting winning records in his first two seasons with Greensboro and Winter Haven, Gabriele ran into some control problems at Class AA New Britain in 1988 when he walked 32 batters in 29 innings pitched. Boston was quick to send Dan back to Class A Lynchburg to finish the season, but at twenty-three years of age, don't expect Gabriele to be held back much longer. The Bosox let him pitch through some rough Eastern League outings in 1989 and should assign the right-hander to Pawtucket this season.

Gabriele has a fluid, loose, natural motion on the mound and a good command of his pitches most of the time. He throws a rising fastball in the 90 mph range and complements it with an effective curve. Boston hopes Dan's tenure in the minor leagues will result in at least one additional pitch. However, scouts seem to feel that if Gabriele can harness his curve and throw it for strikes, he already has the stuff to be a dominant major league starter.

height	weight	bats	throws	birthplace	birthdate
6'2"	190	L	R	Detroit, MI	12/11/66

year	team	league	g	ip	h	so	bb	gs	cg	sho	sv	w	l	era
1985	Elmira	NYP	11	57	37	38	29	11	1	1	0	2	3	1.89
1986	Greensboro	SAL	27	159	157	149	114	27	2	0	0	11	6	5.32
1987	Winter Haven	FSL	26	179	164	150	105	26	6	0	0	13	8	3.42
1988	New Britain	EL	7	29	34	25	32	7	0	0	0	1	6	8.07
1988	Lynchburg	CAR	18	107	78	91	62	18	1	0	0	10	6	2.93
1989	New Britain	EL	26	125	126	82	65	22	3	1	0	5	11	4.67

With an aging tandem of catchers at the major league level, Boston is looking to twenty-three-year-old Todd Pratt as their catcher of the future. Selected sixth by the Red Sox in the June 1985 draft, Todd will probably begin at Class AAA Pawtucket in 1990. Pratt was left unprotected by Boston in 1987 and wound up being selected in the Rule 5 draft by the Cleveland Indians. They felt, however, that Todd was two to three years away from being a major league player and returned him to the Bosox.

Although Pratt performed admirably as a first baseman and designated hitter before a sore right shoulder forced him out from behind the plate in 1988, Boston is looking at him as a catcher. At that position, Todd has shown a strong arm with a good, quick release, as well as a talent for handling pitchers. Offensively, his main asset is power. Pratt hits the ball a long way when he makes contact. However, his long swing has a few holes in it, which lead to a high number of strikeouts.

Todd Pratt
Catcher/First Base

There is little doubt that Todd will be a good defensive major league catcher, but he will spend at least one more season in the minors to work on his swing. Red Sox fans should see Pratt in "Beantown" about 1991.

height	weight	bats	throws	birthplace	birthdate
6'3"	195	R	R	Bellevue, NB	2/9/67

year	team	league	g	ab	r	h	2b	3b	hr	rbi	sb	bb	so	avg
1985	Elmira	NYP	39	119	7	16	1	1	0	5	0	10	27	.134
1986	Greensboro	SAL	107	348	63	84	16	0	12	56	0	74	114	.241
1987	Winter Haven	FSL	118	407	57	105	22	0	12	65	0	70	94	.258
1988	New Britain	EL	124	395	41	89	15	2	8	49	1	41	11	.225
1989	New Britain	EL	109	338	30	77	17	1	2	35	1	44	66	.228

The Red Sox number-one selection in the June 1987 free agent draft, Harris has been less than impressive statistically in his first three professional seasons. After opening with a 2-3 mark and a 5.01 ERA at Elmira in the New York-Penn League in 1987, Reggie was a combined 4-14 in 1988 at lower-level classifications. What makes Harris a top prospect is potential, an excellent attitude and a willingness to learn. He is a fine athlete who won the Virginia Class AA High School Player of the Year Award in 1987, and passed up a basketball scholarship to Virginia Tech in order to sign with Boston.

Harris has the finest arm in the farm system. It's long and loose and can fire a fastball upwards of 90 mph. He has excellent movement on all his pitches, but tends to struggle with his control. What Reggie needs is some work on his mechanics. Expect him to spend one or two more years in the minors before contributing to the big club. He could be well worth the wait.

Reggie Harris
Pitcher

height	weight	bats	throws	birthplace	birthdate
6'2"	190	R	R	Waynesboro, VA	8/12/68

year	team	league	g	ip	h	so	bb	gs	cg	sho	sv	w	l	era
1987	Elmira	NYP	9	47	50	25	22	8	1	0	0	2	3	5.01
1988	Lynchburg	CAR	17	64	86	48	34	11	0	0	0	1	8	7.45
1988	Elmira	NYP	10	54	56	46	28	10	0	0	0	3	6	5.30
1989	Winter Haven	FSL	29	153	144	85	77	26	1	0	0	10	13	3.99

Tom Fischer
Pitcher

Fischer attracted attention in 1987 by striking out a Big Ten record 19 Iowa batters in a seven-inning game for the University of Wisconsin. It was that kind of potential, plus the fact that his Uncle Bill is the Red Sox pitching coach, that led Boston to draft him in the first round of the June 1988 free agent draft. In his first two professional seasons, Tom has been consistent, if not spectacular. And he is the type of pitcher who could move up in the system quickly.

This young left-hander has a good idea of how to pitch. He wastes little time on the mound—throwing strikes and challenging hitters. Fischer's out pitch is a rising mid-to-high 80 mph fastball. In addition, he throws a curve and a slider. The latter two pitches are only average, but they present enough variation in speed and movement to be effective. After two years of Class A ball, Tom may make the jump to Pawtucket in 1990.

height	weight	bats	throws	birthplace	birthdate
5'11"	190	L	L	West Bend, WI	3/23/67

year	team	league	g	ip	h	so	bb	gs	cg	sho	sv	w	l	era
1988	Lynchburg	CAR	14	77	72	63	25	14	2	0	0	7	4	3.52
1989	Lynchburg	CAR	28	171	178	138	79	27	7	2	0	12	13	4.78

Bob Zupcic
Outfield

Drafted first by the Red Sox in the June 1987 free agent draft, Zupcic has not shown the home run power that he was selected for—yet. Bob's production tailed off at New Britain in 1989 after two fine seasons with Elmira and Lynchburg when he hit .303 and .297 respectively and was selected as an All-Star right fielder.

Offensively, Zupcic is not the one-dimensional threat you'd expect from a man of his size. He collects doubles and triples with his strong line-drive swing and can hit for average as well. The only knock on Zupcic is that he tends to be selective and defensive at the plate. Scouts feel that seasoning will rid him of that tendency and that his power numbers will increase. Bob is a fine defensive player as well. He keeps his head in the game and positions himself well, gets a good jump on the ball and has a fine throwing arm.

With all the tools to be a big league outfielder, the question remaining is where Bob will play. The Red Sox outfield situation is crowded and doesn't look to be any less complicated in the years to come. If Zupcic doesn't begin producing more home runs soon, he may reach the majors with another team.

height	weight	bats	throws	birthplace	birthdate
6'3"	215	R	R	Pittsburgh, PA	8/18/66

year	team	league	g	ab	r	h	2b	3b	hr	rbi	sb	bb	so	avg
1986	Elmira	NYP	66	238	39	72	12	2	7	37	5	17	36	.303
1988	Lynchburg	CAR	135	482	69	143	33	5	13	97	10	60	64	.297
1989	New Britain	EL	94	346	37	75	12	2	2	28	15	19	55	.217
1989	Pawtucket	IL	27	94	8	24	7	1	1	11	1	3	15	.255

Draft Analysis

Top Ten Picks:
- 1a. Greg Blosser, Outfield (Sarasota High School, Sarasota, FL)
- 1b. Maurice Vaughn, First Base (Seton Hall University)
- 1c. Kevin Morton, Left-hand Pitcher (Seton Hall University)
- 2. Jeff McNeely, Outfield (Spartanburg Methodist Junior College, Spartanburg, SC)
- 3. Eric Wedge, Catcher (Wichita State University)
- 4. Jeff Bagwell, Third Base (University of Hartford)
- 5. Tim Mitchell, First Base (Culver City High School, Los Angeles, CA)
- 6. Paul Quantrill, Right-hand Pitcher (University of Wisconsin)
- 7. Paul Anicki, Right-hand Pitcher (Sandwich High School, Sandwich, MA)
- 8. Stoney Burke, Catcher (Avon High School, Danville, IN)
- 9. Cedric Santiago, Left-hand Pitcher (Youco, P.R.)
- 10. Greg Hansell, Right-hand Pitcher (Kennedy High School, La Palma, CA)

The loss of Class A free agent Bruce Hurst before last season gave the Red Sox three of the first twenty-nine picks last June. With the sixteenth choice overall, Boston took high school outfielder Greg Blosser (Sarasota, FL). In 68 games, he hit .275 with 4 home runs and earned a promotion to the Florida State League. Next came first baseman Maurice Vaughn from Seton Hall. Vaughn went straight to Class AA New Britain and belted 8 round-trippers in 73 games to go with a .278 average. The club's final first-rounder was another Seton Hall product, pitcher Kevin Morton. This left-hander moved through three leagues on his way to a 6-6 record, 2.08 ERA and 111 strikeouts in 95 innings pitched.

Of the twelve players taken by Boston in the first ten rounds, there were five pitchers, three infielders, two catchers and two outfielders. Ten of them signed with the organization and all had solid professional debuts last summer. Overall, the Red Sox drafted forty-two players—an all-time high for the organization, but also the lowest number of any team. The emphasis was on the traditional power-type hitter for which the organization is known. However, Boston did find twenty pitchers they liked, many of which came cheaply in the lower rounds.

This club regularly gets more out of its draft picks than most other teams. They have a strong player development program and excellent minor league coaching. On the surface, however, this year's crop of talent looks good already. Watch for the first round picks to move up quickly.

DETROIT TIGERS

1989 Farm System Record
350-352 (.499)

Toledo	IL	AAA	69	76	.476
London	EL	AA	63	76	.453
Lakeland	FSL	A	77	59	.566
Fayetteville	SAL	A	70	69	.504
Niagara Falls	NYP	A	43	33	.566
Bristol	APPY	Rookie	28	39	.418

The Tigers have not had much help from their minor league system over the past decade. Only three regular season major league players have been produced in the Tiger system throughout the last decade. The Tigers have the worst farm contribution in the game, and there is little hope that any Triple A player will make the jump this year. However, Detroit has taken steps which should pay off handsomely in the near future. The organization has recently expanded its number of affiliates, added to its number of minor league coaches/instructors and increased the level of spending to sign top draft picks.

As it is with so many clubs these days, the strength of the Tiger farm system is speed and defense. Their lack of power-hitting prospects is evidenced by the fact that Scott Livingstone led all Detroit farmhands with 14 home runs and 71 RBIs. Also of paramount concern to the Tigers is the development of successors to Alan Trammell and Lou Whitaker. They form one of the older double-play combinations in the game, yet there are no heirs apparent on the horizon. The Detroit organization may be on the rise, but it still has a way to go.

The Tigers' top prospects are:

Phil Clark	Rob Richie
Milt Cuyler	Steve Searcy
Rico Brogna	Scott Aldred
Shawn Holman	Scott Livingstone
Torey Lovullo	Randy Nosek

Selected by the Tigers in the first round of the June 1986 free agent draft out of Crockett High School in Texas, Phil has been an All-Star performer in each of his four professional seasons. A fine all-around athlete and accomplished batsman, Clark led the Appalachian League in both average (.332) and hits (82) in 1986; he's been at or near the top of his circuit in doubles, triples, slugging percentage and game-winning RBIs since then. His lifetime .300 average and youth—he's only twenty-one years old—make Phil the organization's top prospect.

As his statistics indicate, Clark has adjusted well offensively at each step up the farm system. However, his defensive skills are still not sharp. Despite above-average arm strength, Phil has had difficulty throwing out runners and is generally rather stiff behind the plate. The Tigers have been using him as a DH with greater regularity over the past two seasons and may try to use his speed and arm in the outfield this year. Wherever Clark plays in the field, it's his bat that will earn him a trip to the major leagues—probably by 1991.

Phil Clark
Catcher

height	weight	bats	throws	birthplace	birthdate
6'0"	175	R	R	Crockett, TX	5/6/68

year	team	league	g	ab	r	h	2b	3b	hr	rbi	sb	bb	so	avg
1986	Bristol	APP	66	247	40	82	4	2	4	36	12	19	45	.332
1987	Fayetteville	SAL	135	542	83	159	26	9	8	79	24	25	43	.293
1988	Lakeland	FSL	109	403	60	120	17	4	8	66	16	15	43	.298
1989	London	EL	104	373	43	108	15	4	8	42	2	31	49	.290

An outstanding prospect, Richie got his first taste of the major leagues this past fall after posting good power figures in a brief stint with Class AAA Toledo. A former second round draft pick in 1987 and the 1988 Eastern League MVP, Rob is an outfielder with above-average speed, arm strength and batting skills. He should open the 1990 campaign in Detroit.

Offensively, Richie is a disciplined hitter with a quick, solid stroke. He drives the ball well to the alleys and has the strength to hit 15-20 home runs per season in the big leagues. Rob's potential as a run-producer is best illustrated by his Class AA campaign at Glens Falls, which saw him lead the league in hits, total bases and RBIs, while finishing among the top four in runs, doubles, triples and home runs.

In the field, Rob has shown vast improvement over the past two seasons. However, his defensive skills are still raw. For a player at such an advanced level of professional baseball, Richie's instincts on fly balls are not what they should be—nor is his hustle. Although he may not fit the mold of a typical DH, that is where the Tigers may start their young talent.

Rob Richie
Outfield

height	weight	bats	throws	birthplace	birthdate
6'2"	190	R	R	Reno, NV	9/5/65

year	team	league	g	ab	r	h	2b	3b	hr	rbi	sb	bb	so	avg
1987	Bristol	APP	7	12	2	3	0	0	0	5	1	1	2	.250
1987	Lakeland	FSL	60	204	31	60	8	3	1	32	4	22	27	.294
1988	Glens Falls	EL	137	501	75	155	24	7	14	82	24	60	69	.309
1989	Toledo	IL	69	215	42	63	9	3	6	26	3	30	40	.293

Milt Cuyler
Outfield

Combining the skills of Milt Cuyler with those of fellow prospect Rob Richie would produce a perennial All-Star outfielder. Although Milt won't hit for a high average or produce many extra-base hits, his defense will certainly garner plenty of Gold Glove Awards. Detroit's second round choice in the June 1986 draft, the twenty-one-year-old Cuyler may already be the finest center fielder in the organization—including Gary Pettis. He has excellent instincts on fly balls and covers incredible amounts of territory with blazing speed—6.3 seconds in the 60-yard dash.

To reach the major leagues, however, Milt will need to perfect the role of a table setter by getting on base and using his speed to create runs. To that end, he has worked on shortening his stroke to make more consistent contact and has practiced long hours to become a proficient bunter. The necessity for this hard work was evidenced by a 1989 season that saw Cuyler overmatched by Triple A pitching and only moderately successful at the Double A level. Tiger fans can expect Milt to spend at least one more year in the minors before joining the major league squad.

height	weight	bats	throws	birthplace	birthdate
5'10"	175	B	R	Macon, GA	10/7/68

year	team	league	g	ab	r	h	2b	3b	hr	rbi	sb	bb	so	avg
1986	Bristol	APP	45	174	24	40	3	5	1	11	12	15	35	.230
1987	Fayetteville	SAL	94	366	64	107	8	4	2	34	25	34	78	.292
1988	Lakeland	FSL	132	483	100	143	11	3	2	32	50	71	83	.297
1989	London	EL	98	366	69	96	8	7	7	34	32	47	74	.262
1989	Toledo	IL	24	83	4	14	3	2	0	6	4	8	27	.169

Steve Searcy
Pitcher

Detroit's third round selection in 1985 out of the University of Tennessee, Steve has been among the organization's top prospects for several years. Unfortunately, a variety of injuries have as yet prevented this hard-throwing lefty from making a contribution on the major league level. In his only two full seasons—1986 and 1988—Searcy posted a combined 24-13 mark with Glens Falls and Toledo and struck out an average of better than 8 batters per 9 innings pitched. He was named the International League's Most Valuable Pitcher in 1988.

Steve's repertoire includes four excellent pitches. In addition to a 90 mph fastball, he throws a hard slider, sharp-breaking curve and straight change-up. At twenty-five years of age, Searcy is proficient at varying the speed and location of his pitches and the movement on his ball is so good that hitters often have difficulty laying off pitches out of the strike zone. With nothing left to prove in the minor leagues, Steve is expected to take a spot in the Tiger rotation this spring. 1990 could be the year he finally lives up to his advance billing.

height	weight	bats	throws	birthplace	birthdate
6'1"	185	L	L	Knoxville, TN	6/4/64

year	team	league	g	ip	h	so	bb	gs	cg	sho	sv	w	l	era
1985	Bristol	APP	4	22	15	24	2	4	2	1	0	1	1	2.05
1985	Birmingham	SL	7	37	39	19	23	7	0	0	0	2	2	3.19
1986	Glens Falls	EL	27	172	166	139	74	27	3	0	0	11	6	3.30
1987	Toledo	IL	10	53	49	54	32	10	0	0	0	3	4	4.22
1988	Toledo	IL	27	170	131	176	79	27	3	0	0	13	7	2.59
1988	Detroit	AL	2	8	8	5	4	0	0	0	0	0	0	5.63
1989	Lakeland	FSL	9	52	40	44	33	9	0	0	0	2	3	2.56
1989	Toledo	IL	9	37	41	26	37	9	0	0	0	2	3	7.54
1989	Detroit	AL	8	22	27	11	12	2	0	0	0	1	1	6.04

Rico Brogna
First Base/Outfield

Although Rico is only twenty years old and the opening of the 1990 season will probably find him at the Double A level, he is being touted by scouts as one of the game's future stars. The Tigers lured Brogna away from a football scholarship at Clemson when they selected him in the first round of the 1988 draft; they were very pleased with the young first baseman's production at Bristol in the Appalachian League that summer. A former High School All-American in both baseball and football, he certainly has the tools to reach the big leagues.

Offensively, Rico is a power hitter and run-producer. His quick wrists and long swing can send balls over the fence to any field and produce plenty of line drives as well. While Detroit would rather not tamper with his natural ability at the plate, coaches may work with Brogna to shorten his stroke in order to produce more contact. Defensively, Rico can play adequately in the outfield. However, his quickness and sure hands make him more valuable as a first baseman. His work ethic and maturity make Brogna a good candidate for rapid advancement and he may reach Detroit by 1992.

height	weight	bats	throws	birthplace	birthdate
6'2"	190	L	L	Turner Falls, MA	4/18/70

year	team	league	g	ab	r	h	2b	3b	hr	rbi	sb	bb	so	avg
1988	Bristol	APP	60	209	37	53	11	2	7	33	3	25	42	.254
1989	Lakeland	FSL	128	459	47	108	20	7	5	51	2	38	82	.235

Scott Aldred
Pitcher

Detroit's sixteenth round selection in the June 1986 free agent draft, Scott's responsive attitude to coaching has resulted in improved performances in each of his three professional seasons. In jumping one classification per year, Aldred has posted two consecutive winning campaigns and improved his walks-to-innings-pitched ratio enough to earn a Triple A assignment in 1990.

As a professional, this young left-hander has worked primarily with two pitches. His lively 90 mph fastball and tight curve yield few hits to opposing batters, and have given Scott an average of more than 7 strikeouts per 9 innings pitched. Aldred's work in the farm system should focus on the development of a third pitch. He will not make it as a starter in the major leagues without one. Even with another pitch, however, the question of Scott's stamina may mean a middle relief assignment. He has averaged only slightly better than five-and-a-half innings per start over a three-year career.

height	weight	bats	throws	birthplace	birthdate
6'4"	190	L	L	Flint, MI	6/12/68

year	team	league	g	ip	h	so	bb	gs	cg	sho	sv	w	l	era
1987	Fayetteville	SAL	21	111	101	91	69	20	0	0	0	4	9	3.81
1988	Lakeland	FSL	25	131	122	102	72	25	1	1	0	8	7	3.56
1989	London	EL	20	122	98	97	59	20	3	1	0	10	6	3.84

A live arm and plenty of experience make Shawn a good bet to start the 1990 season with a job in the Tiger bull pen. In the past two seasons with Glens Falls (1988) and Toledo (1989), Holman notched double figures in saves, posted sub-2.00 ERAs and recorded consecutive winning campaigns. Acquired by Detroit in the trade that sent Terry Harper to the Pirates, Holman's recent emergence is surprising for a pitcher originally drafted in 1982—in the fourteenth round by Pittsburgh.

Shawn Holman
Pitcher

The resurrection of Shawn's career can be traced directly to the development of an outstanding split-fingered fastball. At 90 mph, his splitter is nearly indistinguishable from his regular fastball, and he mixes it well with an improving hard slider. In addition to his new pitch, Holman has also found greater control. On the whole, Shawn has the ingredients necessary to take on the stopper's role in many organizations. The presence of Mike Henneman, however, will most likely dictate a middle relief role for Holman this summer.

height	weight	bats	throws	birthplace	birthdate
6'2"	186	R	R	Sewickley, PA	11/10/64

year	team	league	g	ip	h	so	bb	gs	cg	sho	sv	w	l	era
1982	Bradenton	GCL	7	47	35	33	11	7	2	0	0	5	1	2.68
1983	Greenwood	SAL	22	103	126	60	49	20	1	0	1	5	9	5.79
1984	Macon	SAL	9	47	48	32	25	6	1	1	0	3	2	1.93
1984	Prince William	CAR	15	78	74	47	49	14	1	0	0	7	4	4.06
1985	Prince William	CAR	24	142	123	65	53	23	4	2	0	10	11	3.54
1985	Nashua	EL	2	8	10	2	7	2	0	0	0	0	1	4.50
1986	Nashua	EL	25	109	108	39	67	17	1	1	0	4	3	4.77
1987	Harris./Glen Falls	EL	45	104	116	49	60	5	0	0	3	5	6	4.66
1988	Glen Falls	EL	52	92	82	44	26	0	0	0	10	8	3	1.87
1989	Toledo	IL	51	89	74	38	36	0	0	0	1	3	1	1.91

With the platoon of Doug Strange and Jim Walewander at third base, Scott should have a good chance to make the Tigers' roster within two years. A former Pan American team member and the Southwest Conference's all-time leader in hits (301), doubles (75), home runs (50) and RBIs (228), Livingstone was selected by Detroit in the second round of the June 1988 free agent draft.

Although Scott has yet to make a major offensive impact as a professional, he definitely has the tools to be a big league hitter. His short, quick swing allows Livingstone to handle fastballs and breaking pitches with equal effectiveness and he'll hit the ball where it's pitched. He also shows excellent patience at the plate and could develop 15-20 home run power as an everyday player.

Scott Livingstone
Third Base

Defensively, Scott rates better than average at third base because of his hard work and desire. He's well-equipped to battle ground balls with a powerful upper body and sure hands, while his throwing arm is strong enough to gun down the fastest runners. 1990 should find Scott at Class AAA Toledo.

height	weight	bats	throws	birthplace	birthdate
6'0"	185	L	R	Dallas, TX	7/15/65

year	team	league	g	ab	r	h	2b	3b	hr	rbi	sb	bb	so	avg
1988	Lakeland	FSL	53	180	28	51	8	1	2	25	1	11	25	.283
1989	London	EL	124	452	46	98	18	1	14	71	1	52	67	.217

Torey Lovullo
Second Base/Third Base

Twenty-four-year-old Torey Lovullo should earn a spot as a utility infielder with the Tigers this season. A fifth round draft choice in 1987 out of UCLA, and a veteran of only three professional campaigns, he may not have the bat to replace Lou Whitaker at second base—his regular position—but Torey is certainly on par with other Detroit fill-ins Doug Strange and Jim Walewander.

Lovullo is a switch-hitter with some power from both sides of the plate. Although he hasn't hit for a high average at any level in the farm system, Torey collects more than his share of extra-base hits, has a good eye and knows how to get on base. Without a great deal of speed, he projects as a pesky bottom-of-the-order-type hitter. Defensively, he makes up for limited range with outstanding hustle and hard work. He has sure hands and an arm that is playable from either second or third base. In essence, Lovullo is an overachiever who should develop as a major league role player for Detroit.

height	weight	bats	throws	birthplace	birthdate
6'0"	180	B	R	Santa Monica, CA	7/25/65

year	team	league	g	ab	r	h	2b	3b	hr	rbi	sb	bb	so	avg
1987	Fayetteville	SAL	55	191	34	49	13	0	8	32	6	37	30	.257
1987	Lakeland	FSL	18	60	11	16	3	0	1	16	0	10	8	.267
1988	Glens Falls	EL	78	270	37	74	17	1	9	50	2	35	44	.274
1988	Toledo	IL	57	177	18	41	8	1	5	20	2	9	24	.232
1988	Detroit	AL	12	21	2	8	1	1	1	2	0	1	2	.381
1989	Toledo	IL	112	409	48	94	23	2	10	52	2	44	57	.230
1989	Detroit	AL	29	87	8	10	2	0	1	4	0	14	20	.115

Randy Nosek
Pitcher

The Tigers' number-one pick in the June 1985 free agent draft, Randy didn't even play baseball in high school because there was no team. Now in his fifth season as a professional, Nosek has enjoyed little success on the mound. He has posted only one winning season with an ERA low of 3.82 in 1988. The fact remains, however, that this young right-hander has an excellent, live arm and could help an aging Detroit rotation in the next few years.

Randy's primary pitch is a 90 mph fastball that shows excellent movement. He complements his heater with an average curve and change-up, but has difficulty throwing them for strikes. The organization has been puzzled by Nosek's lack of control—more than 7 walks per 9 innings pitched. His delivery is as smooth and natural as any in the system. Therefore, coaches feel he suffers from a lack of concentaration on the mound. If he is to reach the major leagues, Randy will need to refine his offspeed pitches and learn to get ahead of batters more frequently. He has good enough stuff to succeed, but doesn't seem to know it yet.

height	weight	bats	throws	birthplace	birthdate
6'4"	216	R	R	Omaha, NE	1/8/67

year	team	league	g	ip	h	so	bb	gs	cg	sho	sv	w	l	era
1986	Gastonia	SAL	12	52	56	37	49	10	0	0	0	4	5	6.02
1986	Bristol	APP	11	63	58	48	45	11	2	0	0	6	4	4.55
1987	Lakeland	FSL	10	39	63	16	30	10	0	0	0	2	4	7.38
1987	Fayetteville	SAL	16	78	69	57	63	16	0	0	0	4	11	4.64
1988	Lakeland	FSL	8	31	29	11	16	8	0	0	0	4	3.82
1989	London	EL	22	132	113	62	100	22	3	1	0	8	10	4.95
1989	Toledo	IL	1	1	2	0	4	1	0	0	0	0	0	36.00
1989	Detroit	AL	2	5	7	4	10	2	0	0	0	0	2	13.50

Draft Analysis

Top Ten Picks:
1. Greg Gohr, Right-hand Pitcher (University of Santa Clara)
2. Brad Wilson, Catcher (Towns County High School, Hiawassee, GA)
3. Gino Tagliaferry, Shortstop (Kennedy High School, Granada Hills, CA)
4. Paul Carey, Outfield (Stanford University)
5. David Keating, Outfield (University of California at Los Angeles)
6. Doug Mirabelli, Catcher (Valley High School, Las Vegas, NV)
7. Eric Albright, Catcher (Texas A&M University)
8. John DeSilva, Right-hand Pitcher (Brigham Young University)
9. Kelley O'Neal, Second Base (Belleville High School, Belleville, MI)
10. Jody Hurst, Outfield (Mississippi State University)

It would seem obvious that this organization would be looking for middle infield candidates to replace their aging double-play combo. Yet, until last June, few steps had been taken to do that. That changed when Detroit used eleven of their picks to select shortstops and second basemen in 1989. Ten more choices were used to get outfielders with some power, and twenty-five were spent on pitching. The Tigers also recognized the need to draft players who could provide help to the major league club in a hurry. Two-thirds of their draftees came from college programs.

Among the top ten picks, number-one Greg Gohr had the most attention leading up to the draft. Yet, his 1989 professional performance was overshadowed by those of some other new Tigers. Fellow pitcher John DeSilva recorded a 5-2 mark, with a 2.47 ERA and 78 strikeouts in 76.2 innings of work. And Eric Albright and Jody Hurst showed outstanding power potential at the organization's New York-Penn League affiliate. Albright hit 9 home runs and drove home 42 runs in 66 games, only to be topped by Hurst's 10 round trippers in 55 outings.

Even though the club was unable to sign their fourth and sixth round picks, 1989 would appear to have been a successful one for Detroit. They filled several glaring weak spots with promising talent and should see several more members of the class advance to the big leagues within two years.

NEW YORK YANKEES

1989 Farm System Record
391-309 (.559)

Columbus	IL	AAA	77	69	.527
Albany	EL	AA	92	48	.657
Prince William	CAR	A	72	66	.522
Ft. Lauderdale	FSL	A	61	77	.442
Oneonta	NYP	A	48	27	.640
Sarasota	GCL	Rookie	41	22	.651

Since the coming of George Steinbrenner, no major league team has spent more freely in the big-name free agent market than the Yankees. As a result, New York has forfeited their rights to first-round draft choices in nine of the last ten years. The club has also traded away such former prospects as Willie McGee, Jose Rijo, Fred McGriff, Jim Deshaise, Al Leiter and Jose Uribe. In fact, of the current major league players developed by the farm system, less than 20% actually play for the Yankees.

There is little or no way to predict the future course of the club's player development program. General Managers and Farm Directors come and go so quickly under Steinbrenner that no plan of action is ever seen through. Despite this lack of continuity, however, the Yankees have always managed to stock their minor league affiliates with fine athletes and hot prospects. Whether or not today's prospects end up in pinstripes remains to be seen.

In addition to keeping an eye on the players detailed in this section, New York fans should also watch the progress of several other young pitchers. Last summer at Albany, the Yankees' Class AA team won 92 games on the strength of three young starters—Rodney Imes, Royal Clayton and Steve Adkins. All three won at least 15 games and Adkins paced the organization with 180 strikeouts.

The Yankees' top prospects are:

Bernie Williams	Cullen Hartzog
Deion Sanders	Hensley Meulens
Kevin Maas	Vince Phillips
Ricky Rhodes	Todd Malone
Tony Morrison	Pat Kelly

Bernie Williams
Outfield

Williams signed with the Yankees as a free agent on September 13, 1985 (his seventeenth birthday). Bernie was the 1988 Carolina League batting champion with a .338 average, despite missing the final 48 games of the season because of a wrist injury suffered when he ran into an outfield wall on July 14.

Bernie is a line-drive hitter who makes solid contact from both sides of the plate. Although he has shown only occasional power in the minor leagues, his size, quick reflexes, and patience should dictate 15-20 home runs a season when he matures.

On the base paths, Williams is a true threat. He possesses sprinter's speed—6.4 seconds in the 60—and is adept at reading pitchers. He is capable of stealing 40-50 bases per year.

Bernie has the tools to develop into one of the finest center fielders in the game. He covers enormous amounts of territory with his long, galloping stride and can catch the ball once he runs it down. His arm is only average, but strong enough to keep him out of left field.

height	weight	bats	throws	birthplace	birthdate
6'2"	180	B	R	San Juan, PR	9/13/68

year	team	league	g	ab	r	h	2b	3b	hr	rbi	sb	bb	so	avg
1986	Sarasota	GCL	61	230	45	62	5	3	2	25	33	39	40	.270
1987	Oneonta	NYP	25	93	13	32	4	0	0	15	9	10	14	.344
1987	Ft. Lauderdale	FSL	25	71	11	11	3	0	0	4	9	18	22	.155
1988	Prince William	CAR	91	334	72	113	16	7	7	45	29	65	65	.338
1989	Albany	EL	91	314	63	79	11	8	11	42	26	60	72	.252
1989	Columbia	IL	50	162	21	35	8	1	2	16	11	25	38	.216

Cullen Hartzog
Pitcher

Selected by the Yankees in the thirty-ninth round of the June 1987 free agent draft, and signed on May 24, 1988 following the college baseball season, Cullen has emerged as the organization's top pitching prospect after two solid professional campaigns. He has averaged better than one strikeout per inning in stints with Sarasota and Ft. Lauderdale, and may have the best pure arm of any pitcher in the New York farm system since Jose Rijo came up in the mid-1980s.

Hartzog works with three excellent pitches. His change-up and big-breaking curve are effective in, and of, themselves when thrown for strikes, but are used primarily to set up Cullen's outstanding fastball. Reaching speeds of better than 90 mph, the young right-hander's heater shows outstanding movement into the strike zone and can be difficult to catch, let alone hit. Even with a live ball, however, Hartzog's control is above-average. He shows good poise on the mound for a twenty-year-old and has an exemplary work ethic and attitude.

If Cullen manages to stay off the trading blocks, he could reach the big time with the Yankees by 1991—just four years out of high school. New York fans should look for him to open the 1990 campaign at Class AA Albany.

height	weight	bats	throws	birthplace	birthdate
6'2"	200	R	R	Pensacola, FL	11/11/69

year	team	league	g	ip	h	so	bb	gs	cg	sho	sv	w	l	era
1988	Sarasota	GCL	13	76	65	82	23	13	1	0	0	5	2	2.00
1989	Ft. Lauderdale	FSL	17	109	92	106	40	17	3	0	0	7	7	3.38

Deion Sanders
Outfield

A standout cornerback at Florida State University, Deion regards football as his top priority. He signed with the Yankees as a free agent in June of 1988 for $60,000, even though he'll only play through July. In his brief baseball career, Sanders has shown that he could be developed into a fine major league player. Deion adds about 20 points to his average by speed alone. He goes from home to first in 3.6 seconds and can beat out almost any ball that bounces twice. With his slashing swing, Sanders is projected as a singles hitter in the majors.

Once on base, Deion is a true threat. During his 28 games as a professional in 1988, Sanders reached base 37 times and stole successfully 14 times. If he can combine the ability to read pitchers with his big lead and sprinter's speed, Deion may be impossible to throw out.

Sanders has the speed and natural instincts to be a fine center fielder. However, his lack of arm strength and the presence of Roberto Kelly and Bernie Williams in the Yankee outfield could dictate a future in left field. But wherever Deion plays, he'll be exciting to watch.

height	weight	bats	throws		birthplace				birthdate		
6'1"	195	L	L		Ft. Meyers, FL				8/9/67		

year	team	league	g	ab	r	h	2b	3b	hr	rbi	sb	bb	so	avg
1988	Sarasota	GCL	17	75	7	21	4	2	0	6	11	2	10	.280
1988	Ft. Lauderdale	FSL	6	21	5	9	2	0	0	2	2	1	3	.429
1988	Columbus	IL	5	20	3	3	1	0	0	0	1	1	4	.150
1989	Albany	EL	33	119	28	34	2	2	1	6	17	11	20	.286
1989	Columbus	IL	70	259	38	72	12	7	5	30	16	22	48	.278
1989	New York	AL	14	47	7	11	2	0	2	7	1	3	8	.234

Hensley Meulens
Third Base

A product of outstanding scouting by the Yankees, Meulens became the first major league player ever to come from the Netherlands Antilles when he was called up from Albany last August. Signed by the club as a free agent in October 1985, Hensley has been selected to three All-Star squads in his four professional seasons. Although Hensley has yet to match the 28 home runs and 103 RBIs he put together at Class A Prince William, the young third baseman is still recognized as one of the top power-hitting prospects in the game.

Defensively, Meulens has shown signs of being a smooth glove man at third. Yet, his propensity for errors—37 in 1987 and 23 in 1988—coupled with his size and strong throwing arm could dictate a future in right field. It's certain that New York will find a place for Hensley to play in order to get his bat into the lineup.

With a quick, powerful stroke, Meulens can drive the ball over the fence to any part of the field and hard work with minor league instructors has improved his abilities to turn on the inside pitch and wait on the breaking ball. At twenty-two, he is still far from reaching his potential as a hitter, but he may already be good enough to earn a major league job.

height	weight	bats	throws		birthplace				birthdate		
6'3"	190	R	R		Curacao, Netherlands Antilles				6/23/67		

year	team	league	g	ab	r	h	2b	3b	hr	rbi	sb	bb	so	avg
1986	Sarasota	GCL	59	219	36	51	10	4	4	31	6	28	66	.233
1987	Prince William	CAR	116	430	76	129	23	2	28	103	14	53	124	.300
1987	Ft. Lauderdale	FSL	17	58	3	10	3	0	0	2	0	7	25	.172
1988	Albany	EL	79	278	50	68	9	1	13	40	3	37	96	.245
1988	Columbus	IL	55	209	27	48	9	1	6	22	2	14	61	.230
1989	Albany	EL	104	335	55	86	8	2	11	45	3	61	108	.257
1989	Columbus	IL	14	45	8	13	4	0	1	3	0	8	13	.289
1989	New York	AL	8	28	2	5	0	0	0	1	0	2	8	.179

Kevin was selected by the Yankees as the twenty-second pick in the June 1986 free agent draft out of the University of California at Berkeley, and has progressed quickly in the New York farm system. He was named the organization's Minor League Player of the Year in 1988, and was selected to All-Star teams in each of his first three professional seasons.

An excellent fastball hitter, Maas has a quick, short swing, which provides good coverage of the plate and plenty of power. Over his first two-and-a-half years as a professional, nearly 40% of Kevin's hits went for extra bases, including 28 home runs in 1988. If there has been a problem with Maas' offense, it's that his hits come at the expense of too many strikeouts. He has a tendency to be very selective at the plate and often falls behind in the count.

Kevin Maas
First Base/Outfield

Whichever position Kevin plays in the field, his defense will need some work. He entered the system as a first baseman. However, the presence of Don Mattingly suggests that Maas may be used in the outfield or as the Yankees' long-sought left-handed designated hitter.

height	weight	bats	throws	birthplace	birthdate
6'3"	195	L	L	Castro Valley, CA	1/20/65

year	team	league	g	ab	r	h	2b	3b	hr	rbi	sb	bb	so	avg
1986	Oneonta	NYP	28	101	14	36	10	0	0	18	5	7	9	.356
1987	Ft. Lauderdale	FSL	116	439	77	122	28	4	11	73	14	53	108	.278
1988	Prince William	CAR	29	108	24	32	7	0	12	35	3	17	28	.296
1988	Albany	EL	109	372	66	98	14	3	16	55	5	64	103	.263
1989	Columbus	IL	83	291	42	93	23	2	6	45	2	40	73	.320

Selected by the Yankees in the thirteenth round of the June 1987 free agent draft, Phillips signed for a reported $100,000 bonus. In three seasons at John Muir High School, Vince never hit less than .550. He is an excellent athlete who almost certainly would have gone in the first round, but scouts had thought he would accept a scholarship to play football at the University of Southern California.

Phillips shows outstanding potential as an offensive player. He generates a great deal of bat speed with his quick swing. And for a young player, he shows a good sense of the strike zone. Some Yankee insiders feel that Vince could develop into a .300 hitter with some power.

Vince Phillips
Outfield

Although not quite as fast as Deion Sanders or Bernie Williams, Phillips can run the 60-yard dash in 6.7 seconds, showing enough speed to steal bases, as well as patrol center field. He has a fine natural instinct as an outfielder; and, as he develops, he could further complicate the Yankees' plans in the early 1990s.

height	weight	bats	throws	birthplace	birthdate
6'2"	180	L	L	Pasadena, CA	4/9/69

year	team	league	g	ab	r	h	2b	3b	hr	rbi	sb	bb	so	avg
1988	Ft. Lauderdale	FSL	106	356	44	95	11	1	1	42	8	52	43	.267
1989	Prince William	CAR	132	437	63	116	19	2	6	60	22	77	84	.265

Ricky Rhodes
Pitcher

Rhodes was selected by the Yankees in the thirty-fifth round of the June 1988 free agent draft solely on the basis of his potential. He is a big right-hander out of Navarro Junior College in Corsicana, Texas. In his first professional season with the Gulf Coast League Yankees (1988), Ricky teamed with other top pitching prospects Cullen Hartzog and Todd Malone. While the organization likes his raw arm, Rhodes is not as advanced as his counterparts in the art of pitching.

Coming straight over the top, Ricky can sometimes dominate hitters with a sharp downward-breaking curve and a 90+ mph fastball. When his game is on, Rhodes strikes out more than one batter per inning. However, his lack of solid mechanics leads to inconsistency in his control, velocity and ball movement.

Because Rhodes is such a low draft pick, the Yankees can afford to be patient with him. Fans can expect him to spend at least one year at each classification while coaches work on his consistency and control. The payoff may be a solid right-handed closer.

height	weight	bats	throws	birthplace	birthdate
6'4"	200	R	R	Waco, TX	5/28/68

year	team	league	g	ip	h	so	bb	gs	cg	sho	sv	w	l	era
1988	Sarasota	GCL	12	70	43	76	27	12	1	1	0	6	3	2.33
1989	Oneonta	NYP	12	53	46	52	35	12	0	0	0	2	3	4.70

Todd Malone
Pitcher

Todd was the Yankees' first selection in the June 1988 draft and the 105th player chosen overall. It's likely that he would have been taken sooner if he hadn't signed a letter of intent to attend the University of Nevada-Las Vegas. In 1988, Malone was named the Northern California High School Player of the Year when he was a student at Casa Robles High School in Orangeville, California. With the Gulf Coast League Yankees in his first professional season, he went on to earn the Yankee organization's Minor League Pitcher of the Year honors by averaging 11 strikeouts and 2.9 walks per 9 innings.

Unlike most young strikeout pitchers, Todd doesn't throw really hard. At 85 mph, his fastball is only of average velocity. He relies on excellent ball movement with his pitches. Malone throws a fine straight change-up, a tight downward-breaking curve and a fastball that moves quickly and unpredictably into the strike zone. His tenure in the minor leagues should produce an additional pitch and/or the ability to change speeds with those he already throws. Todd could be ready to challenge other pitchers for a spot in the Yankee rotation by 1992.

height	weight	bats	throws	birthplace	birthdate
6'2"	195	R	L	Folsom, CA	5/16/69

year	team	league	g	ip	h	so	bb	gs	cg	sho	sv	w	l	era
1988	Sarasota	GCL	12	66	55	81	21	12	2	1	0	6	1	1.64
1989	Oneonta	NYP	18	51	78	50	29	5	0	0	1	3	5	6.45

Selected by the Yankees in the fifth round of the June 1987 free agent draft out of High Point College in North Carolina, Tony is regarded as one of the finest athletes in the New York farm system. Morrison's time of 6.35 seconds in the 60-yard dash ranks him as one of the fastest players in the organization, along with Deion Sanders and Bernie Williams.

On the mound, Tony can be an overpowering pitcher. His number-one pitch is a fastball that reaches 90 mph and explodes into the strike zone. He also throws a hard, late-breaking slider and has been working on a straight change. Like many other young hard-throwers, Morrison's main problem has been his control. Several years of work in the minor leagues may be required to stabilize suspect mechanics, which led to 149 walks in 224 innings over his first two professional campaigns.

Tony Morrison
Pitcher

The question remains as to how Morrison will be used if or when he reaches the major leagues. Some scouts feel that he would make a fine short reliever if he could improve his control. The decision will most likely hinge on the progress of his third pitch and the depth of the Yankees' starting pitching at the time.

height	weight	bats	throws	birthplace	birthdate
6'1"	210	R	L	Rockingham, NC	10/18/65

year	team	league	g	ip	h	so	bb	gs	cg	sho	sv	w	l	era
1987	Oneonta	NYP	15	86	60	79	57	15	0	0	0	4	6	3.57
1988	Ft. Lauderdale	FSL	22	128	90	116	80	16	3	1	0	9	7	2.81
1988	Albany	EL	3	10	15	6	12	3	0	0	0	1	1	9.90
1989	Did Not Play													

A shortstop at West Chester State University of Pennsylvania in college, Pat Kelly was picked by the Yankees in the ninth round of the June 1988 free agent draft for his ability at second base. In his professional debut with Oneonta (NY-Penn League), Kelly was selected to the All-Star team as he led the league in games played (69), total chances (344), putouts (122), assists (206) and double plays (32).

Offensively, Pat is mainly a threat as a base stealer. He reads pitchers well and has the speed to succeed in a high percentage of his attempts. However, there is some question about his ability with the bat. Although he was not overwhelmed by his first encounter with professional pitching, Kelly strikes out more than a batter with his lack of power should. His future as a major league player may depend on learning simply to make contact.

Pat Kelly
Second Base

In the field, there are no questions about Pat's ability. He is a slick and graceful glove man with outstanding range and soft hands. His progression to the big leagues will depend solely on his offense.

height	weight	bats	throws	birthplace	birthdate
6'0"	180	R	R	Philadelphia, PA	10/14/67

year	team	league	g	ab	r	h	2b	3b	hr	rbi	sb	bb	so	avg
1988	Oneonta	NYP	71	280	49	92	11	6	2	34	25	16	45	.329
1989	Prince William	CAR	124	436	61	116	21	7	3	45	31	32	79	.266

Draft Analysis

Top Ten Picks:
1. No Selection
2. Andy Fox, Third Base (Christian Brothers High School, Sacramento, CA)
3. Jason Robertson, Outfield (Hillcrest High School, Country Club Hills, IL)
4. Adin Lohry, Catcher/Third Base (Winter Park High School, Winter Park, FL)
5. J.T. Snow, First Base (University of Arizona)
6. Larry Stanford, Right-hand Pitcher (Florida International University)
7. Russ Springer, Right-hand Pitcher (Louisiana State University)
8. Scott Romano, Third Base (Hillsborough High School, Tampa FL)
9. Sterling Hitchcock, Left-hand Pitcher (Armwood High School, Seffner, FL)
10. Rich Turrentine, Right-hand Pitcher (Arkansas High School, Texarkana, AR)

1989 marked the ninth time in the last ten years that New York did not have a first round draft pick. Last year's selection went to the Dodgers as compensation for signing Class 'A' free agent Steve Sax. When the Yankees' turn finally did come around, they took third baseman Andy Fox with the forty-fifth pick overall. Fox, like third and fourth round picks Robertson and Lohry, is a left-handed hitter with the type of power that could be productive in Yankee Stadium. Among the club's top ten draftees, however, J.T. Snow collected the most home runs last summer—8 in 73 games with Oneonta.

New York's 1989 draft may well be remembered for the pitching it brought to the organization. Many considered it a steal when LSU product Russ Springer was still available in the seventh round; and his 3-0 record in the Gulf Coast League last summer backed that up. The finest performance by a Yankee newcomer, though, came from left-hander Sterling Hitchcock. His line for 1989 read: 9-1, 1.64 ERA and 98 Strikeouts in 76.2 innings pitched for the Gulf Coast Yankees.

Overall, New York selected sixty players. Pitchers topped the list with twenty-four, followed by outfielders with fifteen. Other positions the Yankees emphasized included catcher, which warranted seven choices, and third base, five. With New York's need for help at the major league level, it's no surprise that over 50% of the club's draftees came out of college programs.

CALIFORNIA ANGELS

1989 Farm System Record
300-329 (.477)

Edmonton	PCL	AAA	65	76	.461
Midland	TL	AA	70	66	.515
Palm Springs	CAL	A	60	82	.423
Quad City	MWL	A	72	63	.533
Bend	NWL	A	33	42	.440

California is not blessed with a strong talent base in their minor league system. While there is good power potential at first base, third base and in the outfield, the club has failed to develop prospects at the middle infield positions where help is sorely needed. They have had a number of weak drafts in succession, traded away young talent for aging major leaguers and rushed several prospects into the major leagues too quickly. These are not the signs of a strong organization.

If there is a bright spot in the farm system, it would be the number of quality arms working their way up. Mike Fetters, Colin Charland and Mike Erb all have the potential to add depth to the big league rotation, given the proper handling.

In addition to the Angels' top prospects, California fans should monitor the progression of several other young talents. Glenn Carter, the third round pick in 1988, posted a system-high 15 wins to go with a 2.05 ERA and 190 strikeouts at Class A Quad City; first baseman Chris Cron topped the .300 mark and knocked in over 100 runs at Midland; and Bob Rose batted .359 in 99 games at Class AA.

The Angels' top prospects are:

Mike Fetters	Lee Stevens
Dante Bichette	Mark Davis
Colin Charland	Chris Graves
Mike Erb	Bill Vanderwel
John Orton	Cesar de la Rosa

Mike Fetters
Pitcher

Mike was an All-State and All-American performer in his senior year at Iolani High School in Hawaii, and he started at Pepperdine for three seasons before becoming California's fourth number-one draft pick in 1986. The Angels' top minor league prospect, Fetters throws three quality pitches—fastball, curve and slider—and has the arm to be a dominant big league starter. He has been a consistent winner in the farm system and his average of 8+ strikeouts per 9 innings is one of the organization's best.

Until 1989, the only question in the minds of Angel management and coaches was Fetters' intensity and desire. Whether it was an added year of maturity or the success of the club's major league starters (rookie Jim Abbott), Mike showed his true competitive nature by lasting an average of 7 innings per start and tossing 4 complete games for Class AAA Edmonton. This season, Mike will be given a real shot at making the big league rotation and should spend quite a bit of time in Anaheim.

height	weight	bats	throws	birthplace	birthdate
6'4"	200	R	R	Van Nuys, CA	12/19/64

year	team	league	g	ip	h	so	bb	gs	cg	sho	sv	w	l	era
1986	Salem	NWL	12	72	60	72	51	12	1	0	0	4	2	3.38
1987	Palm Springs	CAL	19	116	106	106	73	19	2	0	0	9	7	3.57
1988	Midland	TL	20	114	116	101	67	20	2	0	0	8	8	5.92
1988	Edmonton	PCL	2	14	8	11	10	2	1	0	0	2	0	1.93
1989	Edmonton	PCL	26	168	160	144	72	26	6	2	0	12	8	3.80
1989	California	AL	1	3	5	4	1	0	0	0	0	0	0	8.10

Lee Stevens
First Base/Outfielder

Another of the Angels' first round picks in the June 1986 free agent draft, Lee was named an All-Star in 1987 at first base with the California League and in 1986 at left field in the Northwest League in his four seasons as a pro. Although his fielding at either position would be adequate at the major league level, California is more impressed by Stevens' bat than his glove.

At 6'4" and 205 lbs., Lee packs plenty of power in his long, left-handed swing. In each of the last three seasons, he has reached double figures in home runs—including a high of 23 at Class AA Midland—and collected at least 25 doubles. Stevens has learned to go with the pitch instead of trying to pull every ball, and shows power to all fields. Lee also has good speed for a big man. He'll take the extra base and could steal 10-15 bases per season.

With Wally Joyner and a host of talented outfielders in front of him, the Angels will probably give the twenty-two-year-old Stevens another year at Edmonton. His best chance at the big leagues could be a DH role in 1991.

height	weight	bats	throws	birthplace	birthdate
6'4"	205	L	L	Kansas City, MO	7/10/67

year	team	league	g	ab	r	h	2b	3b	hr	rbi	sb	bb	so	avg
1986	Salem	NWL	72	267	45	75	18	2	6	47	13	45	49	.281
1987	Palm Springs	CAL	140	532	82	130	29	2	19	97	1	61	117	.244
1988	Midland	TL	116	414	79	123	26	2	23	76	0	58	108	.297
1989	Edmonton	PCL	127	446	72	110	29	9	14	74	5	61	115	.247

In a brief stint with the Angels at the start of the 1989 season, Dante became a fan favorite in Anaheim. Unfortunately for Bichette and California, his production didn't match his popularity and he was sent back to Edmonton in late May. Dante's status as a prospect is linked to his versatility in the field and his power potential at the plate.

California's seventeenth pick in the June 1984 free agent draft, Bichette is capable of playing nearly every defensive position. Primarily a right fielder and third baseman in the minor leagues, his strong arm and durable build have caused speculation in the Angel organization that he could be the club's future big league catcher.

Dante Bichette
Outfield/Third Base

Offensively, the twenty-six-year-old Bichette has reached double figures in home runs five times during his professional career and has a composite batting average of .270. Despite his quick, powerful swing, Dante sometimes tries to muscle the ball too often. This leaves him vulnerable to the inside fastball and constitutes the major adjustment Bichette must make to be a regular major league player.

height	weight	bats	throws	birthplace	birthdate
6'3"	210	R	R	W. Palm Beach, FL	11/18/63

year	team	league	g	ab	r	h	2b	3b	hr	rbi	sb	bb	so	avg
1986	Midland	TL	62	243	43	68	16	2	12	36	3	18	49	.284
1986	Palm Springs	CAL	68	290	39	79	15	0	10	73	2	21	53	.272
1987	Edmonton	PCL	92	360	54	108	20	3	13	50	3	26	68	.300
1988	Edmonton	PCL	132	509	64	136	29	10	14	81	7	25	78	.267
1988	California	AL	21	46	1	12	2	0	0	8	0	0	7	.261
1989	Edmonton	PCL	61	226	39	55	11	2	11	40	4	24	39	.243
1989	California	AL	48	138	13	29	7	0	3	15	3	6	24	.210

Acquired in a trade with the White Sox last August, Mark was originally Chicago's second round pick in the June 1986 draft. In four years of minor league baseball, he has been a steady, if unspectacular, performer and could develop into an everyday major league outfielder. Davis' best season came at Class A Peninsula in 1987, when he hit .294 and led his club in home runs, runs scored, doubles and total bases (233) on the way to a Carolina League All-Star selection.

Mark is known as a consistent, intelligent batter who reads pitchers well and hits hard line drives. Although he does not have tremendous power, Davis hits the ball solidly enough to collect 10-15 homers per year on the major league level. As a base runner, Mark uses technique and above-average speed to steal bases in bunches and to take the extra base on singles to right field.

Mark Davis
Outfield

If Davis hadn't been traded, he probably would have reached the big leagues this season. The talent in California, however, will mean another Triple A assignment for Mark—this time in Edmonton.

height	weight	bats	throws	birthplace	birthdate
6'0"	170	R	R	Lemon Grove, CA	11/25/64

year	team	league	g	ab	r	h	2b	3b	hr	rbi	sb	bb	so	avg
1986	Appleton	MWL	77	272	37	62	10	4	3	22	19	54	70	.228
1987	Peninsula	CAR	134	507	91	149	24	6	16	72	36	63	115	.294
1988	Birmingham	SL	66	248	52	72	18	3	6	27	32	38	55	.290
1988	Vancouver	PCL	68	241	24	51	9	2	4	29	8	28	65	.212
1989	Vancouver	PCL	39	123	13	16	4	1	0	8	6	13	38	.130
1989	Birmingham	SL	56	192	35	49	10	3	5	26	16	25	52	.255
1989	Midland	TL	19	58	9	14	1	0	1	7	6	6	18	.241

Colin Charland
Pitcher

Selected by the Angels in the sixth round of the June 1986 draft, Colin suffered through a difficult 1989 after jumping from Class A Palm Springs to Triple A Edmonton. In 1988, Charland led the California League with 17 wins and 14 complete games while finishing second in the circuit with 183 strikeouts and a 2.51 ERA. The hope is that a dismal campaign last year will not damage the young left-hander's confidence and that 1990 will bring a return to top form.

Charland works with a three-pitch repertoire. The best of these is a tight, biting curve that always seems to find the strike zone. As complements, Colin throws a moving fastball in the low-to-mid 80 mph range and a straight change that is still improving. He shows good concentration on the mound and his control has been sound. Colin's second season at Edmonton should be an improvement on 1989. The Angels' will not make the mistake of rushing their young prospect twice, but Charland's name could be on the 1991 spring training roster.

height	weight	bats	throws	birthplace	birthdate
6'3"	205	L	L	New York, NY	11/13/65

year	team	league	g	ip	h	so	bb	gs	cg	sho	sv	w	l	era
1986	Salem	NWL	5	31	16	49	15	5	0	0	0	4	0	1.45
1986	Quad City	MWL	10	59	55	61	29	10	1	1	0	3	4	3.49
1987	Palm Springs	CAL	27	147	159	150	87	27	6	1	0	6	12	5.38
1988	Palm Springs	CAL	27	204	187	183	71	27	12	0	0	17	5	2.51
1989	Edmonton	PCL	25	136	150	107	75	21	2	0	0	5	10	5.49

Chris Graves
Outfield

The Angels' third round pick in the June 1986 draft, twenty-two-year-old Chris Graves is ranked among California's top prospects due to excellent speed and defensive abilities. Built along the lines of a Joe Morgan or Jim W'nn, scouts feel he may have the ability to drive the ball. However, he had difficulty making contact on the professional level until a late season surge at Class AA Midland in 1989. Given the fact that he can steal as many as 40 bases per season, if Graves is able to hit anywhere near .250, he'll be a starter in the major leagues.

As a center fielder, Chris has incredible potential. Quad City manager Eddie Rodriguez went so far as to say that the young Texan would be a better defensive outfielder than Gary Pettis one day. With his speed, quickness and sheer athleticism, Graves makes catches in the outfield that no one else can. 1990 should find Chris at Midland to open the season. The organization is hoping that their young burner shows continued production verses Double A pitching. If so, he could make his way to Triple A Edmonton by mid-season.

height	weight	bats	throws	birthplace	birthdate
5'9"	165	R	R	Houston, TX	8/11/67

year	team	league	g	ab	r	h	2b	3b	hr	rbi	sb	bb	so	avg
1986	Salem	NWL	12	36	7	8	2	0	0	6	3	6	10	.222
1987	Quad Cities	MWL	74	247	31	41	4	2	2	13	14	35	102	.166
1988	Quad Cities	MWL	115	359	45	69	6	3	6	31	28	50	106	.192
1989	Palm Springs	CAL	68	254	49	66	9	4	0	20	19	33	65	.260
1989	Midland	TL	55	201	37	52	6	5	5	18	13	23	49	.259

Mike Erb
Pitcher

The Angels' number-two draft choice in 1987, Mike has shown the ability to dominate hitters in his three years as a professional. With a fastball clocked in the low 90 mph range, an outstanding slider, a big-breaking curveball and a developing straight change, Erb has averaged slightly better than one strikeout per inning over his brief career. His three consecutive winning campaigns, variety of pitches and raw physical ability rate Mike among the organization's top prospects.

If there has been any concern about this young right-hander, it would be his bad attitude. Erb tends to put as much emphasis on his off-the-field activities as he does on his job and has a reputation for being a bad influence on the clubhouse. One rather memorable incident involved spiking balls during a water polo game in the hotel pool during a period in which he was sidelined with tendonitis in his pitching arm. The Angels hope that maturity will catch up with the twenty-four-year-old's considerable pitching talent this season. Mike will most likely begin the 1990 campaign at Class AA Midland.

height	weight	bats	throws	birthplace	birthdate
6'4"	210	R	R	San Diego, CA	3/19/66

year	team	league	g	ip	h	so	bb	gs	cg	sho	sv	w	l	era
1987	Salem	NWL	12	85	65	98	20	12	4	1	0	6	23	2.44
1988	Palm Springs	CAL	19	108	102	86	62	19	3	1	0	10	7	4.40
1989	Quad City	MWL	25	147	113	161	43	24	4	3	0	11	4	2.67

Bill Vanderwel
Pitcher

Originally picked as a starter in the fourth round of the January 1986 free agent draft out of the University of Houston, Bill's best shot at the major leagues may come as a reliever. After his limited success in the rotations at Salem in the Northwest League and Palm Springs in the California League in his first two professional seasons, management decided to move Vanderwel into a middle relief role, where his fiery, competitive nature could be put to better use. The presence of a solid major league staff and three excellent starting prospects in the farm system were also most certainly a contributing factor in this decision.

Bill works with a four-pitch repertoire and moves the ball around in the strike zone well. Although he doesn't have great velocity, Vanderwel's fastball has good movement and he throws his curve for strikes. The focus of his remaining minor league tenure should be the refinement of his split-finger fastball and straight change-up. Their effectiveness will dictate his progression through the system. California fans can expect to find Bill in Class AA Midland for the 1990 season.

height	weight	bats	throws	birthplace	birthdate
6'4"	210	R	R	Toronto, Ontario	9/24/66

year	team	league	g	ip	h	so	bb	gs	cg	sho	sv	w	l	era
1986	Salem	NWL	13	83	73	87	35	13	3	0	0	8	3	3.38
1987	Palm Springs	CAL	25	121	100	103	105	25	0	0	0	3	8	4.76
1988	Palm Springs	CAL	25	69	65	45	96	14	0	0	0	2	7	7.60
1989	Quad City	MWL	22	48	43	37	42	9	0	0	0	1	6	4.84

A product of Cal Poly-San Luis Obispo, Orton was California's first round selection in the 1987 June draft and saw his first major league action in 1989. His best season at the plate came as a first year pro for Salem in the Northwest League. That summer, John hit 8 home runs and posted a .261 batting average. If Orton is able to make that much contact on the major league level, he should be the Angels' starting catcher for many years to come.

Recognized as the catcher with the best arm in the California League in 1988 and as the top defensive backstop in his circuit while playing for Midland in 1989, John is truly accomplished behind the plate. Only twenty-four years of age, he handles pitchers well and calls a smart game. Both agile and durable at 6'1" and 195 lbs., Orton can block balls in the dirt and make quick, accurate throws to any base.

John Orton
Catcher

John will certainly be given an opportunity to make the major league roster this spring. But, with a healthy Lance Parrish in front of him, the Angels will most likely give Orton another year of seasoning at the minor league level.

height	weight	bats	throws	birthplace	birthdate
6'1"	195	R	R	Santa Cruz, CA	12/8/65

year	team	league	g	ab	r	h	2b	3b	hr	rbi	sb	bb	so	avg
1987	Salem	NWL	51	176	31	46	8	1	8	36	6	32	61	.261
1987	Midland	TL	5	13	1	2	1	0	0	0	0	2	3	.154
1988	Palm Springs	CAL	68	230	42	46	6	1	1	28	5	45	78	.200
1989	Midland	TL	99	344	51	80	20	6	10	53	2	37	102	.233
1989	California	AL	16	39	4	7	1	0	0	4	0	2	17	.179

De la Rosa was originally signed by the Phillies as a seventeen-year-old free agent in 1986. He was released after two dismal offensive seasons in the Philadelphia farm system and picked up by California in November of 1987. Cesar's calling card is an outstanding glove at the shortstop position. Scouts say that this young Dominican has the quickest hands of any infielder in the organization and the range to make plays both in the hole and behind second base. He makes the spectacular and routine plays consistently and has a strong, accurate arm.

Cesar's progress in the Angel farm system will be dictated by his bat. Even Class A pitchers have been able to dominate de la Rosa with hard, inside pitches, but he began to make better contact in 1988 at Quad City and even showed some power last year at Palm Springs. If he is to make the major leagues, Cesar will

Cesar de la Rosa
Shortstop

have to show that he can make consistent contact and use his speed. Since de la Rosa is only twenty-two, California won't push him, but 1990 should find him at the Double A level for the first time.

height	weight	bats	throws	birthplace	birthdate
6'1"	170	B	R	Santo Domingo, Dom. Rep.	2/1/68

year	team	league	g	ab	r	h	2b	3b	hr	rbi	sb	bb	so	avg
1986	Utica	NYP	64	198	13	35	4	0	0	10	3	13	60	.177
1987	Spartanburg	SAL	17	47	1	7	0	0	0	4	2	3	11	.149
1987	Bend	NWL	68	232	22	54	9	1	2	29	4	6	65	.233
1988	Quad Cities	MWL	112	384	31	85	7	3	0	28	17	33	104	.221
1989	Palm Springs	CAL	127	445	37	94	11	3	3	35	7	17	139	.211

Draft Analysis

Top Ten Picks:

1. Kyle Abbott, Left-hand Pitcher (Long Beach State University)
2. Joe Grahe, Right-hand Pitcher (University of Miami)
3. Tim Salmon, Outfield (Grand Canyon College)
4. Erik Bennett, Right-hand Pitcher (Cal State Sacramento)
5. Terry Taylor, Second Base (Texas, A & M University)
6. Dave Staydohar, Outfield (American River Junior College)
7. Marvin Cobb, Right-hand Pitcher (University of Oklahoma)
8. Rick Hirtensteiner, Outfield (Pepperdine University)
9. Fili Martinez, Left-hand Pitcher (Cal State Northridge)
10. Ron Lewis, Outfield (Florida State University)

For the second year in a row, California took a left-handed pitcher by the name of Abbott in the first round. Although the 1989 version, Kyle, is no relation to Jim, this Long Beach State product is definitely a power pitching prospect. In his first professional season, Kyle Abbott struckout 95 Midwest League batters in 73.2 innings of work on his way to a 5-4 record and a 2.57 ERA. The Angels also fortified their strength in quality arms with the selection of University of Miami standout Joe Grahe. This right-hander saw his first action in the Instructional League last winter.

What the organization failed to do, however, was shore up a deficiency at the middle infield positions. Of their top ten picks, only number-five, Terry Taylor, was neither a pitcher nor an outfielder. In fact, only seven of the Angels' fifty-one draft choices have experience at second base or shortstop.

If Abbott and Grahe do not develop as planned, 1989 could prove to be a very weak draft for this organization. Few of their picks showed home runs, power or speed last summer and Rick Hirtensteiner paced the top five position players with a .248 batting average. Certainly a better evaluation will be possible after a year or two, but on the surface, California's organization would appear to have taken a step back.

OAKLAND ATHLETICS

1989 Farm System Record
347-340 (.505)

Tacoma	PCL	AAA	77	66	.538
Huntsville	SL	AA	82	61	.573
Modesto	CAL	A	56	86	.394
Madison	MWL	A	59	72	.450
So. Oregon	NWL	A	45	30	.600
Scottsdale	ARIZ	Rookie	28	25	.528

You can't argue with the success enjoyed by the Athletics' major league club over the past two seasons. They've posted the best record in baseball and have a solid, set lineup which includes three consecutive Rookie of the Year Award winners—Canseco, McGwire and Weiss. However, Oakland has also built a formidable talent base in their minor league system through good scouting and excellent drafts. While their prospects may have a difficult time earning a starting job with the big club anytime soon, the A's will have a ready supply of trade material, reserves and role players as near as Tacoma.

There are no shortcomings in this organization. Oakland's top minor league players include four pitchers, three outfielders and three infield-ers—one of whom can catch as well. The position players are all fine athletes with good power, speed and defensive skills and each of the pitchers can throw strikes. In addition, however, A's fans should watch the progress of 15-game winner Bryan Clark (Tacoma), 14-game winner Tony Ariola (Huntsville) and Dann Howitt, who hit 26 home runs and collected 111 RBIs last summer in the Southern League. Each of these players could attain top prospect status this year.

The Athletics' top prospects are:

Dave Otto	Scott Hemond
Felix Jose	Stan Royer
Lance Blankenship	Scott Chiamparino
Will Schock	Steve Howard
David Veres	Lee Tinsley

Dave Otto
Pitcher

With the addition of Mike Moore and Rick Honeycutt to the Oakland staff in 1989, the Athletics' brass saw fit to return Otto to Class AAA Tacoma for another season. Dave was the club's second round pick in the June 1985 free agent draft and is, without question, the top pitching prospect in the organization.

Statistically, Otto's professional career has not been overly impressive. He has missed portions of several seasons with knee injuries and his game has suffered from the lack of work. However, big, strong, hard-throwing left-handed starters don't come along often, and Dave has the potential to be a great one.

Otto's repertoire includes a 90 mph fastball, a hard slider, a straight change-up and a good-moving split-finger pitch, each of which is rated above-average. Moreover, Dave has no trouble throwing any one of them for strikes. At 6'7", the young hurler fields his position well and 1989 produced an improved pickoff move to first base. Dave looks to be ready for a major league starting job in 1990. The only question is whether Oakland will trade one of their current pitchers or Otto.

height		weight		bats		throws			birthplace			birthdate	
6'7"		210		L		L			Chicago, IL			11/12/64	

year	team	league	g	ip	h	so	bb	gs	cg	sho	sv	w	l	era
1986	Madison	MWL	26	169	154	125	71	26	6	1	0	13	7	2.66
1987	Madison	MWL	1	3	2	2	0	1	0	0	0	0	0	0.00
1987	Huntsville	SL	9	50	36	25	11	9	1	0	0	4	1	2.34
1987	Oakland	AL	3	6	7	3	1	0	0	0	0	0	0	9.00
1988	Tacoma	PCL	21	128	123	80	63	21	2	0	0	4	9	3.52
1988	Oakland	AL	3	10	9	7	6	2	0	0	0	0	1	1.80
1989	Tacoma	PCL	29	169	164	122	61	28	2	1	0	10	13	3.67
1989	Oakland	AL	·1	7	6	4	2	1	0	0	0	0	0	2.70

Scott Hemond
Third Base/Catcher

Originally drafted as a catcher in the first round of the June 1986 free agent draft, the A's moved Hemond to third base in 1988 to preserve his speed. The 6'0", 205-pounder's stocky build belies the fact that he is an excellent all-around athlete with outstanding quickness, strength and agility. Scott has shown the potential to be a standout both offensively and defensively.

At the plate, Hemond generates a great deal of bat speed with his quick, short swing. His stroke has few holes in it and could yield a high average, with plenty of extra-base hits as he matures. Once on base, Scott is a true threat to steal. A quick-start runner, he gets a good jump and reads pitchers well. Defensively, Hemond can play second base and catcher, but will probably remain at third. Despite a rocky transition to "The Hot Corner," Scott's quickness, strength and tremendous arm make him a natural for the position.

With a solid lineup at the major league level, Oakland is in no hurry to push their young prospect into the big league. They will most likely assign Hemond to Triple A Tacoma for the 1990 season, but he could make his debut in an Athletic uniform next year.

height		weight		bats		throws			birthplace			birthdate	
6'0"		205		R		R			Taunton, MA			11/18/65	

year	team	league	g	ab	r	h	2b	3b	hr	rbi	sb	bb	so	avg
1986	Madison	MWL	22	85	9	26	2	0	2	13	2	5	19	.306
1987	Madison	MWL	90	343	60	99	20	4	8	52	23	40	79	.289
1987	Huntsville	SL	33	110	10	20	3	1	1	8	5	4	30	.182
1988	Huntsville	SL	133	482	51	106	22	4	9	53	28	48	114	.220
1989	Huntsville	SL	132	490	89	130	26	6	5	62	45	62	77	.265
1989	Oakland	AL	4	0	2	0	0	0	0	0	0	0	0	.000

The most likely addition to the Oakland "Bash Brigade" is young, powerful Felix Jose. Signed as a non-drafted free agent in January of 1984, this 6'4", 210 lb. outfielder is already a proven star at the Triple A level and needs only a chance to play regularly in the major leagues to prove his worth.

Jose is a dangerous offensive player. In the past two seasons, he has learned to harness a quick-wristed swing that produces power from both sides of the plate. The result has been a dramatic increase in average and extra-base hits. To go with his power, Felix has excellent speed. Although he hasn't learned the art of stealing bases, the ability to go from home to first in 4.0 seconds from the left side does translate into many infield hits.

Felix Jose
Outfield

On defense, Felix is an excellent, natural outfielder. He has the speed to cover any one of the three positions and a strong, accurate throwing arm. Although the addition of Ricky Henderson complicated the Oakland outfield picture, Jose should get a shot at a starting position in 1990.

height	weight	bats	throws	birthplace	birthdate
6'2"	200	B	R	Santo Domingo, Dom. Rep.	5/8/65

year	team	league	g	ab	r	h	2b	3b	hr	rbi	sb	bb	so	avg
1985	Madison	MWL	117	409	46	89	13	3	3	33	5	18	37	.217
1986	Modesto	CAL	127	516	77	147	22	8	14	77	14	36	89	.285
1987	Huntsville	SL	91	296	29	67	11	1	5	42	3	28	61	.226
1988	Tacoma	PCL	133	504	71	160	28	5	12	83	16	53	75	.317
1988	Oakland	AL	8	6	2	2	1	0	0	1	1	0	1	.333
1989	Tacoma	PCL	103	383	58	110	25	0	14	62	11	41	81	.287
1989	Oakland	AL	20	57	3	11	2	0	0	5	0	4	13	.193

The Athletics' number-one selection in the June 1988 free agent draft, Stan is another solid third base prospect in an organization laden with young infielders. Although he doesn't have the natural physical ability of Scott Hemond, Royer is a hard-working perfectionist who some scouts feel will push Hemond to another infield position.

In his first season as a professional, Stan was named the top prospect in the Northwest League when he hit .318 with 6 home runs and 48 RBIs in a short 73 game campaign. Royer is projected to post similar numbers in the major leagues. He is a line-drive hitter with a beautiful compact swing and power that should increase as he matures.

Stan Royer
Third Base

As a runner and a fielder, Stan relies on good judgement and awareness to be effective. He is not fast, but has good quickness and a strong throwing arm from the left side of the infield. Royer will reach the major leagues on the strength of his batting stroke and steady play. His arrival should be in 1992.

height	weight	bats	throws	birthplace	birthdate
6'3"	195	R	R	Olney, IL	8/31/67

year	team	league	g	ab	r	h	2b	3b	hr	rbi	sb	bb	so	avg
1988	So. Oregon	NWL	73	287	48	92	19	3	6	48	1	33	71	.321
1989	Modesto	CAL	127	476	54	120	28	1	11	69	3	58	132	.252
1989	Tacoma	PCL	6	19	2	5	1	0	0	2	0	2	6	.263

Lance Blankenship
Second Base/Third Base/ Outfield

Originally drafted in the second round by the Red Sox in June 1985, Lance returned to the University of California for his senior year and became the first player in Pac-10 history to be named to the All-League squad four times. He signed with Oakland as the club's tenth round selection in 1986 and begins his fifth season as a professional this year.

Blankenship has spent most of his career as a second baseman, but he is a fine natural athlete capable of playing steady defense at third base and either left or right field. Lance's versatility on defense carries over to his offensive game as well. A patient hitter with an extremely quick bat, decent power and a good eye, he excels at getting on base. Once there, Blankenship has such good speed and technique that he's considered the finest base-runner in the organization. In only 131 games, Lance stole 40 bases for the 1988 Tacoma Tigers.

Even if Blankenship is unable to crack the A's starting lineup as a second baseman in 1990, it's likely that he will stick with the club as a utility player. He does too many things too well to spend another season in the minor leagues.

height	weight	bats	throws	birthplace	birthdate
6'0"	185	R	R	Portland, OR	12/6/63

year	team	league	g	ab	r	h	2b	3b	hr	rbi	sb	bb	so	avg
1986	Medford	NWL	14	52	22	21	3	0	2	17	9	17	0	.404
1986	Modesto	CAL	55	171	47	50	5	3	6	25	15	41	39	.292
1987	Modesto	CAL	22	84	14	23	9	2	0	17	12	12	29	.274
1987	Huntsville	SL	107	390	64	99	21	3	4	39	34	67	60	.254
1988	Tacoma	PCL	131	437	84	116	21	8	9	52	40	96	75	.265
1989	Tacoma	PCL	25	98	25	29	8	2	2	9	5	19	15	.296
1989	Oakland	AL	58	125	22	29	5	1	1	4	5	8	31	.232

Scott Chiamparino
Pitcher

Scott may have the best raw talent of any pitcher in the Oakland farm system. The A's number-four pick in the June 1987 draft, Chiamparino throws a big league fastball in the low 90 mph range and a hard, tight breaking pitch. His live arm brings excellent movement to his pitches and hitters have a difficult time making solid contact against him. In three professional seasons, Scott has shown the potential to be a true strike-out artist, setting down 8.14 batters on strikes per 9 innings pitched. That kind of talent is hard to overlook. However, Chiamparino does have his critics.

The young right-hander is known to be less than responsible in his dealings with teammates and boasts a bit too much self-confidence. Oakland hopes that several years in the farm system and the maturity that comes with age will help bring Scott's attitude under control. If so, Chiamparino could find himself in an A's uniform by 1992. If not, it could mean expulsion from the organization.

height	weight	bats	throws	birthplace	birthdate
6'2"	190	L	R	San Mateo, CA	8/22/66

year	team	league	g	ip	h	so	bb	gs	cg	sho	sv	w	l	era
1987	Medford	NWL	13	68	64	65	20	11	3	0	0	5	4	2.53
1988	Modesto	CAL	16	107	89	117	56	16	5	0	0	5	7	2.70
1988	Huntsville	SL	13	84	88	49	26	13	4	0	0	4	5	3.21
1989	Huntsville	SL	17	101	109	87	29	17	2	1	0	8	6	4.60

Steve Howard
Outfield

It has taken this Oakland native, who was the Athletics' eighth round selection in the January 1983 free agent draft, a long time to reach the awesome potential the club saw in him. After struggling for four years at the lower levels of the minor leagues, Howard finally put together a solid season at Class AA Huntsville in 1987. Although he continues to show a propensity for striking out, Steve's 1989 power numbers should give him an outside chance to earn a spot on the big league roster this season.

Aside from Jose Canseco, Howard may have as much power as any hitter in the organization. With a 6'2", 215 lb. frame and a long swing, he produces outstanding bat speed and can hit the ball out of the park to any field. He has improved at hitting the breaking pitch in the past two years and has also shown improved skills on the base paths.

Coupled with Steve's outstanding power is his blazing speed. He consistently runs the 40-yard dash in 4.5 seconds and has no difficulty covering any outfield position. Even though his arm is average at best and his skills as a player are still raw, Howard's potential remains great.

height	weight	bats	throws	birthplace	birthdate
6'2"	215	R	R	Oakland, CA	12/7/63

year	team	league	g	ab	r	h	2b	3b	hr	rbi	sb	bb	so	avg
1985	Modesto	CAL	110	349	59	77	15	3	14	64	10	68	138	.221
1986	Modesto	CAL	98	302	64	70	11	4	9	53	13	100	128	.232
1987	Huntsville	SL	133	439	79	112	17	4	13	66	9	76	142	.255
1988	Huntsville	SL	128	461	70	114	18	6	17	78	29	64	134	.247
1989	Tacoma	PCL	107	341	51	83	10	2	13	60	15	64	135	.243

Will Schock
Pitcher

One of the few lower round picks to be included in our list of top prospects, Will was selected in the twenty-third round by Oakland in the June 1987 free agent draft. As a native of the Bay Area and a graduate of nearby Cal Berkeley, the Athletics had ample opportunity to evaluate Schock's talent. Upon entering the farm system, a change was made in the young right-hander's delivery to alleviate strain on his shoulder and he's now on track to reach the big leagues within two years.

Even before the adjustments to his mechanics were made, it was evident that Will knew how to pitch. He has excellent judgement and presence on the mound and rarely gets into trouble. Schock throws a 90 mph fastball with plenty of movement and a good late-breaking curve. He changes speeds well and works the ball in all areas of the strike zone.

While other teams shied away from Will in the 1987 draft due to shoulder trouble in his final two years of college, Oakland looked past the problem and may just have found themselves a gem.

height	weight	bats	throws	birthplace	birthdate
6'3"	190	R	R	San Francisco, CA	10/31/64

year	team	league	g	ip	h	so	bb	gs	cg	sho	sv	w	l	era
1987	Medford	NWL	7	21	29	15	6	7	0	0	0	1	1	5.14
1988	Madison	MWL	17	123	96	75	37	17	3	0	0	10	6	2.71
1988	Huntsville	SL	11	69	49	29	32	11	2	0	0	0	5	3.15
1989	Huntsville	SL	29	178	193	98	69	29	1	0	0	9	7	4.74

Lee Tinsley
Outfield

A four-sport star at Shelby County High in Kentucky, Lee has outstanding physical ability, though his baseball skills are still raw. The Athletics selected him in the first round of the June 1987 free agent draft for his long-range potential rather than any immediate impact. Tinsley is built along the lines of Tim Raines and Ricky Henderson. His 4.3 speed in the 40-yard dash is the best in the organization and he shows a natural talent for center field. Lee turned down a football scholarship at Purdue University to sign with Oakland.

Tinsley will probably remain in Class A ball for at least another season while he's learning to play the game. At the plate, Lee is a line-drive switch-hitter who could develop some power as he fills out. His main problem has been making contact with the ball. In his two-and-a-half years as a professional, Tinsley has struck out once in every 2.3 at bats. When he does reach base, the young outfielder is a daring and exceptional base stealer. If he gets any kind of jump, Lee is impossible to throw out.

Oakland is looking at Tinsley as a project. With plenty of solid outfielders at both the major and minor league levels, the club can afford to wait for what could be an exceptional star of the future.

height	weight	bats	throws	birthplace	birthdate
5'10"	180	B	R	Shelyville, KY	3/4/69

year	team	league	g	ab	r	h	2b	3b	hr	rbi	sb	bb	so	avg
1987	Medford	NWL	45	132	22	23	3	2	0	13	9	35	57	.174
1988	So. Oregon	NWL	72	257	56	64	8	3	3	28	41	66	106	.249
1989	Madison	MWL	123	397	51	72	10	2	6	31	19	67	177	.181

David Veres
Pitcher

A former participant in the Little League World Series, Veres hopes to be a member of a major league championship team in Oakland. Selected in the fourth round of the June 1986 free agent draft, David has progressed steadily in the A's farm system and is considered one of the organization's top pitching prospects. He should begin the 1990 season in Class AAA Tacoma.

Although David's won-loss record has been less than spectacular in his four professional seasons, he has actually pitched very well. His ERA has been below 3.50 in two seasons and his walks-to-innings-pitched ratio has continued to drop. With a 1988 Modesto club that finished the season with a 54-88 mark, Veres was on the losing side of several close decisions. However, of his four victories, two were by shutout.

David shows good poise on the mound. He works quickly and is not afraid to challenge hitters. With a fastball clocked in the mid-to-high 80 mph range, a hard, biting slider and an above-average curve, Veres should reach the big leagues within two years.

height	weight	bats	throws	birthplace	birthdate
6'2"	195	R	R	Montgomery, AL	10/19/66

year	team	league	g	ip	h	so	bb	gs	cg	sho	sv	w	l	era
1986	Medford	NWL	15	77	58	60	57	15	0	0	0	5	2	3.26
1987	Medford	NWL	26	148	124	124	108	26	2	0	0	8	9	4.79
1988	Modesto	CAL	19	125	100	91	78	19	3	2	0	4	11	3.30
1988	Huntsville	CAL	8	39	50	17	15	8	0	0	0	3	4	4.15
1989	Huntsville	SL	29	159	160	105	83	28	2	1	0	8	11	4.86

Draft Analysis

Top Ten Picks:

1. No Selection
2. Scott Lydy, Outfield (South Mountain Community College)
3. Mike Grimes, Right-hand Pitcher (University of Michigan)
4. Darin Kracl, Right-hand Pitcher (Brigham Young University)
5. Scott Erwin, Right-hand Pitcher (Georgia Tech University)
6. Steve Chitren, Right-hand Pitcher (Stanford University)
7. Scott Schockley, First Base (Pepperdine University)
8. Craig Paquette, Third Base (Golden West Junior College)
9. Gavin Osteen, Left-hand Pitcher (Allegany Community College)
10. Todd Smith, Right-hand Pitcher (Lassen Junior College)

The signing of free agent Mike Moore last winter meant that the Athletics didn't have a pick in the draft until fifty-five players were already gone. However, the team had a clear-cut strategy that seems to have filled their needs completely. After power-hitting outfielder Scott Lydy, Oakland selected right-hand pitchers with four straight picks. Each one of them posted winning percentages of .500 or better in their pro debuts, paced by Darin Kracl who went 10-1 in the Northwest League. Overall, the A's took pitchers with thirty-three of their fifty-nine draft picks.

Next came more of the organization's trademark sluggers. Ten selections were spent on outfielders, eleven on infielders and five on catchers. All are fine athletes with good speed and strong throwing arms who know how to hit. Led by eighth round choice Craig Paquette (14 HRs and 56 RBIs in 71 games), Oakland draftees in the Northwest League alone combined for more than fifty round-trippers. A surprise pick included third baseman Rodney Peete. The former USC quarterback, and current field general for the Detroit Lions, is considered a can't miss prospect if he concentrates on baseball.

This organization clearly favors the more developed college product. All but nine of Oakland's selections came out of major or junior college programs. They have the ability to help the club in the near future and can be assessed more quickly than their high-school counterparts.

SEATTLE MARINERS

1989 Farm System Record
340-345 (.496)

Calgary	PCL	AAA	70	72	.493
Williamsport	EL	AA	63	77	.450
San Bernardino	CAL	A	83	59	.585
Wausau	MWL	A	66	68	.493
Bellingham	NWL	A	32	43	.427
Tempe	ARIZ	Rookie	26	26	.500

Last summer, Seattle's minor league system produced several solid major league players as well as some of the finest statistical performances in baseball. The emergence of Ken Griffey, Jr., Greg Briley and Erik Hanson can only bode well for the M's. But the organization's highlights for the 1989 campaign came from Calgary standouts Jim Wilson (26 HRs and 133 RBIs) and Bruce Fields (.351). Unfortunately for Seattle fans, both Wilson and Fields are journeyman minor leaguers who may not fit into future plans.

Over the years, the club's farm system has been fruitful in grooming players for the big leagues—Alvin Davis, Jim Presley and Mark Langston among others—but has not provided the base that successful teams need. 1990 should give some indication as to whether the current crop of talent will prove to be superior to those of the past; however, the minor league system cannot be deemed successful until the Mariners start to win in the big leagues.

In addition to the prospects profiled in this section, Seattle fans should watch the progress of Williamsport pitchers Jim Blueberg (12 wins, 156 Ks and a 2.88 ERA) and David Burba (11-7 with a 3.16 ERA), as well as young Ruben Gonzalez, who led the organization with 27 home runs and knocked in 101 runs.

The Mariners' top prospects are:

Erik Hanson	Greg Briley
Greg Pirkl	Gene Harris
Tino Martinez	Clint Zavaras
Rich Balabon	Mark Merchant
Lee Hancock	Jim Bowie

Two solid minor league campaigns earned Erik a spot in the Mariners' rotation to begin the 1989 season. However, Seattle's 1986 second round pick suffered through several rough outings and found himself back in Calgary by late July. Hanson is a big, powerful, right-handed pitcher with stuff good enough to have thrown a no-hitter and to have led the PCL in strikeouts during 1988; he's also got the solid work habits necessary to stay in the big leagues this year.

Erik has excellent control and throws three above-average pitches—a good, moving fastball that will reach 90 mph, an offspeed screwball and a big, sharp-breaking curve. While known primarily as a power pitcher, Hanson often uses his curve as a strikeout pitch.

At twenty-four years old, Hanson has already proven himself in the farm system. Look for the Mariners to give him a full season as a starter in 1990. He has the tools to be an effective major league pitcher, given another chance.

Erik Hanson
Pitcher

height	weight	bats	throws	birthplace	birthdate
6'6"	205	R	R	Kinnelon, NJ	5/18/65

year	team	league	g	ip	h	so	bb	gs	cg	sho	sv	w	l	era
1986	Chattanooga	SL	3	9	10	11	4	2	0	0	0	0	0	3.86
1987	Chattanooga	SL	21	131	102	131	43	21	1	0	0	8	10	2.60
1987	Calgary	PCL	8	47	38	43	21	7	0	0	0	1	3	3.61
1988	Calgary	PCL	27	162	167	154	57	16	2	1	0	12	7	4.23
1988	Seattle	AL	6	42	35	36	12	6	0	0	0	2	3	3.24
1989	Calgary	PCL	8	38	51	37	11	8	1	0	0	4	2	6.87
1989	Seattle	AL	17	113	103	75	32	17	1	0	0	9	5	3.18

The performance of rookie Greg Briley was overshadowed by the debut of Ken Griffey, Jr. The Mariners' first round selection in the secondary phase of the June 1986 free agent draft, Briley hits for average, plays solid defense and shows good power potential. In four professional seasons—at four different levels of the organization—Greg has been a steady, productive contributor. His 1989 numbers should earn him a starting role in Seattle this year.

The Mariners like Briley for both his on-the-field skills and his Spartan work ethic. He shapes up as an excellent lead-off man with his 4.1 speed from home to first, his ability to draw walks and penchant for stealing bases. But Greg also has good power to the gaps and should pick up quite a few doubles. Defensively, Briley is a natural second baseman. However, Seattle tried him in the outfield and was impressed by how smoothly he made the transition. A very fast learner, Greg could fill in almost anywhere with his speed, quickness and strong, accurate arm. He should be around the major leagues for many years to come.

Greg Briley
Second Base/Outfield

height	weight	bats	throws	birthplace	birthdate
5'9"	170	L	R	Bethel, NC	5/24/65

year	team	league	g	ab	r	h	2b	3b	hr	rbi	sb	bb	so	avg
1986	Bellingham	NWL	63	218	52	65	12	4	7	46	26	50	29	.298
1987	Chattanooga	SL	137	539	81	148	21	5	7	61	34	41	58	.275
1988	Calgary	PCL	112	444	74	139	29	9	11	66	27	40	51	.313
1988	Seattle	AL	13	36	6	9	2	0	1	4	0	5	6	.250
1989	Calgary	PCL	25	94	27	32	8	1	4	20	14	13	10	.340
1989	Seattle	AL	115	394	52	105	22	4	13	52	11	39	82	.266

As Seattle's second round draft pick in 1988, Greg has shown excellent raw potential in his first two seasons as a professional. The Mariners decided to give their young catcher another year at the Class A level in 1989 because he was only eighteen; and Pirkl's numbers showed improvement over the 1988 season when he was named the Northwest League's number-three prospect.

At 6'5" and 225 lbs., Greg should develop into an awesome power hitter. He has a long, smooth stroke and can hit the ball out of sight. The challenge for Mariner coaches will be convincing him to be more selective at the plate. Defensively, Pirkl also has the physical ability to be a top-flight catcher. With his size, it may take several years to perfect proper mechanics and technique behind the plate, but Greg does have a strong throwing arm and a very durable build. Good young catchers have been scarce in recent years and Seattle will take their time molding Pirkl into a major leaguer.

Greg Pirkl
Catcher

height	weight	bats	throws	birthplace	birthdate
6'5"	225	R	R	Long Beach, CA	8/7/70

year	team	league	g	ab	r	h	2b	3b	hr	rbi	sb	bb	so	avg
1988	Bellingham	NWL	65	246	22	59	6	0	6	35	1	12	59	.240
1989	Bellingham	NWL	70	265	31	68	6	0	8	36	4	23	51	.257

Acquired by the Mariners in the deal that sent Mark Langston to Montreal, Gene is already considered one of the finest all-around athletes in the organization. He was originally a sixth round pick in 1986 out of Tulane University. In college, Harris was a starting defensive back in football as well as the ace of the Green Wave's pitching staff. This young right-hander has progressed quickly and should open the 1990 season with the big league club.

Gene is comfortable as either a starter or a reliever. Some scouts believe that his competitive nature can be well-used in the role of a stopper, but the Mariners like the fact that Harris threw 7 complete games in both 1987 and 1988 and they will probably use him in middle relief or as a spot starter. Control problems early in Gene's career seem to have disappeared and he has shown improved command over two top-notch pitches— a tight curve and a fastball with outstanding movement that clicks radar guns at up to 94 mph.

In the long run, Harris' role on the Mariner staff will be determined by the progress of a change-up he began working on in 1988. Three solid pitches would mean a spot in the rotation, while two would label Gene as bull pen material. Either way, he is a solid major league prospect.

Gene Harris
Pitcher

height	weight	bats	throws	birthplace	birthdate
5'11"	185	R	R	Sebring, FL	12/5/64

year	team	league	g	ip	h	so	bb	gs	cg	sho	sv	w	l	era
1986	Jamestown	NYP	7	20	15	16	11	4	0	0	0	0	2	2.21
1986	Burlington	MWL	7	53	37	32	15	6	4	3	0	4	2	1.35
1986	W. Palm Beach	FSL	2	11	14	5	7	2	0	0	0	0	0	4.09
1987	W. Palm Beach	FSL	26	179	178	121	77	26	7	1	0	9	7	4.37
1988	Jacksonville	SL	18	127	95	103	45	18	7	0	0	9	5	2.63
1989	Indiana	AA	6	11	4	9	10	0	0	0	2	2	0	0.00
1989	Calgary	PCL	5	6	4	4	1	0	0	0	2	0	0	0.00
1989	Seattle	AL	10	33	47	14	15	6	0	0	1	1	1	6.48

Tino Martinez
First Base

Tino gained national recognition as the hero of the 1988 U.S. Gold Medal Olympic team when he hit two home runs in a 5-3 victory over Japan in the championship game. His performance came on the heels of a superb college career at the University of Tampa where he was a three-time NCAA Division II All-American. Selected in the first round of the June 1988 free agent draft by the Mariners, Martinez put together a solid campaign as a first-year pro at Class AA Williamsport in 1989 and will probably begin this season in Calgary.

On the field, Tino shows outstanding baseball skills. With an extremely quick bat, he handles pitches on any part of the plate and hits the ball to all fields. Although Martinez has shown some power, he's more dangerous when hitting the ball into the gaps than swinging for the fences. He has the patience and swing to be a consistent .300 hitter.

Defensively, Martinez is a smooth, almost graceful, first baseman. He has good range, soft hands and keeps his head in the game at all times. Seattle fans could see this former Olympian with the big league club when the rosters expand in September.

height	weight	bats	throws	birthplace	birthdate
6'2"	195	L	R	Tampa, FL	12/7/67

year	team	league	g	ab	r	h	2b	3b	hr	rbi	sb	bb	so	avg
1989	Willaimsport	EL	137	509	51	131	29	2	13	64	7	59	54	.257

Clint Zavaras
Pitcher

A sixth-year professional out of Denver, Colorado, Clint has consistently ranked among the top prospects in his respective leagues. In 1987 and 1988, he finished runner-up to the strikeout leader, in the California and the Eastern Leagues respectively. Although Zavaras has not been impressive in terms of won-loss records, he has shown flashes of the form that made him Seattle's third round pick in the June 1985 free agent draft. He pitched well enough in Calgary to earn a promotion to the major league club last summer and could make the team to open the 1990 season.

The Mariners see Clint as a basic power pitcher. He has excellent movement on a fastball that reaches speeds of 88-90 mph and also throws a fine hard slider. However, he has yet to develop a consistent offspeed pitch, and has had difficulties with his mechanics off and on throughout his career—over 6 walks per 9 innings pitched. Although he has been a starting pitcher to this point, if Zavaras is unable to shore up his shortcomings, he may end up in the bull pen.

height	weight	bats	throws	birthplace	birthdate
6'1"	175	R	R	Denver, CO	1/4/67

year	team	league	g	ip	h	so	bb	gs	cg	sho	sv	w	l	era
1985	Bellingham	NWL	12	56	49	62	47	11	0	0	0	4	7	5.59
1986	Wausau	MWL	17	91	69	92	67	17	0	0	0	6	6	3.45
1987	Salinas	CAL	26	140	102	180	101	26	2	2	0	7	12	4.45
1988	Vermont	EL	24	129	115	120	54	24	2	1	0	10	7	3.92
1989	Calgary	PCL	21	110	105	89	56	19	1	0	0	6	9	6.04
1989	Seattle	AL	10	52	49	31	30	10	0	0	0	1	6	5.19

Rick Balabon
Pitcher

Rick came over to the Mariner organization, along with Jay Buhner and Troy Evers, in the deal that sent Ken Phelps to the Yankees on July 21, 1988. He was originally New York's first round pick in the June 1985 draft and is considered a top pitching prospect by Seattle.

Balabon has struggled at times with his mechanics and was stalled in 1987 by a bone spur in his pitching arm, but he has a big league arm and is capable of throwing a 90 mph fastball. He also has an average big league curve and a good hard slider. Aside from Rick's physical ability, the Mariners have also been impressed by his maturity and competitive nature. He is very coachable and has shown signs of developing into a pitcher, rather than just a thrower. Although it may take two to three more seasons of minor league work, this young right-hander should reach the big leagues.

height	weight	bats	throws	birthplace	birthdate
6'2"	180	R	R	Philadelphia, PA	4/26/67

year	team	league	g	ip	h	so	bb	gs	cg	sho	sv	w	l	era
1985	Oneonta	NYP	12	72	50	68	39	12	3	2	0	5	2	1.74
1986	Ft. Lauderdale	FSL	15	75	81	58	57	15	1	1	0	4	7	5.64
1987	Prince William	CAR	11	48	58	40	40	11	0	0	0	1	6	7.17
1987	Albany	EL	1	4	4	3	1	1	0	0	0	0	1	4.15
1988	Ft. Lauderdale	FSL	7	30	27	22	12	1	1	0	1	1	1	4.50
1988	San Bernardino	CAL	7	47	43	29	20	7	1	0	0	3	2	3.28
1989	San Bernardino	CAL	22	157	142	129	41	22	2	0	0	10	6	2.57
1989	Williamsport	EL	4	22	20	14	12	4	1	1	0	1	0	4.84

Mark Merchant
Outfield

Acquired from Pittsburgh, along with pitchers Mike Dunne and Mike Walker, in the Rey Quinones deal last spring, Merchant spent his first year in the Mariner organization at San Bernardino of the California League. Although the potential that made him the Pirates' first round draft pick in June of 1987 has yet to manifest itself fully, coaches in both farm systems have raved about Mark's attitude, work ethic and raw physical ability.

Merchant is a switch-hitter with a quick bat and the power to produce 15-20 home runs per season as he matures. His problems in making consistent contact with the ball have been largely due to swinging at pitches out of the strike zone. His progression through the ranks of the Seattle organization will depend mostly on learning to become more selective at the plate. In the outfield, Mark is already solid. He has good speed—6.6 seconds in the 60-yard dash—fine instincts, a strong accurate arm and he knows how to position himself. Still only twenty-one years old, Merchant will be given time to develop. His good head for the game complements his talent and he could reach the major leagues by 1992.

height	weight	bats	throws	birthplace	birthdate
6'2"	184	B	R	Dunkirk, NY	1/23/69

year	team	league	g	ab	r	ho	2b	3b	hr	rbi	sb	bb	so	avg
1987	Bradenton	GCL	50	185	32	49	5	1	3	17	33	30	29	.265
1988	Augusta	SAL	60	211	36	51	6	0	2	19	14	41	38	.242
1989	Augusta	SAL	15	59	11	19	6	1	0	8	3	7	13	.322
1989	San Bernardino	CAL	119	429	65	90	15	2	11	46	17	61	101	.210

Lee Hancock
Pitcher

Hancock opened some eyes in Seattle when he posted a 6-5 record for a 1988 Bellingham club in the Northwest League that won only 25 of 76 contests. In his first year pro—he was Seattle's fourth pick in the 1988 draft—Hancock finished the campaign with a league-high of 16 games started; he led Bellingham in wins, innings pitched and strikeouts. In a year-end poll of league managers, Lee was voted the NWL's eighth-best prospect.

At a big 6'4" and 225 lbs., Hancock has good velocity on his fastball. However, his main weapon is a nasty hard slider. Lee also has excellent control. His walks-to-strikeouts ratio was among the best in the Seattle organization in 1988 and he rarely loses his composure.

With another strong season at San Bernardino in 1989, Hancock has put himself in a position to jump Class AA ball and pitch in Calgary this year. Continued progress should bring Lee to Seattle in 1991.

height	weight	bats	throws	birthplace	birthdate
6'4"	225	L	L	No. Hollywood, CA	6/27/67

year	team	league	g	ip	h	so	bb	gs	cg	sho	sv	w	l	era
1988	Bellingham	NWL	16	100	83	102	31	16	2	0	0	6	5	2.60
1989	San Bernardino	CAL	26	173	131	119	82	26	5	0	0	12	7	2.60

Jim Bowie
First Base/Outfield

A two-sport star at Armijo High School in Fairfield, California and an All-SEC first baseman at LSU, Jim was selected by Seattle in the twelfth round of the June 1986 free agent draft. In four professional seasons, he has excelled at every stop in the system and has proven to be a top-notch run-producer. Bowie's best campaign to date came at San Bernardino in the California League in 1988. That year, he led his club in games, at bats, hits, doubles, home runs and game-winning RBIs, while his total of 102 RBIs was the sixth-highest total in all of the minor leagues.

Jim makes solid contact with his short, compact swing. His home run power is generally to right field, but he can hit the ball to the gaps as well and could collect plenty of doubles in the big leagues. Defensively, Bowie is capable at either first base or in the outfield. He has a good arm, but his average speed should limit his play to left field.

Considering his steady, productive play over the past four seasons, Jim will most likely get a shot at making the Mariners in 1990. Twenty-five years old, he'll have to make his mark soon, if he's going to make it at all.

height	weight	bats	throws	birthplace	birthdate
6'0"	200	L	L	Tokyo, Japan	2/17/65

year	team	league	g	ab	r	h	2b	3b	hr	rbi	sb	bb	so	avg
1986	Bellingham	NLW	72	274	47	76	12	1	5	68	4	38	53	.277
1987	Wausau	MWL	127	448	56	119	26	0	10	66	8	56	67	.266
1988	San Bernardino	CAL	139	529	76	155	28	0	15	102	8	58	84	.293
1989	Williamsport	EL	11	112	3	11	5	0	0	1	0	5	7	.262
1989	Calgary	PCL	100	336	28	90	12	0	4	37	2	17	45	.268

Draft Analysis

Top Ten Picks:

1a. Roger Salkeld, Right-hand Pitcher (Saugus High School, Saugus, CA)
1b. Scott Burrell, Right-hand Pitcher (Hamden High School, Hamden, CT)
2. No Selection
3. No Selection
4. Kyle Duke, Left-hand Pitcher (Newman Smith High School, Carrollton, TX)
5. Jim Gutierrez, Right-hand Pitcher (Burlington-Edison High School, Burlington, WA)
6. David Evans, Right-hand Pitcher (San Jacinto Junior College)
7. Scott Ledgek, Right-hand Pitcher (University of North Carolina)
8. Sean Twitty, Outfield (McClancy Memorial High School, Astoria, NY)
9. William Kostich, Left-hand Pitcher (Taylor Center High School, Taylor, MI)
10. Fred McNair, Shortstop (Bleckley County High School, Cochran, GA)

Seattle was without its second and third round choices last June as a result of signing free agents Tom Neidenfuer and Jeffrey Leonard. However, the club did receive an extra first round pick for the loss of Mike Moore. The end result was that the Mariners selected pitchers with their first six picks, and eight of the first ten. However, they were unable to sign right-hander Scott Burrell away from a scholarship at the University of Connecticut.

The main figure in Seattle's draft was Roger Salkeld. This hard-throwing seventeen-year-old was one of the top-rated high schoolers in the country after a 10-0, 0.65 ERA senior season. He showed why with a 2-2 record and a 1.29 ERA at Bellingham last summer. Salkeld issued only 10 walks while striking out 55 in 42 innings of work.

Offensively, the bright spots among Seattle's draftees were first baseman Lash Bailey and second baseman Brian Turang. They hit .287 and .285 respectively, while combining for 10 home runs, 47 RBIs and 10 stolen bases in the short Northwest League season.

Overall, the Mariners chose seventy-one players. Despite the clubs' affinity for pitchers in the early rounds, only thirty hurlers made the Seattle list. They were joined by twenty-two infielders, fourteen outfielders and five catchers. Thirty-seven of the draftees came from college programs.

TEXAS RANGERS

1989 Farm System Record
372-314 (.542)

Oklahoma City	AA	AAA	59	86	.407
Tulsa	TL	AA	73	63	.537
Port Charlotte	FSL	A	75	64	.540
Gastonia	SAL	A	92	48	.657
Butte	PIO	Rookie	41	25	.621
Rangers	GCL	Rookie	32	28	.533

Despite the fact that Texas traded away top prospects Sam Sosa and Wilson Alvarez to acquire slugger Harold Baines from Chicago, there is still plenty of talent left in the Rangers' farm system. The organization has made a firm commitment to develop home-grown talent by nearly doubling the money spent in the minor leagues over the last five years. Prospects abound at nearly every position and there are some good power pitchers in the system for the first time in years.

If there is one hole Texas needs to fill, it would be at catcher. They still have perennial hope John Gibbons in Triple A, but he is not the answer. In bypassing a backstop in the high rounds of last June's draft, it appears as though the Rangers may fill their hole via free agency or a trade.

Along with watching the prospects detailed in this section, Ranger fans should keep an eye on relief pitcher Jim Hvizda (8-2, 35 saves and a 1.19 ERA at Class A Gastonia) and outfielder Trey McCoy (.280 with 18 HRs and 89 RBIs for Gastonia). Both could move into the club's list of top prospects with solid campaigns in 1990.

The Rangers' top prospects are:

Kevin Brown	Juan Gonzalez
Monty Fariss	Darren Oliver
Scott Coolbaugh	Timmie Morrow
Robb Nen	Rey Sanchez
Dean Palmer	Rob Mauer

Kevin Brown
Pitcher

While other AL rookie pitchers Tom Gordon, Gregg Olson and Jim Abbott grabbed all the attention in 1989, Kevin quietly compiled some fine numbers in his inaugural major league season. The Rangers' number-one pick out of Georgia Tech in 1986, Brown made the jump from Class AA Tulsa to record double-figures in victories, 7 complete games and a fine ERA. Aside from Nolan Ryan, this young right-hander was arguably the steadiest pitcher in the Texas rotation and should be a force in the league for years to come.

Along with an incredible array of pitches, Brown has excellent poise and control. Over the past two years, he's averaged only slightly more than 3 walks per 9 innings. Kevin's best pitch is a 95 mph fastball. However, his complement pitches—a tight curve, hard slider and straight change-up—are above-average as well. He goes after hitters, gets ahead in the count and isn't afraid to come inside.

Kevin has proven himself to be a big league-quality starter already. He has all the tools expected of a former number-one pick and should only improve with the young, strong Ranger lineup behind him. 1990 could be a big season for Brown.

height	weight	bats	throws	birthplace	birthdate
6'4"	190	R	R	McIntyre, GA	3/14/65

year	team	league	g	ip	h	so	bb	gs	cg	sho	sv	w	l	era
1986	Tulsa	TL	3	10	9	10	8	2	0	0	0	0	0	4.50
1986	Texas	AL	1	5	6	4	0	1	0	0	0	1	0	3.60
1987	Tulsa	TL	8	42	53	25	18	8	0	0	0	1	4	7.29
1987	Oklahoma City	AA	5	24	32	9	17	5	0	0	0	5	0	0.00
1987	Port Charlotte	FSL	6	36	33	21	17	6	1	0	0	0	2	2.72
1988	Tulsa	TL	26	174	174	118	61	26	5	0	0	12	10	3.51
1988	Texas	AL	4	23	33	12	8	4	1	0	0	1	1	4.24
1989	Texas	AL	28	191	167	104	70	28	7	0	0	12	9	3.35

Juan Gonzalez
Outfield

Only twenty years old, Juan is already a veteran of four professional seasons in the Texas organization. He was signed by the club as a free agent on May 30, 1986 for a bonus of $109,000. Gonzalez finished third in the Gulf Coast League with 36 RBIs in 1986 and led his Gastonia team in home runs and RBIs as a Southern League All-Star in 1987. Although his excellent season at Port Charlotte was cut short by a knee injury, Juan bounced back with his finest performance to date in Tulsa last year.

Juan could develop into a bona-fide power hitter as he matures. He generates outstanding bat speed with a solid, compact swing and can hit the ball hard to all parts of the field. Although Gonzalez still chases low-breaking pitches at times, he became more selective at the plate in 1989 and showed signs of maturing as a player. Defensively, he has all the talent needed to be a spectacular outfielder. With good speed and a great arm, Juan could play any of the three positions, but is being groomed for center field by Texas. Don't be surprised to see him roaming the wide open spaces of Arlington Stadium later this year.

height	weight	bats	throws	birthplace	birthdate
6'4"	185	R	R	Vega Baja, Puerto Rico	10/16/69

year	team	league	g	ab	r	h	2b	3b	hr	rbi	sb	bb	so	avg
1986	Rangers	GCL	60	233	24	56	4	1	0	36	7	21	57	.240
1987	Gastonia	SAL	127	510	69	135	21	2	14	73	9	30	92	.265
1988	Port Charlotte	FSL	77	277	25	71	14	3	8	43	5	25	64	.256
1989	Tulsa	TL	133	502	73	147	30	7	21	85	1	31	98	.293
1989	Texas	AL	24	60	6	9	3	0	1	7	0	6	17	.150

The Rangers' first round selection in the June 1988 free agent draft, Monty so dominated the Pioneer League that year that he earned a promotion to Class AA Tulsa after only 17 games. In 53 at bats for Butte, Fariss collected 21 hits, including 4 home runs, and knocked in 22 runs. Although he seemed overmatched by Texas League pitching after being called up that summer, his average increased 50 points in 1989 and should provide the young shortstop with a springboard for this year's Triple A assignment at Oklahoma City.

Some scouts feel that Monty is too big to play effectively as a major league shortstop. However, Texas feels that even at 6'4", Fariss has the quickness and instincts and strong arm to cover the position. Production at the plate will determine Fariss' major league future. He is a very disciplined hitter with occasional power and a solid, compact stroke. Still, scouts see

Monty Fariss
Shortstop

Monty as a bottom-of-the-lineup hitter since he can be dominated by inside heat.

Up the middle, defense wins baseball games. With that in mind, Fariss should be a productive major league player. Texas may give him an extra season at Triple A to work on his hitting, but Monty is the Rangers' shortstop of the 90s.

height	weight	bats	throws	birthplace	birthdate
6'4"	185	R	R	Cordell, OK	10/13/67

year	team	league	g	ab	r	h	2b	3b	hr	rbi	sb	bb	so	avg
1988	Butte	PIO	17	53	16	21	1	0	4	22	2	20	7	.396
1988	Tulsa	TL	49	165	21	37	6	6	3	31	2	22	39	.224
1989	Tulsa	TL	132	497	72	135	27	2	5	52	12	64	112	.272

Although Oliver has yet to reach Class AA in two professional seasons, the Rangers' number-three draft choice has opened eyes in Texas with a pair of solid campaigns. The son of former big leaguer Bob Oliver, Darren is a long, lean left-hander with four above-average pitches in his repertoire. In addition to an 90 mph fastball, he throws two types of change-ups and a sharp, downward-breaking, overhand curve. Oliver led the Rangers' Gulf Coast League rookie squad with 59 strikeouts in 54 innings pitched in 1988 and teamed with fellow prospect Robb Nen to pace Gastonia's South Atlantic League title team.

Only nineteen years old, Darren has a good idea of how to pitch. With several years of work in the farm system perfecting his control, he could be a solid major league starter. 1990 should find Oliver at Class AA Tulsa.

Darren Oliver
Pitcher

height	weight	bats	throws	birthplace	birthdate
6'1"	170	R	L	Kansas City, MO	10/6/70

year	team	league	g	ip	h	so	bb	gs	cg	sho	sv	w	l	era
1988	Gulf Coast	GCL	12	54	39	59	18	9	0	0	0	5	1	2.15
1989	Gastonia	SAL	24	122	86	108	82	23	2	1	0	8	7	3.16

Following an excellent career at the University of Texas where he was named an All-Southwest Conference performer and Team MVP in 1987, Scott was selected by the Rangers in the third round of the June 1987 free agent draft. In three professional seasons, Coolbaugh's steady play at third base and good power figures have resulted in two All-Star selections. He should be given a chance to win a major league job this spring.

Although he's not the most physically impressive prospect in the Texas organization, Scott does everything well and is a dedicated worker. His short, solid stroke is the result of hours and hours of practice in a backyard batting cage and it produces powerful line drives to all parts of the field. Coolbaugh's home run power is mainly to center and right fields.

Scott Coolbaugh
Third Base

Defensively, Scott is more than adequate at the "Hot Corner." He shows good first step quickness, charges the ball well and has a strong, accurate throwing arm. Coolbaugh won't make the spectacular plays in the field, but he should be steady and durable.

height	weight	bats	throws	birthplace	birthdate
5'11"	185	R	R	Binghamton, NY	6/13/66

year	team	league	g	ab	r	h	2b	3b	hr	rbi	sb	bb	so	avg
1987	Port Charlotte	FSL	66	233	27	64	21	0	2	20	0	24	56	.275
1988	Tulsa	TL	136	470	52	127	15	4	13	75	2	76	79	.270
1989	Oklahoma	AA	144	527	66	137	28	0	18	74	1	57	93	.260
1989	Texas	AL	25	51	7	14	1	0	2	7	0	4	12	.275

Twenty-year-old Morrow is a product of Southern High School in Graham, North Carolina, where he played football and basketball and ran track—in addition to starring for the school's baseball team as both a pitcher and outfielder. He is a fine physical talent with good speed, power potential and excellent arm strength. Projected as a center fielder and top-of-the-order hitter by the Rangers, Timmie shows good instincts as a defender and base stealer.

Since being drafted in the second round of the June 1988 free agent draft, Morrow has played with both Texas rookie league clubs—the Gulf Coast Rangers and Butte. While his combined batting average is only slightly better than .250, Timmie is still filling out his 6'3" frame and should begin hitting the ball with more authority over the next two seasons. Ranger fans should look for Morrow to open the 1990 campaign at either Gastonia in the South Atlantic League or Charlotte in the Florida State League.

Timmie Morrow
Outfield

height	weight	bats	throws	birthplace	birthdate
6'3"	180	R	R	Chapel Hill, NC	2/7/70

year	team	league	g	ab	r	h	2b	3b	hr	rbi	sb	bb	so	avg
1988	Gulf Coast	GCL	32	113	15	28	2	4	2	9	3	9	30	.248
1989	Butte	PIO	60	225	40	61	7	2	4	27	13	12	44	.271

Robb Nen
Pitcher

The son of former Washington Senator first baseman Dick Nen, Robb lasted into the thirty-second round of the 1987 draft because most teams felt he would accept a scholarship to play college ball. Nen had difficulty in his first two professional seasons because he was trying to be too fine. In 1989, however, Nen seemed to realize that his arm was good enough to dominate most Class A hitters and his success improved dramatically.

A lean 6'4" and 180 lbs., Robb's fastball can push radar guns to 96 mph and shows good movement. Plus, his curve is developing nicely. But, if he's going to be a big league starter, the challenge for Nen will be to fine-tune his control and come up with a third pitch. Since Robb is only twenty years old, the Rangers will give him ample opportunity to do that, but they may be eyeing this young right-hander as a reliever. 1990 should find Nen with Class AA Tulsa.

height	weight	bats	throws	birthplace	birthdate
6'4"	180	R	R	San Pedro, CA	11/28/69

year	team	league	g	ip	h	so	bb	gs	cg	sho	sv	w	l	era
1987	Gulf Coast	GCL	2	2	4	4	3	0	0	0	0	0	0	7.71
1988	Gastonia	SAL	14	48	69	36	45	10	0	0	0	0	5	7.45
1988	Butte	PIO	14	48	65	28	45	13	0	0	0	4	5	8.75
1989	Gastonia	SAL	24	138	96	146	76	24	1	1	0	7	4	2.41

Rey Sanchez
Shortstop

Until Rey reached the Triple A level with Oklahoma City in 1989, he had been his club's standout offensive performer in each of his three professional seasons. A former All-American at Live Oak High School in Morgan Hill, California, and the Rangers' thirteenth round pick in the June 1986 draft, Sanchez began last season with a composite .300 career average. With his drop off in average and on-base percentage, it's safe to assume that Rey will spend the 1990 season in Oklahoma once again.

Sanchez is a slap hitter with good speed. He occasionally shows some power to the gaps, but is more likely to beat out an infield grounder than rip a line drive to the wall. His main asset as an offensive player is speed. Once on base, Rey is a true threat to steal. But, this young shortstop's ticket to the major leagues is his glove. With exceptional quickness, soft hands and a strong arm, Sanchez makes difficult plays look routine. He's a gutsy performer who can turn the double play and he should be a durable big league infielder.

height	weight	bats	throws	birthplace	birthdate
5'10"	180	R	R	Rio Piedras, Puerto Rico	10/5/67

year	team	league	g	ab	r	ho	2b	3b	hr	rbi	sb	bb	so	avg
1986	Rangers	GCL	52	169	27	49	3	1	0	23	10	41	18	.290
1987	Gastonia	SAL	50	161	19	35	1	2	1	10	6	22	17	.217
1987	Butte	PIO	49	189	36	69	10	6	0	25	22	21	11	.365
1988	Port Charlotte	FSL	128	418	60	128	6	5	0	38	29	35	24	.306
1989	Oklahoma City	AA	134	464	38	104	10	4	1	39	4	21	50	.224

Dean Palmer
Third Base

Right behind Scott Coolbaugh on the Ranger's third base depth-chart is young Dean Palmer. This player shows the ability to drive the ball well to all fields. He generates good bat speed and has learned more discipline at the plate in his four years as a professional. In 1989 at Class AA Tulsa, Dean blossomed into the power hitter that Texas anticipated when he was a number-three draft choice in 1986. He easily outdistanced fellow prospect Juan Gonzalez as the club's leading home run hitter and put up superb numbers in the RBI and doubles categories as well.

On defense, Dean needs to become more consistent. He has a good build for a third baseman, sure hands and a strong arm, but often seems uptight in the field. The Rangers are in no hurry to push Dean into the big leagues, however, and will probably assign him to Oklahoma City for the 1990 campaign. If or when Palmer does arrive in Arlington, he should be a fan favorite. He's a hard-nosed player who always gives 100%.

height	weight	bats	throws	birthplace	birthdate
6'1"	175	R	R	Tallahassee, FL	12/27/68

year	team	league	g	ab	r	h	2b	3b	hr	rbi	sb	bb	so	avg
1986	Rangers	GCL	50	163	19	34	7	1	0	12	6	22	34	.209
1987	Gastonia	SAL	128	484	51	104	16	0	9	54	4	36	126	.215
1988	Port Charlotte	FSL	74	305	38	81	12	1	4	35	0	15	69	.266
1989	Tulsa	TL	133	498	82	125	31	5	25	90	15	41	152	.251
1989	Texas	AL	16	19	0	2	2	0	0	1	0	0	12	.105

Rob Mauer
First Base

Rob was a teammate of 1988's first overall draft pick, Andy Benes, at the University of Evansville, but he made some headlines of his own with a .391 batting average at Butte that same summer. His mark was good enough to lead the Pioneer League and stands as the highest average ever for a Ranger rookie league player. Mauer was the Rangers' sixth round selection in the June 1988 draft.

As a first baseman, Rob still has to learn the finer points of his position. He tends to place himself too close to the right-field line and has difficulty reaching routine ground balls toward the hole. On the positive side, Mauer has shown good quickness, sure hands and an accurate arm starting the double play. Offensively, he has the potential to hit for power as well as average. Rob's solid left-handed stroke sends line drives to all parts of the park and he has the strength and quickness to turn on the inside pitch.

With two productive minor league seasons and three years of college ball behind him, Mauer should move up through the system rapidly. 1990 could find Rob at Tulsa to begin the season, but he'll probably reach Triple A before the end of the campaign.

height	weight	bats	throws	birthplace	birthdate
6'3"	200	L	L	Evansville, IN	1/7/67

year	team	league	g	ab	r	h	2b	3b	hr	rbi	sb	bb	so	avg
1988	Butte	PIO	63	233	65	91	18	3	8	59	0	35	34	.391
1989	Port Charlotte	FSL	132	456	69	126	18	9	6	51	3	86	109	.276

Draft Analysis

Top Ten Picks:
1. Donald Harris, Outfield (Texas Tech University)
2. No Selection
3. Dan Peltier, Outfield (Notre Dame University)
4. Joey Eischen, Left-hand Pitcher (Pasadena Community College)
5. Jason Ayala, Right-hand Pitcher (Brighton High School, Sandy, UT)
6. Ken Powell, Outfield (Poly High School, Long Beach, CA)
7. David Giberti, Left-hand Pitcher (Alhambra High School, Martinez, CA)
8. Jay Franklin, Right-hand Pitcher (Oral Roberts University)
9. Randy Marshall, Outfield/First Base (LeMoyne College)
10. Steve Rowley, Right-hand Pitcher (Tulane University)

The Rangers got their man when they selected outfielder Donald Harris in the first round last June, but at what price? Many teams had rated Harris far below the fifth overall position he commanded. Few can argue with the numbers he put up in the Pioneer League (.284 with 6 HRs, 37 RBIs and 14 stolen bases in 65 games), yet, Texas may have been able to pick Donald in the third round had they been patient.

Among the remaining top ten picks, only third round selection Dan Peltier distinguished himself last summer. Peltier hit a stellar .405 with Butte and collected 7 home runs in only 121 at bats. The next best average was Randy Marshall's .267 mark—also at Butte.

On the mound, the most impressive Ranger draftee was Clearwater High School standout Mike Arner. This right-hander posted a 7-0 record in 13 games with the Gulf Coast Rangers and allowed only 47 hits in 63 innings of work. Arner's walks-to-strikeouts ratio was an excellent 1 to 8.5.

Overall, Texas selected fifty-eight players in the amateur draft. Exactly half were pitchers; while fourteen play the outfield and seven catch. In an effort to develop help for the big league club quickly, the Rangers chose thirty-nine players from the college ranks.

KANSAS CITY ROYALS

1989 Farm System Record
356-346 (.507)

Omaha	AA	AAA	74	72	.507
Memphis	SL	AA	59	84	.413
Baseball City	FSL	A	78	61	.561
Appleton	MWL	A	67	68	.496
Eugene	NWL	A	43	33	.566
Boardwalk	GCL	Rookie	35	28	.556

The biggest concern in Kansas City these days is acquiring a replacement for catcher Bob Boone. Ed Hearn wasn't the answer and neither is Rey Palacios. A look through the Royals' farm system would suggest that the club will need to go elsewhere in search of their man. Unfortunately, it would not be the first time. Kansas City has developed only three regular players since Willie Wilson joined the team in 1974—Bo Jackson, Kevin Seitzer and Don Slaught—and the Triple A affiliate in Omaha has an older roster than most major league teams. The majority of the Royals' position player prospects are at least two years away from the show.

Kansas City has shown the ability to develop pitchers, however. Many of the better arms are gone now with Dave Cone in New York, Danny Jackson in Cincinnati and Scott Bankhead in Seattle. But, Tom Gordon was only the first of several strong prospects who should make their way to the American League soon.

In addition to following the Royals' top prospects, Kansas City fans should watch the progress of Southern League standout Harvey Pulliam (.285, 10 HRs and 69 RBIs) as well as Class A hurler Greg Harvey (13-7 with 115 strikeouts). Both could figure in the club's future plans with solid outings in 1990.

The Royals' top prospects are:

Bob Hamelin	Kevin Appier
Jose DeJesus	Hugh Walker
Luis de los Santos	Kevin Shaw
Aquedo Vasquez	Terry Shumpert
Victor Cole	Gary Thurman

Bob Hamelin
First Base

Holder of the single-season Junior College records for both home runs (31) and RBIs (105), Hamelin was selected by Kansas City in the second round of the June 1988 free agent draft. Bob has been named an All-Star twice, and there's no doubt he has the potential to be a major league star. Playing for Eugene of the Northwest League in 1988, he paced the circuit with 17 round-trippers and a .604 slugging percentage in a short 70-game season.

Although he lacks polish around first base, Bob is a hard worker and the Royals feel that with proper coaching he can become an adequate big league fielder. But Hamelin's skills with a bat far outweigh any concerns about his defense. Like all good, young, power hitters, Bob can put a charge into the baseball with his quick, compact stroke. Moreover, he is extremely patient at the plate. He has excellent knowledge of the strike zone and is not afraid to take a base-on-balls.

Hamelin's progression through the Royals' farm system should find him at Triple A Omaha for the 1990 season. It's possible that he may appear in Kansas City later in the year, but it's a safe bet that Bob will be a big league regular by 1991.

height	weight	bats	throws	birthplace	birthdate
6'1"	230	L	L	Elizabeth, NJ	11/29/67

year	team	league	g	ab	r	h	2b	3b	hr	rbi	sb	bb	so	avg
1988	Eugene	NWL	70	235	42	70	19	1	17	61	9	56	67	.298
1989	Memphis	SL	68	211	45	65	12	5	16	47	3	52	52	,308

Kevin Appier
Pitcher

The departure of Tom Gordon to the major leagues in 1989 left Kevin as the top pitching prospect in the Royals' farm system. An unheralded and undrafted high school player, Appier was chosen by Kansas City in the first round of the June 1987 free agent draft out of tiny Antelope Valley Junior College in California. As the club expected, the young right-hander has progressed rapidly in the minors, posting 3 winning campaigns while striking out 7.4 and walking only 2.8 batters per 9 innings.

With a 90+ mph fastball, hard slider, forkball and an excellent straight change-up, Kevin has the tools to be a dominant pitcher. However, Kansas City is more impressed by Appier's polished mound presence than his raw physical ability. At only twenty-two years of age, Kevin shows an advanced knowledge of the art of pitching—changing speeds and moving the ball around the strike zone effectively. He's not afraid to challenge hitters and his solid mechanics translate into good control. Appier could make a major impact in the AL West in 1990.

height	weight	bats	throws	birthplace	birthdate
6'2"	180	R	R	Los Angeles, CA	12/6/67

year	team	league	g	ip	h	so	bb	gs	cg	sho	sv	w	l	era
1987	Eugene	NWL	15	77	81	72	29	15	0	0	0	5	2	3.04
1988	Baseball City	FSL	24	147	134	112	39	24	1	0	0	10	9	2.75
1988	Memphis	SL	3	20	11	18	7	3	0	0	0	2	0	1.83
1989	Omaha	AA	22	139	141	109	42	22	3	2	0	8	8	3.95
1989	Kansas City	AL	6	22	34	10	12	5	0	0	0	1	4	9.14

During his seven years as a professional pitcher, Jose has had some brilliant outings. In 1988 alone, he won 7 straight decisions by striking out 10 or more batters 5 times, while allowing no more than 5 base hits per game. Over the past two seasons, DeJesus has averaged 10.7 strikeouts per 9 innings.

The main reason it has taken DeJesus so long to reach the upper levels of the farm system is a lack of control. He throws a hard slider and a fastball clocked in the mid-to-upper 90 mph range, but the outstanding movement on his pitches makes it difficult for Jose to throw strikes. The fine tuning of his slider was credited for his improved control in 1988. However, problems resurfaced last season.

Jose DeJesus
Pitcher

The Royals haven't quite decided whether to use DeJesus as a starter or out of the bull pen, though his future as a big league contributor might best be served in the role of stopper. Given the chance to come in and challenge two or three hitters, Jose could be quite effective.

height	weight	bats	throws		birthplace			birthdate				
6'5"	175	R	R		Brooklyn, NY			1/6/65				

year	team	league	g	ip	h	so	bb	gs	cg	sho	sv	w	l	era
1984	Charleston	SAL	27	163	152	85	69	27	6	2	0	11	12	4.42
1985	Ft. Myers	FSL	27	130	119	84	59	26	3	1	0	8	10	4.30
1986	Ft. Myers	FSL	22	110	87	97	82	22	1	0	0	4	9	3.44
1987	Memphis	SL	25	130	106	79	99	24	2	0	0	4	11	4.49
1988	Memphis	SL	20	116	88	149	70	20	4	1	0	9	9	3.88
1988	Omaha	AA	7	50	44	57	14	7	3	0	0	2	3	3.44
1988	Kansas City	AL	2	3	6	2	5	0	0	0	0	0	1	0.00
1989	Omaha	AA	31	145	112	158	98	21	2	0	1	8	11	3.78
1989	Kansas City	AL	3	8	7	2	8	1	0	0	0	0	0	4.50

The Royals' number-one selection in the 1988 free agent draft, Walker is an outstanding natural athlete. He showed enough potential as a first-year pro to be named the top prospect in the Rookie Leagues (Florida State and Arizona) for the 1988 season. Hugh was a highly sought-after player out of Jacksonville High School in Arkansas, where he hit .512 with 11 home runs and 37 RBIs in his senior year. He passed up a chance to play at Oklahoma State in order to sign with Kansas City.

Walker's main asset is his speed. From the left side of the plate, he can go from home to first in an amazing 3.9 seconds; and, even without proper technique, is a true threat to steal once on base. Defensively, Hugh has an innate instinct for playing the outfield. With his speed, he can easily cover any of the three positions and his arm is good enough for right field. At the plate,

Hugh Walker
Outfield

Walker needs to become more disciplined. When he stays back on the ball, he makes good contact; and as he fills out, he should develop some power. The Royals will bring Walker—only twenty years old—along slowly. He'll probably make at least two more stops in the farm system before reaching the major leagues.

height	weight	bats	throws		birthplace			birthdate			
6'1"	190	L	R		Columbus, OH			2/9/70			

year	team	league	g	ab	r	h	2b	3b	hr	rbi	sb	bb	so	avg.
1988	Royals	GCL	63	242	41	58	9	6	0	24	27	34	50	.240
1989	Appleton	MWL	103	344	38	88	13	3	6	40	11	35	74	.256

Luis de los Santos
First Base/Third Base/ Outfield

At the age of twenty-three, de los Santos has nothing left to prove in the minor leagues. The Royals' second round pick in the June 1984 draft, Luis owns a lifetime average better than .290 in six professional seasons. He has twice been named to league All-Star teams, and is the winner of the American Association Most Valuable Player Award in 1988. Due to George Brett's injuries the past two seasons, de los Santos has been given some playing time at the major league level, but the young first baseman could be given the chance to win a full-time job this spring.

The weakest link in Luis' game is his play in the field. Although he has good hands, quick reactions and a strong arm, de los Santos failed to adapt to third base or the outfield and is still learning his way around first base. At the plate, he has no such problems. The possessor of a sweet swing and a good eye, Luis makes solid contact and hits the ball with authority to all fields. He is especially tough with men on base and should continue to be a top run-producer at the major league level. While he has not hit many home runs thus far, de los Santos could develop more power as he fills out.

height	weight	bats	throws	birthplace	birthdate
6'5"	190	R	R	San Cristobal, Dom. Rep.	12/29/66

year	team	league	g	ab	r	h	2b	3b	hr	rbi	sb	bb	so	avg
1985	Ft. Meyers	FSL	123	454	44	120	18	2	0	48	2	37	53	.264
1986	Memphis	SL	135	525	72	159	21	5	3	84	5	46	65	.303
1987	Omaha	AA	135	518	53	152	29	6	2	67	2	29	80	.293
1988	Omaha	AA	136	535	62	164	25	4	6	87	2	40	79	.307
1988	Kansas City	AL	11	22	1	2	1	1	0	1	0	4	4	.091
1989	Omaha	AA	99	387	45	115	31	3	3	62	1	29	53	.297
1989	Kansas City	AL	28	87	6	22	3	1	0	6	0	5	14	.253

Kevin Shaw
Pitcher

The Royals' eighth round pick in the June 1987 free agent draft, Kevin almost certainly would have gone higher if teams hadn't felt he was going to accept a scholarship to play at Brigham Young. And, in two-and-a-half seasons as a professional, Shaw has shown that his advance billing was warranted. He has posted three winning records and two ERAs under 2.00. Although a strained tendon in his pitching elbow kept Kevin from seeing full-time action in 1988 and early 1989, his dominance of the farm's lower levels will certainly earn him a Class AA assignment this season.

Shaw is built solidly and should gain velocity with physical maturity. His live arm delivers a mid-to-high 80 mph fastball with good movement and he throws strikes with an above-average curve. Kevin also knows how to pitch. He moves the ball around well in the strike zone and keeps hitters off balance by changing speeds. With several years of seasoning, Shaw could earn a spot in the Kansas City rotation.

height	weight	bats	throws	birthplace	birthdate
6'3"	215	R	R	Yorba Linda, CA	7/2/69

year	team	league	g	ip	h	so	bb	gs	cg	sho	sv	w	l	era
1987	Royals	GCL	7	31	28	15	7	6	0	0	0	3	2	1.44
1988	Appleton	MWL	18	90	83	40	33	18	2	0	0	5	4	1.99
1989	Baseball City	FSL	11	53	42	26	15	11	0	0	0	3	1	2.53

Signed as a non-drafted free agent in November 1985, Aguedo emerged as the dominant relief pitcher in the Royals' farm system with a stellar campaign at Baseball City in 1988. Among his numerous accolades that year were selections to the FSL All-Star game and the post-season All-Star squad, the FSL Rolaids Relief Man Award and the league MVP Award. His 62 appearances paced the circuit and his 33 saves were an all-time league record—as well as the second highest total in minor league history.

Nicknamed "The Terminator," Vasquez had been pitching in the Dominican Republic under contract until mid-1987 when he reported to Sarasota. Although Aguedo is slight in stature, American hitters soon found him to be a dominating force on the mound. His primary weapons are two distinct types of fastballs. When Vasquez throws from over the top, his ball reaches speeds of 88-89 mph. When he drops down to a sidearm delivery, his ball shows excellent movement but has less velocity.

Aguedo has a resilient arm and is capable of pitching every day. He also has the right mentality for a reliever. Although the Royals won't push him through the system, Vasquez could be ready for the big leagues in about two years.

Aguedo Vasquez
Pitcher

height	weight	bats	throws	birthplace	birthdate
5'10"	160	R	R	Puerta Plata, Dom. Rep.	2/5/67

year	team	league	g	ip	h	so	bb	gs	cg	sho	sv	w	l	era
1987	Sarasota	GCL	3	2	1	0	2	0	0	0	1	1	0	0.00
1987	Ft. Myers	FSL	8	16	24	7	8	0	0	0	0	0	1	6.32
1988	Baseball City	FSL	62	81	54	68	30	0	0	0	33	3	2	1.67
1988	Omaha	AA	2	4	9	1	2	0	0	0	0	0	0	9.00
1989	Memphis	SL	64	94	99	48	46	0	0	0	11	8	6	4.02

Selected in the second round of the June 1987 draft, Shumpert is the latest in a long line of heir apparents to the ageless Frank White as the Royals' future second baseman. But Terry is probably still a year away from the major leagues. He made the jump from Class A Appleton in 1988 to Kansas City's Triple A affiliate Omaha in 1989, but he'll need time to establish a comfort zone at the upper level of the farm system.

Defensively, Shumpert is a polished second base-man. He has excellent range, good hands and a strong throwing arm. On offense, Terry's main weapon is speed. He can beat out infield hits with his 4.0 time from home to first and has quickly learned how to steal bases. If Kansas City has any reservation about this young glove man, it's his bat. Terry has a good solid swing and has shown power to the gaps. In fact, he led the Midwest League in doubles in 1988. However, Shumpert will need to learn more discipline in order to raise his average. He has a tendency to go for pitches out of the strike zone and tries to pull everything. When he starts to draw more walks and use the whole field, he may find himself in a Royal uniform.

Terry Shumpert
Second Base

height	weight	bats	throws	birthplace	birthdate
6'1"	190	R	R	Paducah, KY	8/16/66

year	team	league	g	ab	r	h	2b	3b	hr	rbi	sb	bb	so	avg
1987	Eugene	NWL	48	186	38	54	16	1	4	22	16	27	41	.290
1988	Appleton	MWL	114	422	64	102	37	2	7	39	36	56	90	.242
1989	Omaha	AA	113	355	54	88	29	2	4	22	23	25	63	.248

Victor Cole
Pitcher

The fact that Victor was born in Leningrad in the Soviet Union seems to have drawn as much attention to this young right-handed pitcher as his skills on the mound. Selected in the fourteenth round of the June 1988 free agent draft out of Santa Clara University, Cole performed well in his first season as a professional, notching 6 victories without a defeat and picking up 9 saves. Unfortunately, injuries kept Victor out of the Baseball City lineup for much of the 1989 campaign, although he did post a winning record upon his return.

As the 5'10", 150-pounder moves up through the organization, he will probably draw comparisons to 1989 rookie sensation Tom Gordon. Victor has three excellent pitches—including a fastball that hits 90 mph on occasion. To complement his heater, Cole throws a hard curve and a baffling change-up that may be as good as any in the game. With another two seasons in the minors to sharpen his mechanics and control, Victor could arrive in the major leagues as something special.

height	weight	bats	throws	birthplace	birthdate
5'10"	150	B	R	Leningrad, USSR	1/23/68

year	team	league	g	ip	h	so	bb	gs	cg	sho	sv	w	l	era
1988	Eugene	NWL	15	24	16	39	8	0	0	0	9	1	0	1.52
1988	Baseball City	FSL	10	35	27	29	21	5	0	0	1	5	0	2.06
1989	Baseball City	FSL	9	42	43	30	22	9	0	0	0	3	1	3.86
1989	Memphis	SL	13	63	67	52	51	13	0	0	0	1	9	6.36

Gary Thurman
Outfield

Gary Thurman has fallen in and out of favor with the organization several times during his seven years in the Kansas City farm system. But, the fact remains that this 1983 number-one draft pick is still only twenty-five years old and has impressive physical ability. Thurman really has nothing left to prove at the minor league level. He's already been honored as an All-Star three times— leading his league in stolen bases in each of those years—and hit .300 or better twice. 1990 may be Gary's last chance to prove himself to the Royals.

Gary's trademark is his sprinter's speed. He covers enormous amounts of territory in center field and is a standout defender due to his excellent natural instincts on balls hit over his head and a strong, accurate throwing arm. Offensively, Thurman seems cut out for the role of a table setter. He can hit for average, has doubles power to the gaps and knows how to steal bases. However, for Gary to get a legitimate shot at a starting position in 1990, he'll have to prove to Kansas City that he's not overmatched by major league pitching. The tools are there and this could be the season.

height	weight	bats	throws	birthplace	birthdate
5'10"	165	R	R	Indianapolis, IN	11/12/64

year	team	league	g	ab	r	h	2b	3b	hr	rbi	sb	bb	so	avg
1985	Ft. Myers	FSL	134	453	68	137	9	9	0	45	70	68	93	.302
1986	Memphis	SL	131	526	89	164	24	12	7	62	53	54	81	.312
1987	Omaha	AA	115	450	88	132	14	9	8	39	57	48	84	.293
1987	Royals	AL	27	81	12	24	2	0	0	5	7	8	20	.296
1988	Omaha	AA	106	422	77	106	12	6	3	40	35	38	80	.251
1988	Kansas City	AL	35	66	6	11	1	0	0	2	5	4	20	.167
1989	Omaha	AA	17	64	5	14	3	2	0	3	5	7	18	.219
1989	Kansas City	AL	72	87	24	17	2	1	0	5	16	15	27	.195

Draft Analysis

Top Ten Picks:

1. Brent Mayne, Catcher (Cal State Fullerton)
2a. Rick Tunison, First Base (Brevard Junior College)
2b. Lance Jennings, Catcher (El Rancho High School, Pico Rivera, CA)
3. Ed Gerald, Outfield (St. Paul's High School, St. Paul's, NC)
4. Ray Suplee, Outfield (Sarasota High School, Sarasota, FL)
5. Brian Ahern, Right-hand Pitcher (Central Florida University)
6. Bubba Dunn, Right-hand Pitcher (Volunteer State Junior College)
7. Eddie Pierce, Left-hand Pitcher (Orange Coast Junior College)
8. Matt Karchner, Right-hand Pitcher (Bloomsburg State University)
9. Keith Adaway, Outfield (Parkway South High School, Ballwin, MO)
10. Chris Schaefer, Right-hand Pitcher (Indiana State University)

Kansas City's organizational strength throughout the last decade has been the development of young pitching prospects. If last year's draft is any indication, the focus in the Royals' system may not change in the 1990s. Of the club's sixty-one selections, twenty-seven were pitchers— nearly half of them out of the high school ranks. To date, the most dominant of these young hurlers is Eddie Pierce. He opened at Eugene (Northwest League) with a 2-2 mark, a 2.77 ERA, 4 saves and an incredible 71 strikeouts in 39 innings pitched.

Aside from the pitchers, Kansas City made moves to shore up their problems at catcher. In addition to first round pick Brent Mayne, the club selected seven other backstops. Mayne, however, is by far the most polished defensively and could be ready for the major leagues within two seasons.

Two pleasant surprises from the lower rounds were first baseman David King and second baseman Sean Collins. Both began their professional careers at Eugene last summer with King hitting a resounding .348 (7 HRs, 28 RBIs) and Collins reaching .319 (39 RBIs and 32 stolen bases). Their efforts typified a solid draft for the Royals and bode well for the class of 1989.

MINNESOTA TWINS

1989 Farm System Record
337-290 (.537)

Portland	PCL	AAA	72	72	.500
Orlando	SL	AA	79	65	.549
Visalia	CAL	A	76	66	.535
Kenosha	MWL	A	63	66	.488
Elizabethton	APPY	Rookie	47	21	.691

The Twins' farm system hasn't provided the major league club with any players of note since the early-to-mid 1980s when Puckett, Viola, Hrbek, Gaetti and Brunansky made the jump. The club needn't be overly concerned with developing position players in the short term since their everyday lineup is still fairly young; but they must get help quickly for a pitching staff that saw only two men reach double figures in wins last year—Allen Anderson with 17 and Roy Smith with 10. While the acquisition of Rick Aguilera, David West and Kevin Tapani from the Mets last year should help fill this demand, Minnesota is counting heavily on the hard-throwing youngsters in their system. Six of the Twins' top ten prospects are pitchers.

On the positive side, the organization is firmly committed to promoting a winning atmosphere in the minor leagues. In 1989, there was only one losing team among the five affiliates. This may be due, in part, to the increase of the number of roving instructors assigned to the Minnesota system and the significant signing bonuses doled out since the departure of Calvin Griffith. In addition to the following players profiled here, Twins' fans should keep an eye on the progress of PCL All-Star first baseman Kelvin Torve (.291 with 8 HRs and 62 RBIs), relief pitcher Pete Delkus (10 saves and a 1.87 ERA at Class AA Orlando), and starter Doug Simons (who won 13 games and struck out 138 in 178 innings pitched at Orlando).

The Twins' top prospects are:

Johnny Ard	Willie Banks
Derek Parks	Paul Sorrento
Rafael DeLima	Mike Dyer
Chip Hale	Park Pittman
Larry Casian	Paul Abbott

Johnny Ard
Pitcher

The recipient of an $88,000 signing bonus as the Twins' number-one pick in the June 1988 free agent draft, Johnny earned every penny with a 7-1 mark in his first professional season. Ard dominated Appalachian League hitters in 1988, striking out 71 in 59 innings pitched, and was undefeated with a 1.05 ERA after a mid-season promotion to Class A Kenosha. His 1989 campaign at Visalia in the California League brought continued success in the form of 13 victories and 153 strikeouts in 186 innings pitched. This season should find Johnny at Double A Orlando.

Of Minnesota's several young pitching prospects, Ard may be the most polished. He works with two solid pitches—a 90 mph fastball and a hard, biting slider—and is not afraid to challenge batters. In tandem with his live arm, Johnny's proficiency at working the inside of the plate held opposing batters to a .181 average during his rookie campaign.

Ard's tenure in the farm system will likely focus on the development of an offspeed pitch. However, with smooth mechanics that belie his size, Johnny shouldn't have much difficulty. He could reach the major leagues by 1991.

height	weight	bats	throws	birthplace	birthdate
6'5"	220	R	R	Las Vegas, NV	6/1/67

year	team	league	g	ip	h	so	bb	gs	cg	sho	sv	w	l	era
1988	Elizabethton	APP	9	59	40	71	26	8	1	1	0	4	1	1.97
1988	Kenosha	MWL	4	26	14	16	4	3	1	0	0	3	0	1.05
1989	Visalia	CAL	28	186	155	153	84	28	4	0	0	13	7	3.29

Willie Banks
Pitcher

The 1987 Gatorade High School Player of the Year and the Twins' number-one selection in that summer's free agent draft, and the third overall, Willie has made great strides in his three professional campaigns. Not only has he shown his expected potential as a power pitcher, but Banks has improved his mechanics and control more quickly than the club anticipated. From a previous average of nearly 8 walks per 9 innings, Willie dropped to a norm of 4.5 in 1989, while maintaining his status as a strikeout artist.

When Banks gets the ball over the plate, he's dominating. His fastball has been clocked at speeds of anywhere from 95-100 mph and his curve breaks sharply enough to handcuff even the best hitters. If that weren't enough, Willie began working on a straight change in 1989.

Banks is only twenty years old, and Minnesota won't rush the young right-hander into the big leagues. More likely, he will begin the 1990 campaign at Class AA Orlando. Within two years, however, Banks could be the ace of a youthful Twins' rotation.

height	weight	bats	throws	birthplace	birthdate
6'1"	195	R	R	Jersey City, NJ	2/27/69

year	team	league	g	ip	h	so	bb	gs	cg	sho	sv	w	l	era
1987	Elizabethton	APP	13	66	73	71	62	13	0	0	0	1	8	6.99
1988	Kenosha	MWL	24	124	109	113	107	24	0	0	0	10	10	3.73
1989	Visalia	CAL	27	174	122	173	85	27	7	4	0	12	9	2.59
1989	Orlando	SL	1	7	10	9	0	1	0	0	0	1	0	5.14

Derek Parks
Catcher

The past two seasons have been a major disappointment for Derek. After an outstanding campaign at Kenosha in 1987, he struggled offensively in his first encounter with Double A pitching in Orlando in 1988 and went down with an injury after only 90 at bats last year. A former number-one draft choice in 1986, Parks must still be considered among the Twins' top prospects, however. He is a powerful young catcher with the tools to be an impact player on the major league level.

Offensively, Derek's only trouble has been making consistent contact. When he does catch the ball squarely, it jumps off his bat. His strong wrists and long swing generate tremendous bat speed through the hitting zone and Parks may one day be a big run-producer. Defensively, this twenty-one-year-old has the makings of a solid backstop. His arm is on par, or better than, most big league catchers and his build suggests a durable performer. Minnesota will probably allow Derek two more full seasons at the minor league level to shorten his stroke and learn to hit breaking pitches more consistently.

height	weight	bats	throws	birthplace	birthdate
6'0"	200	R	R	Covina, CA	9/29/68

year	team	league	g	ab	r	h	2b	3b	hr	rbi	sb	bb	so	avg
1986	Elizabethton	APP	62	224	39	53	10	1	10	40	1	23	58	.237
1987	Kenosha	MWL	129	466	70	115	19	2	24	94	1	77		.247
1988	Orlando	SL	118	400	52	94	15	0	7	42	1	49	81	.235
1989	Orlando	SL	31	95	16	18	3	0	2	10	1	19	27	.189

Paul Sorrento
Outfield/First Base

Originally the fourth round pick of the California Angels in 1986, Sorrento came to the Minnesota organization in the Bert Blyleven deal last winter. His first season in the Twins' farm system produced a Southern League All-Star selection, as he led the circuit in both home runs and RBIs while playing for Orlando. The Florida State product has hit more than 50 round trippers and driven in nearly 300 runs as a pro.

As his home run totals suggest, Paul is a tremendously powerful hitter. He can hit the ball out to any field and feasts on fastballs. Like many young power hitters, however, Sorrento is prone to the strikeout. He has been sent back to the dugout on strikes an average of once in every 4.5 at bats during his career. Hard work with minor league batting instructors last year taught Paul to take the ball up the middle more often and he should make more consistent contact in 1990.

The Twins will need to find a place for Sorrento to play in the field unless they want to make him a DH. He was an outfielder both in college and with the Angel organization, but looks more comfortable around first base. But, with Kent Hrbek as a solid incumbent, Paul may have to ply his trade with bat alone.

height	weight	bats	throws	birthplace	birthdate
6'2"	210	L	R	Somerville, MA	11/17/65

year	team	league	g	ab	r	h	2b	3b	hr	rbi	sb	bb	so	avg
1986	Quad Cities	MWL	53	177	33	63	11	2	6	34	0	24	40	.356
1986	Palm Springs	CAL	16	62	5	15	3	0	1	7	0	4	15	.242
1987	Palm Springs	CAL	114	370	66	83	14	2	8	45	1	78	95	.224
1988	Palm Springs	CAL	133	465	91	133	30	6	14	99	3	110	101	.286
1989	Orlando	SL	140	509	81	130	35	2	27	112	1	84	119	.255
1989	Minnesota	AL	14	21	2	5	0	0	0	1	0	5	4	.238

Signed as a free agent in 1985 by Twins' scouts in his native Venezuela, Rafael has consistently been singled out by managers as one of the top prospects in his league both as a hitter and outfielder during a four-year minor league career. As a member of the 1988 Orlando Twins, DeLima finished second in the Southern League in hits and batting, led all outfielders with a .985 fielding percentage and earned a selection to the year-end All-Star squad. He has adjusted quickly to higher levels within the farm system each year and could find himself on the major league roster to open the 1990 season.

As one of the fastest players in the Minnesota organization, Rafael should benefit from playing on the artificial surface of the Metrodome. He makes good contact by hitting down on the ball and his occasional gap power could mean plenty of doubles and triples. With his speed, scouts feel that DeLima would be wasted anywhere but center field. He has good instincts breaking back on the ball and an above-average arm. However, with Kirby Puckett firmly entrenched as the starter at that position, Rafael will get his shot in right.

Rafael DeLima
Outfield

height	weight	bats	throws	birthplace	birthdate
5'11"	175	L	L	Valencia, Venezuela	12/21/67

year	team	league	g	ab	r	h	2b	3b	hr	rbi	sb	bb	so	avg
1986	Kenosha	MWL	20	35	2	1	0	0	0	0	0	4	11	.029
1986	Elizabethton	APP	49	136	20	31	7	0	2	21	1	30	26	.228
1987	Kenosha	MWL	131	494	75	135	24	9	9	65	12	86	77	.273
1988	Orlando	SL	137	500	66	143	25	3	3	46	29	77	88	.286
1989	Portland	PCL	127	464	54	127	19	3	3	33	18	37	79	.274

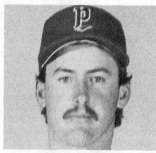

Selected by Minnesota in the fourth round of the June 1986 draft, Mike is a former winner of the Sherry Robertson Award—denoting the organization's Minor League Player of the Year—who reached the major leagues for the first time last year. Though his late season starts were limited, due to the acquisitions of Dave West and Rick Aguilera from the Mets, Dyer pitched well enough that he should earn a return trip to Minneapolis for the 1990 campaign.

Mike has been a starter throughout his four years in professional baseball. However, with a solid three-pitch repertoire and a three-quarters delivery that hides the ball well from hitters, he could just as easily be converted to middle relief. Dyer throws a fastball in the high 80 mph range, that looks faster when teamed with his excellent breaking pitch. His style is to move the ball in and out and constantly vary the speed of his pitches. This formula brought Dyer good success in the farm system and should keep him in the big leagues for many years to come.

Mike Dyer
Pitcher

height	weight	bats	throws	birthplace	birthdate
6'3"	195	R	R	Upland, CA	9/8/66

year	team	league	g	ip	h	so	bb	gs	cg	sho	sv	w	l	era
1986	Elizabethton	APP	14	72	70	62	42	14	3	1	0	5	7	3.48
1987	Kenosha	MWL	27	167	124	163	84	27	2	0	0	16	5	3.07
1988	Orlando	SL	27	162	155	125	86	27	3	0	0	11	13	3.94
1989	Portland	PCL	15	89	80	63	51	15	2	0	0	3	6	4.43
1989	Minnesota	AL	16	71	74	37	37	12	1	0	0	4	7	4.82

Minnesota fans who like Wally Backman will love this young University of Arizona product. A former Academic All-American and Pac-10 Southern Division co-MVP in 1987, Hale is a down-and-dirty scrapper with an outstanding attitude and work ethic. Chip was drafted in the seventeenth round of the June 1987 free agent affair and won the Midwest League batting title in his first professional season with a mark of .345. Although he's been unable to match that lofty standard in his past two campaigns, with a solid contact stroke, Hale projects as a .280 hitter with some power on the major league level.

Chip Hale
Second Base

Chip does not have the great speed, awesome power, or outstanding glove work of some of the other top prospects, but he is a solid fundamental ball player who'll play steady defense and provide leadership on the field for many years to come. He has a strong, accurate arm and can turn the double play as well as anyone. At twenty-six years old, Hale has nothing left to prove in the farm system. Look for him to challenge Backman for the starting job this spring and to open the season with the Twins.

height	weight	bats	throws	birthplace	birthdate
5'10"	180	L	R	Santa Clara, CA	2/16/64

year	team	league	g	ab	r	h	2b	3b	hr	rbi	sb	bb	so	avg
1987	Kenosha	MWL	87	339	65	117	12	7	7	65	3	33	26	.345
1988	Orlando	SL	133	482	62	126	19	1	11	65	8	64	31	.261
1989	Portland	PCL	108	411	49	112	16	9	2	34	3	35	55	.273
1989	Minnesota	AL	28	67	6	14	3	0	0	4	0	1	6	.209

The MVP of the Ohio State baseball team in his senior season and a five-sport star at National Trail High School in Dayton, Ohio, Park was selected by Minnesota in the fourth round of June 1986 free agent draft. Although he's posted only one winning season in four years as a professional, Pittman has shown the potential to be a dominant right-handed starter. On average, he has allowed only 6.5 hits and struck out over 10 batters per 9 innings of work.

Park Pittman
Pitcher

Park throws three top-notch pitches: a straight change-up, big-breaking curve and a fastball that consistently hits 90 mph. When throwing strikes, Pittman seems nearly unhittable. His problem, however, has been finding the plate on a regular basis. His average of almost 7 walks per game leaves plenty of room for improvement, and it was the major reason for a second season at the Double A level in 1989.

Work on Park's mechanics is progressing, but he will not make it in the major leagues without improved consistency and control. He pitched well enough last year to warrant an assignment at Class AAA Portland for the upcoming year, but he may still be a year away from an American League debut.

height	weight	bats	throws	birthplace	birthdate
6'0"	175	R	R	Richmond, IN	8/5/65

year	team	league	g	ip	h	so	bb	gs	cg	sho	sv	w	l	era
1986	Elizabethton	APP	8	44	31	65	23	7	1	0	0	3	1	2.45
1987	Visalia	CAL	31	162	109	198	137	29	1	0	0	4	12	3.17
1988	Orlando	SL	24	104	73	103	84	18	1	0	0	8	7	3.82
1989	Orlando	SL	34	102	82	103	72	15	0	0	11	5	9	4.59

Larry Casian
Pitcher

A teammate of Cubs' prospect Mike Harkey at Cal State-Fullerton, Larry was a second team All-American and PCAC Player of the Year in 1987. He was selected in the sixth round of the June free agent draft that same year and posted a fine 10-3 mark for Visalia in the California League in his first season as a professional. 1988 saw the young left-hander lead his Orlando club in ERAs, and in complete games and innings pitched en route to a Southern League All-Star selection.

Although Casian struck out nearly one batter per inning pitched in 1987, he is not a power pitcher. He relies more on mixing up his pitches, hitting spots in the strike zone, and on varying speeds than on blowing a fastball by hitters. What Larry does have is a fine four-pitch repertoire—a mid 80s fastball, a tight curve, a slider and a change-up—and an excellent competitive nature. Casian's superb concentration and his fine pickoff move display the typical way in which he succeeds. While Larry may start the 1990 campaign in Portland for the second time, he should see some major league action this summer.

height	weight	bats	throws	birthplace	birthdate
6'0"	170	R	L	Lynwood, CA	10/28/65

year	team	league	g	ip	h	so	bb	gs	cg	sho	sv	w	l	era
1987	Visalia	CAL	18	97	89	96	49	15	2	1	2	10	3	2.51
1988	Orlando	SL	27	174	165	103	62	26	4	1	0	9	9	2.95
1988	Portland	PCL	1	3	5	0	0	0	0	0	0	0	1	0.00
1989	Portland	PCL	28	169	201	65	63	27	0	0	0	7	12	4.52

Paul Abbott
Pitcher

Another hard-throwing right-hander in the vein of Park Pittman, Paul became the Twins' third round selection in the June 1985 draft after taking honors as the Orange County Player of the Year in his senior year at Sunny Hills High School in Fullerton, California. With three winning campaigns and a strikeout title to his credit in five professional seasons, Abbott should be in Minnesota's future plans.

Numbers don't lie, and the facts that Paul held opposing batters to a .198 average at Kenosha in 1987 and that he has averaged over one strikeout per inning throughout his career prove that he can be a dominating force on the mound. His fastball, while only reaching 87-88 mph, is well complemented by a tantalizing offspeed pitch. The combination seems too much for minor league hitters, but he may need the addition of one more pitch before reaching the majors.

As with many young hurlers, Abbott needs work on his control. He showed enough improvement in 1989 to earn a spot in Portland for the upcoming season, but will not be considered for a position on the Twins' staff until his walks-to-innings-pitched ratio drops further.

height	weight	bats	throws	birthplace	birthdate
6'2"	175	R	R	Van Nuys, CA	9/15/67

year	team	league	g	ip	h	so	bb	gs	cg	sho	sv	w	l	era
1985	Elizabethton	APP	10	35	33	34	32	10	1	0	0	1	5	6.94
1986	Kenosha	MWL	25	98	102	73	73	15	1	0	0	6	10	4.50
1987	Kenosha	MWL	26	145	102	138	103	25	1	0	0	13	6	3.65
1988	Visalia	CAL	28	172	141	205	143	28	4	2	0	11	9	4.18
1989	Orlando	SL	17	90	71	102	48	17	1	0	0	9	3	4.37

Draft Analysis

Top Ten Picks:
1. Chuck Knoblauch, Shortstop (Texas A&M University)
2. John Gumph, Outfield (Poly High School, Riverside, CA)
3. Denny Neagle, Left-hand Pitcher (University of Minnesota)
4. Scott Erikson, Right-hand Pitcher (University of Arizona)
5. Jay Richardson, Outfield (Northside High School, Ft. Smith, AR)
6. Ken Norman, Outfield (Sweetwater High School, Sweetwater, TX)
7. Ray Ortiz, Outfield, (Oklahoma State University)
8. Jeff Thelen, Right-hand Pitcher (Craig High School, Janesville, WI)
9. Troy Buckley, Catcher (Santa Clara University)
10. Martin Cordova, Third Base (Orange Coast Junior College)

In recent years, most of the Twins' top prospects have been pitchers. The 1989 draft changed that trend. Of the club's fifty-nine selections, only nineteen were hurlers and only three of them were picked in the first ten rounds. Instead, Minnesota moved to replenish their stock of offensive firepower and find a solid catching prospect. Thirteen picks were spent on backstops and three of them reached the Class A level last summer—Ken Briggs, Todd Logan and Joe Siwa. The club got speed in Ken Norman, solid defense in Chuck Knoblauch and power in Martin Cordova (8 HRs and 29 RBIs in 38 games).

Even though the focus of the Twins' draft was not pitching, these pitchers they did pick performed well. Third and fourth round selections Denny Neagle and Scott Erickson combined for a 9-6 mark in limited action as first-year pros, and each notched better than one strikeout per inning. They look like the type of strong-armed peformers this organization favors.

Overall, this was a very balanced draft for Minnesota. Thirty-nine of their picks came from college programs and several could appear on the club's list of top prospects next year.

CHICAGO WHITE SOX

1989 Farm System Record
403-290 (.582)

Vancouver	PCL	AAA	73	69	.514
Birmingham	SL	AA	88	55	.615
South Bend	MWL	A	85	47	.644
Sarasota	FSL	A	79	57	.581
Utica	NYP	A	39	39	.500
Sarasota	GCL	Rookie	39	23	.629

The Chicago White Sox have demonstrated that winning in the minor leagues does not necessarily mean a team has a strong system. The Palehose's affiliates posted the top winning percentage in all of baseball last summer; yet, the club is widely considered to have the least amount of talent in the game. Once past the top prospects, Chicago has little depth at any position. They need middle infielders, catching prospects and more live arms.

The White Sox did pick up two solid prospects from Texas last summer, however. Left-hander Wilson Alvarez became the first player born in the 1970s to appear in the big leagues and outfielder Sam Sosa looks like the genuine article, in addition to Triple A pitcher Tom Drees. Drees turned in three no-hitters over the course of the season, but didn't even earn a call up in September.

The White Sox do have several young players on the rise. The challenge for the organization will be to improve the overall quality of their system before the major league roster grows too old. They should be helped in the next several years with some of the first picks in the draft.

The White Sox' top prospects are:

Robin Ventura	Adam Peterson
Carlos Martinez	Sammy Sosa
Wilson Alvarez	Aubrey Waggoner
Roberto Hernandez	Ed Smith
Ravelo Manzanillo	Brent Knackert

Robin Ventura
Third Base

Chicago's number-one selection in the June 1988 draft, and the tenth player picked overall, Ventura first earned national recognition with a 58-game hitting streak while a junior at Oklahoma State. That season, Robin hit .391 with 26 home runs and 96 RBIs, earning the 1988 Golden Spikes Award as well as a second All-American distinction. He went on to star for the U.S. Gold Medal Olympic Team before making his professional debut with Birmingham in the Southern League in 1989.

The White Sox feel that Ventura can move through the farm system quickly in light of his solid swing and experience. Patient and relaxed at the plate, Robin's quick wrists and compact stroke produce line drives to all fields. His power to the gaps is not of the home run variety, but should translate into plenty of doubles on the big league level.

In the field, Ventura has the skills to be average or slightly better at third base. First-step quickness, fair range and a solid, accurate arm mean that he makes all the plays that should be made and he does so on a consistent basis. Robin will be an improvement over whoever the White Sox have at third by the time he arrives at Comisky. With his solid 1989 campaign fresh in the minds of management, his arrival could be this year.

height	weight	bats	throws	birthplace	birthdate
6'2"	188	L	R	Santa Maria, CA	7/14/67

year	team	league	g	ab	r	h	2b	3b	hr	rbi	sb	bb	so	avg
1989	Birmingham	SL	129	454	75	126	25	2	3	67	9	93	51	.278
1989	Chicago	AL	16	45	5	8	3	0	0	7	0	8	6	.178

Adam Peterson
Pitcher

Peterson had another outstanding season at Triple A Vancouver in 1989, notching career bests in victories and ERAs. The former Southern League All-Star and Birmingham Pitcher of the Year in 1987 has excelled at every level of the Chicago farm system and should be ready to take his place in the major league rotation this year.

Adam was the White Sox' sixth selection in the June 1984 free agent draft and he has all the tools a successful pitcher could ask for. He throws a nasty hard slider to go with a 90 mph fastball and a change-up that has improved greatly in the past two years. Peterson should be a workhorse for Chicago as well. He usually gets ahead of hitters in the count, keeping his number of pitches-per-inning down.

At twenty-four, this young right-hander has nothing left to prove in the minor leagues. With the crop of young talent acquired by Chicago in the past calendar year, Adam could develop into the ace of an exciting club in the years to come.

height	weight	bats	throws	birthplace	birthdate
6'3"	190	R	R	Long Beach, CA	12/11/65

year	team	league	g	ip	h	so	bb	gs	cg	sho	sv	w	l	era
1986	Peninsula	CAR	24	147	150	84	58	23	1	0	0	9	8	4.58
1986	Birmingham	SL	6	32	34	21	16	5	2	0	0	1	3	4.18
1987	Birmingham	SL	26	171	165	124	73	26	2	0	0	12	9	3.90
1987	Chicago	AL	1	4	8	1	3	1	0	0	0	0	0	13.50
1988	Vancouver	PCL	28	171	161	103	81	28	4	1	0	14	7	3.32
1988	Chicago	AL	2	6	6	5	6	2	0	0	0	0	1	13.50
1989	Vancouver	PCL	25	172	141	116	71	24	6	1	0	14	5	2.72
1989	Chicago	AL	3	5	13	3	2	2	0	0	0	0	1	15.19

Carlos Martinez
Third Base

White Sox fans got their first taste of what young Carlos could do on a baseball field in 1989. Called up from Vancouver in the first half of the season, Martinez hit for a fine average and showed some power potential with a quick, short stroke. He also played a fine defensive third base in his inaugural big league campaign, showing the quickness, range, sure hands and arm that could keep him in the Chicago lineup for a long, long time.

Martinez was among the players acquired by the White Sox in the trade that sent Ron Kittle, Joel Skinner and Wayne Tolleson to the Yankees in 1986. The organization likes Carlos' speed and intensity as well as the fact that his 6'5", 186 lb. frame is still filling out. The only doubts about this young Venezuelan have been his maturity, discipline and conduct. He had several ugly encounters with umpires and fans while playing in the minors, and coaches could rarely get through to him. As long as Carlos can produce on the major league level, however, both he and the White Sox should be happy.

height	weight	bats	throws	birthplace	birthdate
6'5"	186	R	R	La Guaria, Venezuela	8/11/65

year	team	league	g	ab	r	h	2b	3b	hr	rbi	sb	bb	so	avg
1984	Sarasota	GCL	31	91	9	14	1	1	0	4	3	6	15	.154
1985	Ft. Lauderdale	FSL	93	311	39	77	15	7	6	44	8	14	65	.248
1986	Albany	EL	69	253	34	70	18	2	8	39	2	6	46	.277
1986	Buffalo	AA	17	54	6	16	1	0	2	6	0	2	12	.296
1987	Hawaii	PCL	83	304	32	75	15	1	3	36	3	14	50	.247
1987	Birmingham	SL	9	30	2	7	1	0	0	0	2	1	6	.233
1988	Birmingham	SL	133	498	66	138	22	3	14	73	24	36	82	.277
1988	Chicago	AL	77	55	5	9	1	0	0	0	0	0	12	.164
1989	South Bend	MWL	3	11	2	6	3	0	0	3	2	1	1	.545
1989	Vancouver	PCL	18	64	12	25	3	1	2	9	2	5	14	.391
1989	Chicago	AL	109	350	44	105	22	0	5	32	4	21	57	.300

Sammy Sosa
Outfield

Acquired by the White Sox in the trade that sent Harold Baines to Texas, Sammy spent parts of the 1989 season in AA Tulsa, AAA Oklahoma City, Texas, AAA Vancouver and Chicago. Throughout his travels, Sosa put up good numbers and showed the ability to be a big-league-impact player. 1990 will mark his fifth professional season, and the young outfielder should have a regular spot in the White Sox starting lineup.

Sammy's seemingly meteoric rise to stardom is a result of a newfound discipline at the plate. He has the power to drive the ball to the gaps and hit 15-20 home runs per year, as well as the speed to steal 50 or more bases. However, until last season, Sosa had a tendency to chase bad pitches. Being selective and drawing walks will make Sammy an outstanding offensive performer.

There have never been any doubts about Sammy's skills as an outfielder. He has the speed to cover any field, good instincts and one of the best arms in the Chicago organization. With Dave Gallagher firmly entrenched in center field, White Sox fans should look for Sosa to showcase his talents in right field this year.

height	weight	bats	throws	birthplace	birthdate
6'0"	170	R	R	San Pedro de Macoris, Dom. Rep.	11/10/68

year	team	league	g	ab	r	h	2b	3b	hr	rbi	sb	bb	so	avg
1986	Rangers	GCL	61	229	38	63	19	1	4	28	11	22	51	.275
1987	Gastonia	SAL	129	519	73	145	27	4	11	59	22	21	123	.279
1988	Port Charlotte	FSL	131	507	70	116	13	12	9	51	42	35	106	.229
1989	Tulsa	TL	66	273	45	81	15	4	7	31	16	15	52	.297
1989	Vancouver	PCL	13	49	7	18	3	0	1	5	3	7	6	.367
1989	Chicago	AL	58	183	27	47	8	0	4	13	7	11	47	.257

Wilson Alvarez
Pitcher

Another of the prospects received in the Baines deal, Alvarez, at eighteen, was the youngest player to appear in the major leagues last season when he started a game for the Texas Rangers. It was a less than auspicious debut, however, as the young left-hander failed to retire a single batter.

The White Sox are very high on Wilson despite his one pitching setback. He pitched extremely well on the Double A level with both Tulsa and Birmingham and is projected as a number-one or -two big league starter by Chicago. Alvarez is seen as a power pitcher with outstanding control. His fastball moves well and consistently registers in the 88-90 mph range. Aggressive and fearless on the mound, he challenges batters by throwing strikes early in the count and is not afraid to work the inside part of the plate. With these traits, it wouldn't be surprising if Chicago experimented by using Wilson as a closer, out of the bull pen.

Still only nineteen years old, Alvarez is probably one or two years away from a full-time big league assignment. He will probably spend the 1990 season at Class AAA Vancouver, but could see action with the White Sox when the rosters expand in September.

height	weight	bats	throws	birthplace	birthdate
6'1"	175	L	L	Marcaibo, Venezuela	3/24/70

year	team	league	g	ip	h	so	bb	gs	cg	sho	sv	w	l	era
1987	Gastonia	SAL	8	32	39	19	23	6	0	0	0	1	5	6.47
1987	Rangers	GCL	10	45	41	46	21	10	0	0	0	2	5	5.24
1988	Gastonia	SAL	23	127	113	134	50	23	1	0	0	4	11	2.98
1988	Oklahoma City	AA	5	17	17	9	6	3	0	0	0	1	1	3.78
1989	Port Charlotte	FSL	13	81	68	51	21	13	3	2	0	7	4	2.11
1989	Tulsa	TL	7	48	40	29	16	7	1	1	0	2	2	2.06
1989	Texas	AL	1	0	3	0	2	1	0	0	0	0	1	——
1989	Birmingham	SL	6	35	32	18	16	6	0	0	0	2	1	3.03

Aubrey Waggoner
Outfield

In four professional campaigns, Aubrey has made seven stops within the White Sox farm system and sustained two season-ending injuries (1987 with leg problems, 1988 with a broken wrist). Although the lack of continuity and health problems have hampered Waggoner's progress, his immense physical abilities still rank this former 1985 number-five draft pick among the organization's top prospects.

At 5'11" and 170 lbs., Aubrey is as solid as a rock and as fast as any player in the system. Although he's had difficulty making contact at the plate throughout his career, his average did climb last season at Class AA Birmingham, and nearly half of his hits went for extra bases. If Waggoner's bat ever starts meeting the ball consistently, he'll be a top major league run-producer.

On the base paths and in the field, Aubrey is ready for the big leagues now. With speed enough to steal 60-70 bases per season, he can cover enormous amounts of territory in center field and is considered the finest at that position in the entire organization. Waggoner will probably open the 1990 season at Vancouver, but Chisox fans should remember his name.

height	weight	bats	throws	birthplace	birthdate
5'11"	170	L	R	Ft. Worth, TX	12/6/66

year	team	league	g	ab	r	h	2b	3b	hr	rbi	sb	bb	so	avg
1986	Appleton	MWL	60	188	25	34	2	0	3	7	29	23	46	.181
1986	White Sox	GCL	34	81	22	23	3	3	1	12	18	27	13	.284
1986	Peninsula	CAR	20	72	7	14	0	3	0	9	4	14	24	.194
1987	Peninsula	CAR	115	426	82	113	15	4	12	51	51	87	88	.265
1988	Tampa	FSL	43	126	19	28	3	6	3	15	11	21	34	.222
1988	Birmingham	SL	13	40	6	8	2	2	0	1	4	11	11	.200
1989	Birmingham	SL	114	302	66	69	23	6	4	35	25	76	74	.228

Roberto Hernandez
Pitcher

Roberto came to the White Sox from the Angels in exchange for minor league outfielder Mark Davis last August. Originally California's top selection in the June 1986 free agent draft, this big right-hander has the ability to dominate hitters at any level of professional baseball with his three quality pitches. His number-one pitch—a hard, sinking fastball—is nearly unhittable at times and, when complemented by an above-average curve and developing forkball, it can make Hernandez look like Mike Scott.

The problems with Roberto have all been health-related. He has difficulty maintaining his weight (à la Sid Fernandez), and was diagnosed in 1988 as having an arthritic pitching arm. Although doctors have told Roberto that pitching will not further damage his arm, he must still learn to perform with pain in order to be effective. Chisox fans should look for the club to try Hernandez out of the bull pen at Birmingham this season in order to cut down on his innings pitched. He has the tools to be a big league pitcher and, with determination, could make it by 1991.

height	weight	bats	throws	birthplace	birthdate
6'4"	220	R	R	Santurce, PR	11/11/64

year	team	league	g	ip	h	so	bb	gs	cg	sho	sv	w	l	era
1986	Salem	NWL	10	55	57	38	42	10	0	0	0	2	2	4.58
1987	Quad City	MWL	7	21	24	21	12	6	0	0	1	2	3	6.86
1988	Quad City	MWL	24	165	157	114	48	24	6	1	0	9	10	3.17
1988	Midland	TL	3	12	16	7	8	3	0	0	0	0	2	6.57
1989	Palm Springs	CAL	7	42	49	33	16	7	0	0	0	1	4	4.64
1989	Midland	TL	12	64	94	42	30	12	0	0	0	2	7	6.89
1989	South Bend	MWL	4	24	19	17	7	4	0	0	0	1	1	3.33

Ed Smith
Third Base

The White Sox selected Ed in the seventh round of the June 1987 free agent draft for his potential as a power hitter. Still only nineteen years old, Smith checks in at 6'4" and 220 lbs.. Although Ed works hard on his defense and shows good hands and an excellent arm at third base, Robin Ventura should be the Sox regular at that position for years to come. Consequently, coaches have worked long hours with Smith to tighten his swing and improve his level of contact for a possible future as a designated hitter.

In 1989, the dedication began to pay off. Ed more than doubled his previous home run output, increased his percentage of extra-base hits and generally hit the ball harder. Being more selective at the plate boosted Smith's on-base percentage last season as well and he even stole a few bases. The next test will be a Class AA assignment in Birmingham in the Southern League. If Ed's numbers improve this season, he should be on track to make the big leagues in 1992.

height	weight	bats	throws	birthplace	birthdate
6'4"	220	R	R	Trenton, NJ	6/5/69

year	team	league	g	ab	r	h	2b	3b	hr	rbi	sb	bb	so	avg
1987	White Sox	GCL	32	114	10	27	3	0	2	18	3	6	28	.237
1988	South Bend	MWL	130	462	51	107	14	1	3	46	5	51	87	.232
1989	South Bend	MWL	115	382	52	94	20	2	8	49	7	43	84	.246

Ravelo Manzanillo
Pitcher

Manzanillo was discovered by the White Sox while he was pitching in a semi-pro league in the Bronx after a less-than-successful career with the Pirates ended in 1986. Since joining Chicago, however, Ravelo has shown improved command of his pitches and a good, live arm. He finished the 1988 season with two starts in the major leagues and, at twenty-five, he still has a good shot to earn a spot in the Chisox rotation within two years.

Ravelo's trademark is a 94 mph fastball. With it, he led the Florida State League in strikeouts (140) in 1988. In addition to the heater, he throws a good curve and a slider—enough variety to succeed in any league. The one problem Manzanillo needs to correct is a tendency to miss high in the strike zone. No matter how hard a pitcher throws, major league hitters will take the high fastball deep.

1990 should find Ravelo in Vancouver to begin the year, but White Sox fans may see him in Comisky Park before the campaign is over.

height	weight	bats	throws	birthplace	birthdate
5'10"	190	L	L	San Pedro de Macoris, Dom. Rep.	10/17/63

year	team	league	g	ip	h	so	bb	gs	cg	sho	sv	w	l	era
1986	played in the Dominican Summer League													
1987	played in the Dominican Summer League													
1988	Tampa	FSL	24	130	93	140	49	20	2	2	0	10	6	3.04
1988	Chicago	AL	2	9	7	10	12	2	0	0	0	0	1	5.79
1989	Birmingham	SL	22	129	105	89	72	22	2	0	0	8	7	3.90

Brent Knackert
Pitcher

Chicago's second round selection in the June 1987 free agent draft, Brent has been a pleasant surprise for the organization in his first three professional seasons. Still only twenty years old, Knackert has notched better than 25 victories, posted three excellent ERAs and shown outstanding control. This young man knows how to pitch and definitely figures into White Sox plans for the early '90s.

Although not overpowering, Brent's fastball does reach 85-87 mph. What makes him effective is the movement of his pitches. The fastball tails in on right-handed hitters and his tight curve breaks sharply. He will need to develop one or two more pitches during his tenure in the minor leagues, but scouts feel that with his solid mechanics this should be no problem.

1990 will probably find Knackert in Class AA Birmingham. The White Sox won't rush their young prospect, but a pitcher with Brent's poise and attitude tends to open eyes. Don't be surprised to find this young right-hander in Chicago when the rosters expand in September.

height	weight	bats	throws	birthplace	birthdate
6'3"	185	R	R	Huntington, CA	8/1/69

year	team	league	g	ip	h	so	bb	gs	cg	sho	sv	w	l	era
1987	White Sox	GCL	12	73	55	60	15	11	1	0	0	6	2	2.85
1988	Tampa	FSL	23	142	132	78	46	23	4	0	0	10	8	3.17
1989	Sarasota	FSL	35	98	85	80	35	12	2	0	12	8	5	2.94

Draft Analysis

Top Ten Picks:
 1. Frank Thomas, First Base (Auburn University)
 2. Don Sheppard, Outfield (Pittsburg High School, Pittsburg, CA)
 3. Todd Martin, Shortstop (Morehead High School, Eden, NC)
 4. Dan Matznick, Right-hand Pitcher (Sterling High School, Sterling, IL)
 5. Mike Eatinger, Third Base (University of California at Riverside)
 6. John Smith, Right-hand Pitcher (Garrett Community College, Garrett, MD)
 7. Mike Mongiello, Right-hand Pitcher (Fairleigh Dickinson University)
 8. John Sutherland, Right-hand Pitcher (University of California at Los Angeles)
 9. Kevin Tolar, Left-hand Pitcher (Mosley High School, Panama City, FL)
 10. Scotty Pugh, First Base (Cooper High School, Abilene, TX)

The White Sox selected first baseman Frank Thomas with the seventh pick overall last June. He promptly moved through two classifications in 72 professional games on his way to a .296 average. Thomas also showed the expected power from his 6'5" frame with 5 home runs and 41 RBIs. Once past the first round, Chicago looked to add a bit of everything to their existing talent base.

Of primary concern was pitching. Of the forty-three players taken by the Palehose, twenty-five were mound men—twenty right-handers and five lefties. Dan Matznick was the first selected, but Kevin Tolar had the finest pro debut. Tolar went 5-2 with a 1.64 ERA and allowed only 26 hits in 55 innings of work in the Gulf Coast League. Next came eight middle infielders with versatility and speed. Shortstop Todd Martin recorded 10 stolen bases in 23 games in the Gulf Coast League and third baseman Mike Eatinger hit .270 with 28 RBIs and 9 stolen bases in 57 games in a season split between the Gulf Coast League, the Midwest League and the NY-Penn League.

Overall, Chicago did a fine job of addressing the problem areas in their organization. The club's main strength is in the outfield; therefore, only four outfielders were drafted. They picked up needed speed and defense, plenty of live arms and secured one of the top power hitting prospects in the draft.

ST. LOUIS CARDINALS

1989 Farm Systems Record
373-330 (.531)

Louisville	AA	AAA	71	74	.490
Arkansas	TL	AA	79	56	.585
Springfield	MWL	A	41	27	.603
St. Petersburg	FSL	A	75	64	.540
Savannah	SAL	A	37	33	.529
Hamilton	NYP	A	32	44	.421
Johnson City	APPY	Rookie	38	32	.543

The Cardinals were one of the most successful teams of the 1980s. They won with strong pitching, solid defense and outstanding team speed. That formula is unlikely to change in the near future. Most of St. Louis' prospects can run like the wind and field their positions with distinction. The club is grooming successors to Ozzie Smith and Tony Pena, plus they have outfield prospects with some power, and their minor league pitching staffs feature some of the finest young arms in the game.

The value of winning in the minor leagues can not be underestimated as a factor in good player development. Yet, many times, the desire to field a winning club stifles the advancement of young prospects. This has not been the case with the Cardinals. While their much publicized streak of promoting a number-one pick to the major leagues for seven straight seasons did come to an end, contributions came in the form of rookies Tim Jones, Cris Carpenter and Todd Zeile. At Class AA Arkansas, outfielder Ray Lankford posted the highest batting average (.317) and RBI total (98) in the system, while placing in the top five with 11 home runs and 37 stolen bases. The Travelers' 79-56 mark paced the Texas League.

The St. Louis organization is among the finest in the game. They have a top-notch scouting staff, excellent minor league coaching and a patient approach with their prospects. By blending new talent with old in a rational, organized manner, the Cardinals should ensure continued success in the 1990s.

The Cardinals' top prospects are:

Todd Zeile	Ray Lankford
Cris Carpenter	John Ericks
Geronimo Pena	Brian Jordan
Alex Cole	Luis Alicea
Mike Fitzgerald	Brad DuVall

Todd Zeile
Catcher

Todd is one of the brightest catching prospects in the game today. In addition to winning the USA Today Minor League Player of the Year Award in 1989, he has been selected to an All-Star team in each of his four professional campaigns. The Cardinals think so much of their 1986 third round selection that they may deal Tony Pena to get Zeile in the starting lineup this spring.

Defense is the overriding concern behind the plate, perhaps more than at any other position, and Todd has all the tools to be a great catcher. Zeile is very agile at 6'1" and blocks well. He also has an outstanding arm— a fact highlighted by his 38% success rate in throwing out American Association base stealers last year. Moreover, this young receiver also has excellent offensive potential. He hits the ball with power to all fields and should average 20 or more home runs per season with the Cardinals when he learns to handle the outside pitch more consistently.

At twenty-four, Zeile has many productive years ahead of him. He has proven to be a steady, sometimes spectacular, player on the minor league level and should be among the top rookies in the Senior Circuit this season.

height	weight	bats	throws	birthplace	birthdate
6'1"	190	R	R	Van Nuys, CA	9/9/65

year	team	league	g	ab	r	h	2b	3b	hr	rbi	sb	bb	so	avg
1986	Erie	NYP	70	248	40	64	14	1	14	63	5	37	52	.258
1987	Springfield	MWL	130	487	94	142	24	4	25	106	1	70	85	.292
1988	Arkansas	TL	129	430	95	117	33	2	19	75	6	83	64	.272
1989	Louisville	AA	118	453	71	131	26	3	19	85	0	45	78	.289
1989	St. Louis	NL	28	82	7	21	3	1	1	8	0	9	14	.256

Ray Lankford
Outfield

Cut in the mold of Whitey Herzog, Ray is an exciting outfielder with excellent speed and athletic ability. A 1987 third round draft pick, Lankford has earned All-Star honors twice in his three years as a professional and led minor league baseball with 16 triples in 1988. He has shown improvement at each level in the Cardinal farm system and should earn a spot on the Triple A Louisville club for the 1990 campaign.

Although he's only 5'11" and 180 lbs., Ray's good power and speed more than compensate for his size. Over 36% of his hits have gone for extra bases and he's belted 11 home runs in each of the past two seasons. Lankford hits left-handed pitching well enough to stay out of a platoon situation, and he will give St. Louis yet another base-stealing threat.

Defensively, Ray is a solid, dependable outfielder. His arm is strong enough to play either right or center and he has the range to almost cover both positions at the same time. While the outfield situation in St. Louis is crowded, another good offensive season with Louisville could force Lankford into the major league lineup in 1991.

height	weight	bats	throws	birthplace	birthdate
5'11"	180	R	R	Modesto, CA	6/5/67

year	team	league	g	ab	r	h	2b	3b	hr	rbi	sb	bb	so	avg
1987	Johnson City	APP	66	253	45	78	17	4	3	32	14	19	43	.308
1988	Springfield	MWL	135	532	90	151	36	16	11	66	33	60	92	.284
1989	Arkansas	TL	134	498	98	158	28	12	11	98	37	65	57	.317

The Cardinals' number-one selection in the June 1987 free agent draft, Cris came out of the University of Georgia with a long list of accomplishments. He was the MVP of the 1987 Pan Am team, a two-time All-American pitcher and an All-SEC performer in both baseball and football. Carpenter reached the major leagues for brief periods in both of his first two professional seasons and seems to be ready to earn a permanent spot on the St. Louis staff this year.

Cris can be used as either a starter or reliever, and his role may not be defined in the near future. The presence of Todd Worrell in the Cardinal bull pen rules out a right-handed closer's job and Carpenter has never thrown the number of innings that come with a spot in the rotation. Whatever his assignment, this twenty-four-year-old has the pitches to succeed. To go with a moving fastball that reaches nearly 90 mph, Cris throws a tight, biting curve and good change-up. His simple delivery has few, if any, mechanical flaws and he is always around the plate. The manner in which Carpenter challenges batters should make him an effective pitcher in the spacious confines of Busch Stadium.

Cris Carpenter
Pitcher

height	weight	bats	throws	birthplace	birthdate
6'1"	185	R	R	St. Augustine, FL	4/5/65

year	team	league	g	ip	h	so	bb	gs	cg	sho	sv	w	l	era
1988	Louisville	AA	13	87	81	45	26	13	1	1	0	6	2	2.87
1988	St. Louis	NL	8	47	44	38	25	8	1	0	0	2	3	4.72
1989	Louisville	AA	27	36	39	29	9	0	0	0	11	5	3	3.19
1989	St. Louis	NL	36	68	70	35	26	5	0	0	0	4	4	3.18

A number-one selection in 1988 out of the University of Illinois, John has the makings of an outstanding power pitcher. He is a fierce competitor, and at 6'7", he's a menacing figure on the mound, with an explosive fastball that has been clocked at up to 98 mph. In his two professional seasons, Ericks has registered nearly 11 strikeouts per 9 innings pitched and has held opposing batters to an average of less than .180. He will most likely spend the 1990 campaign with Class AA Arkansas.

The difficulty for John has been a lack of consistency. His losses are often the result of too many free passes—an average of 5.54 walks per 9 innings—and he needs to mix in more offspeed pitches to be effective at higher levels of the organization. Ericks' mechanics are good for a pitcher of his size; however, smoothing them out will be the club's main concern over the next two years. With the best fastball in the system and a rapidly improving change-up, John could be a force in the major leagues by 1992.

John Ericks
Pitcher

height	weight	bats	throws	birthplace	birthdate
6'7"	215	R	R	Oak Lawn, IL	9/16/67

year	team	league	g	ip	h	so	bb	gs	cg	sho	sv	w	l	era
1988	Johnson City	APP	9	41	27	41	27	9	1	0	0	3	2	3.73
1989	Savannah	SAL	28	167	90	211	101	28	1	0	0	11	10	2.04

Geronimo Pena
Second Base

Signed by the Cardinals as a free agent in August of 1984, the twenty-three-year-old Pena increased his stock as a prospect with a fine performance at Class AA Arkansas in 1989. In addition to raising his average nearly 40 points from his previous campaign, Geronimo showed a great deal of patience at the plate as well as some surprising power. Although he may begin the 1990 season back in the Texas League, Pena should wind up in Triple A Louisville before the year is out.

Offensively, Geronimo is a typical Cardinal player. He is a switch-hitter with outstanding speed—4.1 seconds to first base from the right side and 3.9 from the left—good bunting ability, and line drive power to the alleys. A true base stealer, Pena's 80 thefts in 1987 were the most in the minor leagues and second in the organization.

In the field, this young Dominican has good range and sure hands. His size and strength should make Pena a durable performer, and combined with his strong arm, they allow him to turn the double play effectively. Cardinal fans should look for Geronimo to compete for a starting job in 1991 or 1992.

height	weight	bats	throws	birthplace	birthdate
6'1"	170	B	R	Distrito Nacional, Dom. Rep.	3/29/67

year	team	league	g	ab	r	h	2b	3b	hr	rbi	sb	bb	so	avg
1986	Johnson City	APP	56	202	55	60	7	4	3	20	26	46	34	.297
1987	Savannah	SAL	134	505	95	136	28	3	9	51	79	73	98	.269
1988	St. Petersburg	FSL	130	484	82	125	25	10	4	35	35	88	103	.258
1989	St. Petersburg	FSL	6	21	2	4	1	0	0	2	2	3	6	.190
1989	Arkansas	TL	77	267	61	79	16	8	9	44	14	38	68	.296

Brian Jordan
Outfield

One of two 1988 first round selections received by St. Louis for the loss of free agent Jack Clark, Brian could develop into a solid all-around big league outfielder if the organization can keep him from playing football. Jordan has missed much of his first two seasons due to football related injuries and NFL training camp, but he's been outstanding in limited duty. His career average stands at .325 and Brian has hit one home run for every 19 at bats.

Jordan is a switch-hitter who generates plenty of bat speed from either side of the plate with his powerful upper body and quick wrists. A cornerback and kick-return man with the University of Richmond, Brian has good speed and is capable of stealing 20 or more bases in a season. He's solid defensively, has outstanding range, fine instincts and a strong throwing arm.

If the Cardinals are to lure Jordan away from the NFL, it may have to be done with the promise of life in the big leagues. Although he's not ready to make the jump from Single A to the Cardinals, St. Louis may try Brian at the Triple A level this season.

height	weight	bats	throws	birthplace	birthdate
6'0"	185	B	R	Baltimore, MD	3/29/67

year	team	league	g	ab	r	h	2b	3b	hr	rbi	sb	bb	so	avg
1988	Hamilton	NYP	19	71	12	22	3	1	4	12	3	6	15	.310
1989	St. Petersburg	FSL	11	43	7	15	4	1	2	11	0	0	8	.349

Alex Cole
Outfield

Selected by the Cardinals in the second round of the June 1985 free agent draft, Alex eclipsed the 40 stolen base mark for the fifth time in as many seasons last year. He has the impressive speed—9.3 in the 100-yard dash—and technique to join the "Running Redbirds", and showed enough improvement at the plate in 1989 to warrant a long look this spring.

There has never been any doubt about Cole's ability to run or play defense. His excellent range in center field and his strong, accurate arm have kept him among his league's leaders in assists each year. If there is one statistic that will dictate Alex's success, it's on-base percentage. Last year with Louisville, he reached base at a .379 clip and should hold a job in the big leagues if that pace can be maintained. But Cole has never filled out like the organization hoped he would and looks like a singles hitter all the way.

Alex will turn twenty-five in August. He has proven himself in the minor leagues and deserves a shot at the big time. If there is no room in the Cardinal outfield he could be offered in a trade.

height	weight	bats	throws		birthplace		birthdate	
6'2"	175	L	L		Fayetteville, NC		8/17/65	

year	team	league	g	ab	r	h	2b	3b	hr	rbi	sb	bb	so	avg
1985	Johnson City	APP	66	232	60	61	5	1	1	13	46	30	27	.263
1986	St. Petersburg	FSL	74	286	76	98	9	1	0	26	56	54	37	.343
1986	Louisville	AA	63	200	25	50	2	4	1	16	24	17	30	.250
1987	Arkansas	TL	125	477	68	122	12	4	2	27	68	44	55	.256
1988	Louisville	AA	120	392	43	91	7	8	0	24	40	42	59	.232
1989	St. Petersburg	FSL	8	32	2	6	0	0	0	1	4	3	7	.188
1989	Louisville	AA	127	455	75	128	5	5	2	29	47	71	76	.281

Luis Alicea
Second Base

Alicea may not be as productive offensively as fellow second base prospect Geronimo Pena, but he has the excellent defensive skills that made him a number-one pick in the June 1985 draft. Luis spent the 1989 campaign with Triple A Louisville after a disappointing performance with the major league club the previous summer. Although his average dipped nearly 30 points in 1989, Alicea showed a more aggressive attitude at the plate and posted career-high power figures.

Luis has a solid swing and line drive power to the alleys. Although Alicea is strong enough to turn on the inside pitch and hit an occasional home run, he must hit the ball on the ground more often to be effective. He's a heads-up runner with base stealing speed and makes enough contact to hit near the top of the order.

In the field, Luis is smooth and graceful. He has an accurate arm and turns the double play as well as anyone. This twenty-four- year-old should be given the chance to earn a major league job in the spring.

height	weight	bats	throws		birthplace		birthdate	
5'9"	165	B	R		Santorce, PR		7/29/65	

year	team	league	g	ab	r	h	2b	3b	hr	rbi	sb	bb	so	avg
1986	Erie	NYP	47	163	40	46	6	1	3	18	27	37	20	.282
1986	Arkansas	TL	25	68	8	16	3	0	0	3	0	5	11	.235
1987	Arkansas	TL	101	337	57	91	14	3	4	47	13	49	28	.270
1987	Louisville	AA	29	105	18	32	10	2	2	20	4	9	9	.305
1988	Louisville	AA	49	191	21	53	11	6	1	21	8	11	21	.277
1988	St. Louis	NL	93	297	20	63	10	4	1	24	1	25	32	.212
1989	Louisville	AA	124	412	53	102	20	3	8	48	13	59	55	.248

Mike Fitzgerald
First Base/Catcher

In the two seasons since Mike led the Texas League with 108 RBIs, he has not shown the kind of offensive production needed to warrant a big league job. The Cardinals' first selection in the secondary phase of the June 1984 draft, Fitzgerald opened his professional career by leading the Appalachian League with a .345 average and followed up with four solid seasons. His recent tailspin may be attributable more to the presence of both catcher Todd Zeile and first baseman Pedro Guerrero ahead of him than to the improved Triple A pitching Mike's had to face.

Fitzgerald does have the power potential and solid stroke needed to be an impact player on the major league level, but he must learn more patience at the plate. He tends to chase balls out of the strike zone. Defensively, Mike is primarily a first baseman currently. He made the switch in 1987 and seems to have the work ethic needed to overcome his lack of natural ability at the position. The Cardinals will no doubt give Fitzgerald another season at Louisville in 1990. However, if the club is not in a pennant race in September, he should get the call up then.

height	weight	bats	throws	birthplace	birthdate
6'1"	200	R	R	Savannah, GA	3/28/64

year	team	league	g	ab	r	h	2b	3b	hr	rbi	sb	bb	so	avg
1984	Johnson City	APP	51	171	31	59	11	0	7	31	2	18	25	.345
1985	Springfield	MWL	113	413	58	105	21	0	16	62	1	32	64	.254
1986	Springfield	MWL	126	498	74	148	30	4	19	93	1	19	90	.297
1987	Arkansas	TL	126	447	72	128	36	4	27	108	3	35	94	.286
1988	Louisville	AA	106	382	33	92	14	1	10	50	1	12	69	.241
1988	St. Louis	NL	13	46	4	9	1	0	0	1	0	0	9	.196
1989	Louisville	AA	103	343	22	75	13	0	7	38	0	10	47	.219

Brad DuVall
Pitcher

DuVall signed with St. Louis as the club's first pick in the June 1988 free agent draft. Just one year earlier, he passed up an opportunity to play for Baltimore when that team drafted him number-one. Now a veteran of two professional campaigns, Brad must begin to live up to his advance billing. His composite record is only 5-8 and he's issued 107 bases-on-balls in 142 innings pitched.

Despite DuVall's unimpressive figures, the Cardinals have enough confidence in their young right-hander to give him a shot at Class AA this spring, but will be watching his progress closely. Brad has an exceptionally lively 90 mph fastball and a fine hard slider, but he tends to nibble at the corners of the plate. The organization's minor league pitching instructors will undoubtably work with DuVall on the art of throwing inside and challenging hitters. A tougher attitude and the development of a reliable offspeed pitch could make Brad a big winner at any level.

height	weight	bats	throws	birthplace	birthdate
6'1"	185	R	R	Oxford, MS	5/17/66

year	team	league	g	ip	h	so	bb	gs	cg	sho	sv	w	l	era
1988	Hamilton	NYP	13	76	63	58	40	13	0	0	0	3	3	3.54
1989	Springfield	MWL	13	66	61	49	38	13	0	0	0	2	5	3.95

Draft Analysis

Top Ten Picks:

1. Paul Coleman, Outfield (Frankston High School, Frankston, TX)
2. Mike Milchin, Left-hand Pitcher (Clemson University)
3. Tripp Cromer, Shortstop (University of South Carolina)
4. John Farrell, Outfield/Catcher (Sandalwood High School, Jacksonville, FL)
5. Tony Ochs, Catcher (Memphis State University)
6. Todd Steverson, Outfield (Culver City High School, Venice CA)
7. Tracey Ealy, Outfield (Chaparral High School, Las Vegas, NV)
8. Anthony Lewis, Outfield (Rancho High School, Las Vegas, NV)
9. Jeff Fayne, Outfield (Munford High School, Brighton, TN)
10. John Dempsey, Catcher (Crespi High School, Agoura, CA)

With the sixth overall selection in the draft, St. Louis took outfielder Paul Coleman. While this young man has the speed to fit nicely into the Cardinal game plan, he also has enough power to stand apart from the crowd. As a high school senior, Coleman hit .510 with 7 home runs and 27 RBIs in only 49 at bats. Granted, his performance last summer in the Appalachian League didn't meet these standards (.233, 3 HRs and 24 RBIs), yet, Paul could be a major league impact player within three years.

The remainder of the club's top ten choices also concentrated mainly on outfielders. Tracey Ealy and Anthony Lewis showed offensive promise at St. Louis' Arizona League affiliate, while Jeff Fayne struggled some-what at Johnson City. The big disappointment, however, was the failure to sign Todd Steverson. The Cardinals took a chance on Steverson despite his stated intention to honor a commitment to Arizona State. The gamble didn't pay off.

Among the Cardinals' other top choices, pitcher Mike Milchin was impressive in a split-season with Hamilton and Springfield. Despite a 4-4 record, Milchin recorded a 2.16 ERA and struck out 90 batters in only 83.1 innings. Overall, St. Louis selected fifty-six players—twenty-seven pitchers, fifteen outfielders, eight catchers and six infielders. Twenty-two came from the high school ranks.

CHICAGO CUBS

1989 Farm System Record

404-435 (.482)

Iowa	AA	AAA	62	82	.431
Charlotte	SL	AA	70	73	.490
Winston-Salem	CAR	A	64	71	.474
Peoria	MWL	A	80	59	.576
Charleston (W.Va.)	SAL	A	58	76	.433
Geneva	NYP	A	36	39	.480
Wytheville	APPY	Rookie	34	35	.493

Chicago's success in 1989 was largely due to the contributions of rookies Jerome Walton, Dwight Smith, Joe Girardi and Rick Wrona. All four are home-grown products and represent a new wave of talent sweeping into the Windy City. The strength of this farm system is in the speed and defense evident at the outfield positions, plus the tremendous depth behind the plate. In fact, Girardi and Wrona may not even be the best of Chicago's catching prospects. Rick Wilkins and Kelly Mann are waiting in the wings and Damon Berryhill is already a proven big league performer. With the relative dearth of catching prospects elsewhere in baseball, the Cubs will be in a strong position when it comes time to trade for infield or pitching help.

At this point, there is an excellent base of talent in the Cubs' minor league system; due in a large part to Gordon Goldsberry—the former V.P. of Minor Leagues and Scouting. But, with Goldsberry ousted at the request of Jim Frey, it remains to be seen whether or not Chicago has the administrative personnel to prosper.

The key prospects for the Cubs are Ty Griffin and Mike Harkey. Griffin is an essential element in Chicago's infield plans and Harkey is coming off a disappointing, injury-riddled 1989 campaign. Big things are expected of each player, but there is little hope of help from either player anytime soon.

The Cubs' top prospects are:

Ty Griffin	Rick Wilkins
Mike Harkey	Derrick May
Frank Castillo	Joe Girardi
Shawn Boskie	Kelly Mann
Doug Dascenzo	Laddie Renfroe

The Cubs' need for a regular third baseman places Griffin at the top of their prospect list. Whether he plays at second base and Ryne Sandberg moves to third or vice versa, Ty's exciting game of baseball will be a welcome addition in Wrigley Field. An All-American at Georgia Tech University and the catalyst of the 1988 U.S. Olympic team, this twenty-two-year-old was selected in the first round of the June 1988 draft, and ninth overall. After a fine start in Peoria, Griffin earned a promotion to Class AA Charlotte during his first season as a professional, and he could reach the Triple A level this year.

Ty Griffin
Third Base/Second Base/ Shortstop

Ty is a switch-hitter with line drive abilities from both sides of the plate. The organization was pleasantly surprised by his show of power last season—Griffin could hit as many as 20 home runs per season in Chicago. His main offensive asset, however, is speed. He can take the extra base and has the technique to steal upwards of 50 bases per year. Defensively, Griffin's range is better suited to third base than second, and questions remain about the strength of his arm. His progress in the field will dictate how quickly Ty reaches the majors.

height	weight	bats	throws	birthplace	birthdate
6'0"	185	B	R	Fort Campbell, KY	9/5/67

year	team	league	g	ab	r	h	2b	3b	hr	rbi	sb	bb	so	avg
1989	Peoria	MWL	82	296	45	85	15	6	10	64	16	49	74	.287
1989	Charlotte	SL	45	143	25	33	6	0	3	21	8	25	29	.231

In most other ballclubs, Wilkins would be a likely candidate for the starting catcher's role within two years. However, at that same position are fellow left-handed hitter Damon Berryhill in Chicago and two other solid prospects; thus Rick will have to work hard to earn a Cubs' uniform. A twenty-third round pick out of Florida Junior College in 1986, Wilkins has shown good power and defensive skills in three seasons at Class A and he should move up to Double A Charlotte in 1990.

Offensively, Rick has a quick, strong swing and loves to hit fastballs. He is still learning to wait on breaking pitches and tends to be a bit selective at the plate, but he could be a big run-producer if he finds a comfort zone. Behind the plate, Wilkins provides a good target at 6'2", 210 lbs., and will be a durable performer.

Rick Wilkins
Catcher

His outstanding agility is courtesy of a high school All-State wrestling career; balls in the dirt rarely get by him and Rick has a quick, accurate throw to second base. If Wilkins can't crack the Cubs' lineup, he will certainly play elsewhere in the major leagues.

height	weight	bats	throws	birthplace	birthdate
6'2"	210	L	R	unknown	6/4/67

year	team	league	g	ab	r	h	2b	3b	hr	rbi	sb	bb	so	avg
1987	Geneva	NYP	75	243	35	61	8	2	8	43	7	58	40	.251
1988	Peoria	MWL	137	490	54	119	30	1	8	63	4	67	110	.243
1989	Winston-Salem	CAR	132	445	61	111	24	1	12	54	6	50	87	.249

Mike Harkey
Pitcher

The fourth player chosen in the June 1987 draft, Mike was to have earned a spot in the major league rotation last year. Instead, he suffered an injury-riddled season that saw him throw in only 12 games at Class AAA Iowa. Harkey had tendonitis in his right shoulder in April and twisted his left knee in late June. He underwent arthroscopic surgery on the knee and now the club feels Mike will be ready to pitch in the big leagues this summer.

At 6'5", Mike is an intimidating figure on the mound and throws as hard as any pitcher in baseball. His riding fastball has been clocked anywhere from 95-100 mph and he throws a slider of nearly 90 mph. With these two pitches, Harkey averages 6.6 strikeouts per 9 innings and forces many weak ground balls. If his change-up develops to average major league quality, he could be almost unhittable. While there has been some question about his control, the important factor in Harkey's future is whether or not he will fully recover from his 1989 injuries.

height	weight	bats	throws	birthplace	birthdate
6'5"	210	R	R	San Diego, CA	10/25/66

year	team	league	g	ip	h	so	bb	gs	cg	sho	sv	w	l	era
1987	Peoria	MWL	12	76	81	48	28	12	3	0	0	2	3	3.55
1987	Pittsfield	EL	1	2	1	2	0	0	0	0	0	0	0	0.00
1988	Pittsfield	EL	13	86	66	73	35	13	3	1	0	9	2	1.37
1988	Iowa	AA	12	79	55	62	33	12	3	1	0	7	2	3.55
1988	Chicago	NL	5	35	33	18	15	5	0	0	0	0	3	2.60
1989	Iowa	AA	12	63	67	37	25	12	0	0	0	2	7	4.43

Derrick May
Outfield

Selected by Chicago in the first round of the June 1986 draft, and the ninth player overall, Derrick has compiled a .302 average in three-and-a-half professional seasons. He is a big, strong, athletic twenty-one year old who should develop into a fine everyday player along the lines of his father, Dave, who was a twelve-year major leaguer. After consecutive All-Star campaigns at Winston-Salem and Charlotte, May should get his first taste of Class AAA action at Iowa this year.

Offensively, Derrick can do more than hit for average. He is still maturing physically and has only begun to show the 20-25 home run power that scouts insist is there. May sprays line drives to all parts of the field and has the speed to stretch many of them into extra-base hits. The poise that he shows at the plate and on the base paths, carries over to Derrick's defense as well. He studies hitters, positions himself well, gets a good jump on the ball and displays a strong, accurate arm.

With plenty of young outfielders already on the major league scene, the Cubs will give May plenty of time to develop, if neccessary. His performance so far, however, would indicate that he may be ready by 1991.

height	weight	bats	throws	birthplace	birthdate
6'4"	200	L	R	Rochester, NY	7/14/68

year	team	league	g	ab	r	h	2b	3b	hr	rbi	sb	bb	so	avg
1986	Wytheville	APP	54	178	25	57	6	1	0	23	17	16	16	.320
1987	Peoria	MWL	128	439	60	131	19	8	9	52	5	42	106	.298
1988	Winston-Salem	CAR	130	485	76	148	29	9	8	65	13	37	82	.305
1989	Charlotte	SL	136	491	72	145	26	5	9	70	19	33	76	.295

Just three years out of high school, twenty-one-year-old Frank Castillo has the mound presence of a veteran and the outstanding control needed to reach the big leagues quickly. Selected by Chicago in the sixth round of the June 1987 free agent draft, Castillo has posted a 28-12 record, struck out an average of 7.9 batters per 9 innings and issued less than 2 walks a game. He finished the 1989 season with a 10-game stint at Class AA Charlotte and he should open 1990 there as well.

Castillo is not an overpowering pitcher, but his ball has enough movement to let him challenge hitters. He changes speeds and location very well, can throw his breaking pitches for strikes and has the durability to throw 200 innings a year. The time it takes Frank to reach the major leagues will depend not only on his own performance at Charlotte this year, but also on the progress of Mike Harkey. If Harkey is unable to hold a spot in the rotation, Castillo may be the man called on to fill in.

Frank Castillo
Pitcher

height	weight	bats	throws	birthplace	birthdate
6'1"	180	R	R	El Paso, TX	4/1/69

year	team	league	g	ip	h	so	bb	gs	cg	sho	sv	w	l	era
1987	Wytheville	APP	12	90	86	83	21	12	5	0	0	10	1	2.29
1988	Peoria	MWL	9	51	25	58	8	8	2	0	0	6	1	0.71
1989	Winston-Salem	CAR	18	129	118	114	24	18	8	1	0	9	6	2.51
1989	Charlotte	SL	10	68	73	43	12	10	4	0	0	3	4	3.84

Girardi may be the best defensive backstop of the Cubs' minor league catching triumvirate, and he has the advantage of batting right-handed—Damon Berryhill's weaker side. He has surprising speed for a catcher, and showed a good field presence in his National League stint last summer. With Wilkins and Kelly Mann as starters at the Double and Triple A levels respectively, Joe will probably earn a backup or platoon role with the Cubs this spring.

Selected in the fifth round of the June 1986 draft out of Northwestern University, Girardi's offensive production has been solid in the minor leagues, but he sputtered on the major league level. He is a decent contact hitter who likes to take the ball up the middle and he has some power to the opposite field. Joe will not hit many home runs—a maximum of 10 per season—but he is capable of driving in some clutch runs. Joe is quick and agile behind the plate, gets rid of the ball in a hurry, and calls a good game. Girardi will stay in the big leagues because of his defense.

Joe Girardi
Catcher

height	weight	bats	throws	birthplace	birthdate
5'11"	195	R	R	Peoria, IL	10/14/64

year	team	league	g	ab	r	h	2b	3b	hr	rbi	sb	bb	so	avg
1986	Peoria	MWL	68	230	36	71	13	1	3	28	6	17	36	.309
1987	Winston-Salem	CAR	99	364	51	102	8	8	8	46	9	33	64	.280
1988	Pittsfield	EL	104	357	44	97	14	1	7	41	7	29	51	.272
1989	Iowa	AA	32	110	12	27	4	2	2	11	3	5	19	.245
1989	Chicago	NL	59	157	15	39	10	0	1	14	2	11	26	.248

Shawn Boskie
Pitcher

The Cubs' number-one pick in the January 1986 draft, Shawn was a third baseman at Modesto Junior College. He was immediately converted into a pitcher by Chicago, and has developed very quickly. Boskie posted two consecutive winning campaigns in 1988 and 1989. In addition to this, his walks-to-strikeouts ratio has improved each year; and last summer it stood at an impressive 1 to 2 at Class AA Charlotte. This twenty-three-year-old right-hander should open the 1990 campaign at Triple A Iowa.

Boskie has taken to his new role very well. He's an intelligent young man with a tough competitive nature and a willingness to learn. He has the ability to dominate hitters with his 90+ mph fastball and hard curve, but still needs to improve his control. At Charlotte, in an effort to reduce his number of walks, Shawn threw too many balls in the heart of the strike zone and was touched for 196 hits in 181 innings pitched. If Boskie's going to be a starter in the major leagues, his remaining minor league tenure should concentrate on the development of an offspeed pitch.

height	weight	bats	throws	birthplace	birthdate
6'3"	205	R	R	Hawthorne, NV	3/28/67

year	team	league	g	ip	h	so	bb	gs	cg	sho	sv	w	l	era
1986	Wytheville	APP	14	54	42	40	57	12	1	0	0	4	4	5.33
1987	Peoria	MWL	26	149	149	100	56	25	1	0	0	9	11	4.35
1988	Winston-Salem	CAR	27	186	176	164	89	27	4	2	0	12	7	3.39
1989	Charlotte	SL	28	181	196	164	84	28	5	0	0	11	8	4.38

Kelly Mann
Catcher

The third of Chicago's young catching prospects is Kelly Mann. He will open the 1990 campaign one level ahead of Wilkins at Class AAA Iowa and one level behind Girardi. This is a fitting position for the twenty-first round pick from June 1985, as he is similar to both his counterparts in many areas.

Kelly is a fine defensive catcher with a strong arm and the commanding personality needed to run a game. He's not quite as smooth behind the plate as Girardi, but he was good enough to be rated the top fielding backstop in the Carolina League in 1988 in a poll of managers, and he has regularly thrown out over 40% of would-be base stealers.

Offensively, Mann does not have the power of Wilkins. However, he is a solid line drive hitter capable of driving in 60-70 runs per season and getting the clutch hit. In order to secure a full-time major league job, Mann will have to make more consistent contact and learn to take the ball the other way. He may have a difficult time earning a spot with the Cubs, but could bring good value in a trade.

height	weight	bats	throws	birthplace	birthdate
6'2"	210	R	R	Santa Monica, CA	8/17/67

year	team	league	g	ab	r	h	2b	3b	hr	rbi	sb	bb	so	avg
1986	Geneva	NYP	60	191	17	37	1	0	2	15	3	18	38	.194
1986	Peoria	MWL	3	13	4	6	2	0	0	4	0	0	1	.462
1987	Peoria	MWL	95	287	24	73	16	1	4	45	1	23	66	.254
1988	Winston-Salem	CAR	94	307	32	84	11	0	8	40	5	24	46	.274
1988	Pittsfield	EL	22	51	7	10	3	0	0	3	0	3	14	.196
1989	Charlotte	SL	117	345	37	85	14	1	8	56	1	33	60	.246

Injuries in the Cubs' outfield last year gave Doug a chance to perform at the major league level for the second straight season. While he had difficulty making consistent contact with National League pitching, he did show defensive talent and played hard everyday. Dascenzo may never be a full-time big leaguer, but he should make a living as a platoon player or defensive replacement throughout the '90s.

Dascenzo has shown good offensive versatility in the minor leagues. He is a switch-hitter with some pop in his bat, and has above-average speed and excellent bunting technique. His home run power comes from the right side of the plate and he is very patient in waiting for his pitch. Doug is also adept at stealing bases.

Doug Dascenzo
Outfield

Capable of playing left or center field, Doug goes back on the ball very well, which allows him to play fairly shallow. With an outstanding jump and good instincts, he gets to balls many defenders could never reach. His arm is only average in strength, but very accurate.

height	weight	bats	throws	birthplace	birthdate
5'8"	160	B	L	Cleveland, OH	6/30/64

year	team	league	g	ab	r	h	2b	3b	hr	rbi	sb	bb	so	avg
1985	Geneva	NYP	70	252	59	84	15	1	3	23	33	61	20	.333
1986	Winston-Salem	CAR	138	545	107	178	29	11	6	83	57	63	44	.327
1987	Pittsfield	EL	134	496	84	152	32	6	3	56	36	73	38	.306
1988	Iowa	AA	132	505	73	149	22	5	6	49	30	37	41	.295
1988	Chicago	NL	26	75	9	16	3	0	0	4	6	9	4	.213
1989	Iowa	AA	111	431	59	121	18	4	4	33	34	51	41	.281
1989	Chicago	NL	47	139	20	23	1	0	1	12	6	13	13	.165

Renfro has put together two excellent seasons in Double A ball, but he must prove himself in Iowa this year if he's to reach the major leagues with Chicago. Laddie is being groomed for a middle relief job in the majors, and has the type of resilient arm that allows him to pitch almost every day. In 1989, this twenty-eight-year-old right-hander appeared in a league-high 78 games at Charlotte and notched 15 saves to go with his 19 victories.

Laddie pitches with guile rather than power. He is adept at changing speeds and is always around the plate. However, he has to prove to the Cubs that he has the stuff to pitch in the National League. No hurler can hit the corners every time and Renfro has gotten in trouble in brief stints facing Triple A batters. Still, his recent success certainly warrants close attention from the organization and Laddie could see his first major

Laddie Renfro
Pitcher

league action this September.

height	weight	bats	throws	birthplace	birthdate
5'11"	200	B	R	Natchez, MS	5/9/62

year	team	league	g	ip	h	so	bb	gs	cg	sho	sv	w	l	era
1984	Geneva	NYP	24	39	34	33	10	0	0	0	10	3	3	1.38
1985	Peoria	MWL	57	96	79	56	39	0	0	0	8	10	6	3.20
1986	Winston-Salem	CAR	65	83	84	51	27	0	0	0	21	6	6	2.93
1987	Pittsfield	EL	40	46	56	27	15	0	0	0	16	4	5	4.08
1987	Iowa	AA	8	14	8	9	5	0	0	0	0	0	1	5.02
1988	Pittsfield	EL	29	110	102	57	24	7	1	0	1	9	4	1.96
1988	Iowa	AA	16	24	28	12	11	0	0	0	0	1	3	4.88
1989	Charlotte	SL	78	132	127	85	34	2	1	1	15	19	7	3.14

Draft Analysis

Top Ten Picks:

1. Earl Cunningham, Outfield (Lancaster High School, Lancaster, SC)
2. Gary Scott, Third Base (Villanova University)
3. Billy White, Shortstop (University of Kentucky)
4. Jason Evans, Shortstop (Chatsworth High School, Catsworth, CA)
5. Derrick Duke, First Base (Reagan High School, Houston, TX)
6. Calvin Ford, Outfield (Ontario High School, Ontario, CA)
7. Edgardo Larregui, Outfield (Carolina, P.R.)
8. Travis Willis, Right-hand Pitcher (University of California)
9. Dave Swarzbaugh, Left-hand Pitcher (University of Miami of Ohio)
10. Gordon Sanchez, Catcher (San Marcos High School, San Marcos, CA)

In a year when many top picks passed on substantial bonuses in order to attend college, the Cubs may have been hardest hit. Four of the Cubs' first ten picks would not sign—number-four Jason Evans, number-five Derrick Duke, number-seven Edgardo Larregui and number-ten Gordon Sanchez. This left the organization with only two pitchers, two outfielders, a shortstop and a third baseman to show for their precious selections. With so few opportunities available to infuse young talent into a system, this draft could haunt Chicago for many years to come.

Of those players that did join the organization, the brightest may have been Villanova product Gary Scott. This young third baseman hit .280 and belted 10 home runs in only 48 games at Geneva. Highly-rated Earl Cunningham (Lancaster High School, SC) hit 7 home runs and knocked in 38 in 49 games at Wytheville. On the pitching side, the Cubs' eighth and ninth round picks did not fare as well. Right-hander Travis Willis managed only a 3-7 mark at Geneva while left-hander Dave Schwarzbaugh posted a 2-3 record to go with his 5.09 ERA.

Overall, Chicago selected fifty-four players. Pitchers accounted for twenty-two slots, followed by infielders with sixteen, outfielders with twelve and catchers with four. There may be some diamonds-in-the-rough among the organization's draftees; however, the failure to sign four top picks represents a missed opportunity.

MONTREAL EXPOS

1989 Farm System Record
375-325 (.536)

Indianapolis	AA	AAA	87	59	.596
Jacksonville	SL	AA	68	76	.472
W. Palm Beach	FSL	A	74	64	.536
Rockford	MWL	A	74	59	.556
Jamestown	NYP	A	44	32	.579
Pirate City	GCL	Rookie	28	35	.444

Good talent and good coaching equal success, and the Expos have plenty of all three in their farm system. The last big stop for many of Montreal's prospects before reaching the major leagues is Indianapolis—a club that has won the American Association title each of the last four years as well as both of the newly founded Triple A Classic series. This tradition gives the Expos confident young players who know what it takes to win.

The organization has also helped itself immeasurably by drafting fine young athletes, rather than just experienced college baseball players. Many of the the club's top prospects were two or three-sport stars in high school and almost all of them have good speed and power potential. The dividends of this philosophy will be evident at the major league level this year with the likes of Marquis Grissom, Larry Walker and Jeff Huson. However, there are many others only a season or two away.

In addition to the players detailed below, Expos fans should keep an eye on the progress of pitchers Howard Farmer (12 wins, 151 Ks and a 2.20 ERA at Jacksonville) and Mel Rojas (10 wins, 104 Ks and a 2.49 ERA at Jacksonville), as well as outfielder Terrel Hansen (24 doubles, 16 HRs and 81 RBIs at Rockford).

The Expos' top prospects are:

Marquis Grissom	Delino DeShields
Junior Noboa	Larry Walker
Wilfredo Cordero	Hector Rivera
Yorkis Perez	Mike Blowers
Danilo Leon	Reid Cornelius

Marquis Grissom
Outfield

A third-round selection in the June 1988 free agent draft, Grissom worked his way through two levels of the farm system last summer before ending the season in the major leagues. He showed all the speed, power and baseball instincts Montreal expected, and then some. Marquis is simply a fine athlete and could contend for the National League Rookie of the Year Award in 1990.

Offensively, this twenty-two-year-old product of Florida A&M has the stroke to hit .300 in the big leagues. He can handle the breaking ball or fastball almost anywhere in the strike zone and has extra-base power to all fields. Marquis' base-stealing capabilities are comparable to those of Tim Raines and he projects as a top-of-the-order hitter.

Grissom is also a natural in the field. He has tremendous range, sure hands and an accurate arm. With Otis Nixon and Dave Martinez injured last fall, Marquis stepped into the Expo lineup and delivered solid defense in the midst of a pennant race. It will be difficult to keep him out of the starting nine this year.

height	weight	bats	throws	birthplace	birthdate
5'11"	190	R	R	Atlanta, GA	4/17/67

year	team	league	g	ab	r	h	2b	3b	hr	rbi	sb	bb	so	avg
1988	Jamestown	NYP	74	291	69	94	14	7	8	39	23	35	39	.323
1989	Jacksonville	SL	78	278	43	83	15	4	3	31	24	24	31	.299
1989	Indianapolis	AA	49	187	28	52	10	4	2	21	16	14	23	.278
1989	Montreal	NL	26	74	16	19	2	0	1	2	1	12	21	.257

Delino DeShields
Shortstop/Third Base

The Expos selected Delino in the first round of the June 1987 free agent draft because he was the best athlete available. He has the speed, strength and sure hands needed to advance quickly in the system; moreover, he showed improvement in virtually every offensive category at the Double and Triple A levels last season. He should open the 1990 campaign at Indianapolis.

Only twenty-one years old, Delino can be overpowered by inside fastballs at times. Otherwise, he makes solid contact and has good line drive power to all fields. He has the speed to beat out infield hits and the technique to steal 50+ bases per year. Defensively, DeShields is as quick and agile as any shortstop in the game. His outstanding range actually increases his error totals, as does an erratic arm, but he is improving every day.

With Spike Owen and young Jeff Huson already in the major leagues, Montreal can afford to be patient with Delino. However, another solid campaign in 1990 could find this exciting young shortstop in the National League by next spring.

height	weight	bats	throws	birthplace	birthdate
6'2"	180	L	R	Seaford, DE	1/15/69

year	team	league	g	ab	r	h	2b	3b	hr	rbi	sb	bb	so	avg
1987	Bradenton	GCL	31	111	17	24	5	2	1	4	16	21	30	.216
1987	Jamestown	NYP	34	96	16	21	1	2	1	5	14	24	28	.219
1988	Rockford	MWL	129	460	97	116	26	6	12	46	59	95	110	.252
1989	Jacksonville	SL	93	307	55	83	10	6	3	35	37	76	80	.270
1989	Indianapolis	AA	47	181	29	47	8	4	2	14	16	16	53	.260

At age twenty-five, Junior will begin his tenth season as a professional in 1990 with his third different organization. This time however, it appears as if he's finally ready for a major league assignment. Noboa impressed the Expos last September with the type of solid performance that made him an American Association All-Star and league batting champion earlier in the summer. He'll go to spring training with a legitimate shot at the team's starting second base slot and should open the season with Montreal.

With all his experience, Noboa has certainly learned how to handle the bat. He makes solid contact, has line drive power and executes the hit-and-run play as well as anyone. With most clubs, Junior's above-average speed would mean a spot near the top of the order. With Raines and Grissom occupying the number-one and –two holes, however, Noboa, will probably bat sixth.

Junior Noboa
Second Base

Defensively, Junior is a solid performer. He does not have exceptional range or the strongest throwing arm, but his sure hands and hard work rate him as major league quality.

height	weight	bats	throws	birthplace	birthdate
5'9"	160	R	R	Azua, Dom. Rep.	11/10/64

year	team	league	g	ab	r	h	2b	3b	hr	rbi	sb	bb	so	avg
1981	Batavia	NYP	50	162	15	49	8	0	0	6	11	11	19	.302
1982	Waterloo	MWL	121	385	69	96	12	5	0	23	44	62	61	.249
1983	Waterloo	MWL	132	449	64	115	22	3	1	29	47	48	71	.256
1984	Buffalo	EL	117	383	55	97	18	4	1	45	12	31	28	.253
1984	Cleveland	AL	23	11	3	4	0	0	0	0	1	0	2	.364
1095	Maine	IL	122	403	62	116	11	2	5	32	14	34	28	.288
1986	Maine	IL	108	399	44	114	21	1	4	32	10	15	33	.286
1987	Buffalo	AA	43	149	26	47	6	2	0	14	2	18	16	.315
1987	Cleveland	AL	39	80	7	18	2	1	0	7	1	3	6	.225
1988	Edmonton	PCL	50	159	24	47	6	1	0	17	5	11	12	.296
1988	California	AL	21	16	4	1	0	0	0	0	0	0	1	.063
1989	Indianapolis	AA	117	467	61	159	21	8	2	62	14	21	34	.340
1989	Montreal	NL	21	44	3	10	0	0	0	1	0	1	3	.227

Canadian-born Larry Walker earned a promotion to the major leagues last September with an All-Star campaign at Class AAA Indianapolis. It marked the beginning of a promising comeback for the twenty-three-year-old outfielder who severely damaged his right knee while playing in the Mexican League between the 1987 and 1988 seasons. Big, strong and fast, Walker has a chance to earn a starting spot with the Expos this year.

In what amounts to less than three full seasons, Larry has hit 73 home runs and collected 258 RBIs. He has a short, quick left-handed power stroke and will take the outside pitch to left field. He also has the speed to leg-out plenty of doubles and the savvy to steal bases. The only drawback to Larry's offensive game is a high number of strikeouts.

Larry Walker
Outfield

Defensively, Walker has enough range to cover any of the three outfield positions. However, his arm would be wasted anywhere but in right. With the Expos' crowded outfield situation, it may be difficult to play Larry every day, but he should get a fair number of major league at bats this season.

height	weight	bats	throws	birthplace	birthdate
6'1"	205	R	L	Maple Ridge, B.C.	12/1/66

year	team	league	g	ab	r	h	2b	3b	hr	rbi	sb	bb	so	avg
1985	Utica	NYP	62	215	24	48	8	2	2	26	12	18	57	.223
1986	Burlington	MWL	95	332	67	96	12	6	29	74	16	46	112	.289
1986	West Palm Beach	FSL	38	113	20	32	7	5	4	16	2	26	32	.283
1987	Jacksonville	SL	128	474	91	136	25	7	26	83	24	67	120	.287
1988	Did Not Play													
1989	Indianapolis	AA	114	385	68	104	18	2	12	59	36	50	87	.270
1989	Montreal	NL	20	47	4	8	0	0	0	4	1	5	13	.170

Wilfredo Cordero
Shortstop

The promotion of Delino DeShields to Class AAA Indianapolis last July gave Wilfredo his first taste of Double A action in Jacksonville. Although his average dropped 62 points with the promotion, Montreal has high hopes for this eighteen-year-old shortstop. Cordero has good size and speed for his position and should show improvement with a full season in the Southern League this year.

Signed to an undisclosed six-figure bonus in 1988, Wilfredo has the makings of a power-hitting infielder. His strong right-handed swing sends line drives to all fields and should only get better with physical maturity. Although he can't be considered a base stealer, Cordero runs well and legged-out 17 doubles in 1989.

In the field, Wilfredo has quick reactions and sure hands. And, if DeShields is entrenched at shortstop when Cordero is ready for the major leagues, the Expos feel that Wilfredo could make a smooth adjustment to either second or third base. He'll still need at least two or three more years in the minor leagues, but this young Puerto Rican's potential is unlimited.

height	weight	bats	throws	birthplace	birthdate
6'2"	185	R	R	Mayaguez, PR	10/3/71

year	team	league	g	ab	r	h	2b	3b	hr	rbi	sb	bb	so	avg
1988	Jamestown	NYP	52	190	18	49	3	0	2	22	3	15	44	.258
1989	W. Palm Beach	FSL	78	289	37	80	12	2	6	29	2	33	58	.277
1989	Jacksonville	SL	39	121	9	26	6	1	3	17	1	12	33	.215

Hector Rivera
Pitcher

Signed by the Expos as a free agent out of the Mexican League in February of 1987, twenty-year-old Hector Rivera was among the top pitchers in the Florida State League last summer when he earned a promotion to Class AA Jacksonville. He will most likely open the 1990 campaign back in the Southern League to get a full year in Double A ball, before stopping at Indianapolis on his way to the major leagues.

Hector has a live arm and powerful build. He delivers a good, moving fastball in the 90 mph range and has a hard, tight curve. Although his offspeed pitches are inconsistent, coaches feel that Hector could master a variety of them with his large hands, and will work with the young right-hander toward that end this spring.

Rivera shows good poise for a young pitcher. He challenges hitters, works the inside part of the plate and rarely hurts himself with walks. If Hector can reach the major leagues while still in his early twenties, he'll give Montreal quality pitching for many years.

height	weight	bats	throws	birthplace	birthdate
6'3"	180	R	R	Navohoa, Sonora, Mex.	2/8/70

year	team	league	g	ip	h	so	bb	gs	cg	sho	sv	w	l	era
1987	Bradenton	GCL	14	87	67	62	44	14	3	0	0	5	8	2.70
1988	Did Not Play													
1989	W. Palm Beach	FSL	16	103	85	61	27	16	2	1	0	7	3	1.83
1989	Jacksonville	SL	5	27	24	22	17	5	0	0	0	1	2	5.33

Originally signed by the Twins as a fifteen-year-old free agent, Yorkis came to the Montreal organization in the trade that sent reliever Jeff Reardon to Minnesota. In three seasons with his new team, Perez has worked at the Single and Double A levels compiling a 37-30 record. At only twenty-two years old, this 1989 Florida State League All-Star may see his first Class AAA action this season.

Yorkis has made his mark in the minor leagues as a strikeout pitcher. Over his career, Perez has averaged better than one K per inning pitched. Although slight of stature, this left-hander throws a sailing 91 mph fastball and a big-breaking curve. He generally has pretty good control and isn't afraid to throw offspeed pitches when behind in the count.

Yorkis Perez
Pitcher

Perez has the talent to reach the big leagues but needs to develop more consistency to do so. The Expos will evaluate Yorkis closely in Indianapolis this season and could give him some National League starts in September if he performs well.

height	weight	bats	throws	birthplace	birthdate
6'0"	160	L	L	Bajos de Haina, Dom. Rep.	9/30/67

year	team	league	g	ip	h	so	bb	gs	cg	sho	sv	w	l	era
1986	Kenosha	MWL	31	131	120	144	88	18	3	0	0	4	11	5.15
1987	W. Palm Beach	FSL	15	100	78	111	46	15	3	0	0	6	2	2.34
1987	Jacksonville	SL	12	60	58	60	30	10	1	0	1	2	7	4.05
1988	Jacksonville	SL	27	130	142	105	94	25	2	1	0	8	12	5.82
1989	W. Palm Beach	FSL	18	94	62	85	54	12	0	0	1	7	6	2.76
1989	Jacksonville	SL	20	35	25	50	34	0	0	0	0	4	3	3.60

A University of Washington product, Blowers was selected in the tenth round of the June 1986 draft. After opening his professional career that summer with brief stints in the Gulf Coast and New York-Penn Leagues, Mike has progressed one level in the farm system in each of the last three years. Mike's power potential is underscored by the fact that he has averaged 15 home runs per season during that advancement—however, they've come at the expense of too many strikeouts.

For Blowers to earn a steady job with the major league club, he'll have to make more consistent contact. To that end, he began taking the ball to right field more often last year and raised his average nearly 20 points. Mike is adequate defensively at third base, with good quickness and a very strong arm. He would probably be a plus for many teams at that position, but

Mike Blowers
Third Base/Second Base

will need to work very hard to gain playing time ahead of perennial All-Star Tim Wallach in Montreal. If Blowers' name comes up in winter trade talks, the Expos might be willing to listen.

height	weight	bats	throws	birthplace	birthdate
6'2"	190	R	R	Wurzburg, Germany	4/24/65

year	team	league	g	ab	r	h	2b	3b	hr	rbi	sb	bb	so	avg
1986	Jamestown	NYP	32	95	13	24	9	2	1	6	3	17	18	.252
1986	Expos	GCL	31	115	14	25	3	1	2	17	2	15	25	.216
1987	W. Palm Beach	FSL	136	491	68	124	30	3	16	71	4	48	118	.252
1988	Jacksonville	SL	137	460	58	115	20	6	15	60	6	68	114	.250
1989	Indianapolis	AA	131	461	49	123	29	6	14	56	3	41	109	.267
1989	New York	AL	13	38	2	10	0	0	0	3	0	3	13	.263

Danilo Leon
Pitcher

Danilo works with a standard fastball, slider, and change-up repertoire, and has had good success in his three professional campaigns in the Expo farm system. His fastball has been clocked at 91 mph and has a sinking motion which keeps the ball on the ground and Leon's ERA low. By mixing in the hard slider and straight change effectively, he has averaged better than 7 strikeouts per 9 innings pitched and held opposing batters to a .200 average.

Signed as a free agent in 1986, Leon dominated New York-Penn League hitters in 1987, his first full season as a starter, and proved he was equal to the challenge of Class AA Jacksonville last summer with a 7-4 mark. At only twenty-three years old, he should open the 1990 campaign with Triple A Indianapolis and could see some major league action before the year is out. His fiery, competitive nature and solid mechanics promise better years to come, and Montreal fans should watch for Leon to earn a permanent spot on the Expos' pitching staff within two years.

height	weight	bats	throws	birthplace	birthdate
6'1"	165	R	R	La Concepcion, Venezuela	4/3/67

year	team	league	g	ip	h	so	bb	gs	cg	sho	sv	w	l	era
1986	Bradenton		15	29	32	21	13	0	1	0	2	1	2	4.30
1987	Jamestown	NYP	3	2	4	3	1	0	0	0	0	0	0	16.20
1988	Jamestown	NYP	15	116	75	100	48	15	7	4	0	10	3	1.16
1988	W. Palm Beach	FSL	6	14	12	15	5	0	0	0	0	0	0	3.21
1989	Jacksonville	SL	18	95	85	64	55	18	1	0	0	7	4	4.63

Reid Cornelius
Pitcher

Montreal lured Cornelius away from a scholarship at Mississippi State with a $240,000 bonus in 1988, and then watched their young prospect struggle in his first professional season at Class A Rockford last summer. On the positive side, Reid posted 5 wins and allowed only 71 hits in 84 innings. However, he also showed that he needs to work hard on his control. The organization is unsure whether to assign Cornelius to Double A Jacksonville or move him to West Palm Beach in the pitcher-oriented Florida State League.

A powerfully built right-hander, Reid throws his fastball in the mid-90s and has an outstanding over-hand curve. He's an extremely intelligent young man with the willingness to learn and the talent to succeed, but it may take longer than expected for Cornelius to reach the major leagues. He must overcome the urge to be too fine with his control. He doesn't need to nibble at the corners to get people out, but must be resigned to the fact that he will get hit sometimes.

height	weight	bats	throws	birthplace	birthdate
6'0"	185	R	R	Thomasville, AL	6/2/70

year	team	league	g	ip	h	so	bb	gs	cg	sho	sv	w	l	era
1989	Rockford	MWL	17	84	71	66	63	17	0	0	0	5	6	4.27

Draft Analysis

Nearly the only position devoid of top-notch prospects in the Expos' organization is catcher. Montreal attempted to remedy that situation by drafting backstops with thirteen of their sixty-nine picks and three of their first five. Unfortunately, the would-be jewel in the system got away. High school standout Charles Johnson balked at the Expos' final offer of better than $200,000 and was lost to the organization when he attended his first class at the University of Miami. Montreal was one of only three clubs which failed to sign their top draft pick.

Although few of the other catchers signed by Montreal distinguished themselves last summer, several of their battery mates did. Left-hander Brian Barnes compiled a 6-3 record in a season split between the Florida State and New York-Penn Leagues. He also posted a stellar 0.83 ERA and struck out 87 batters in 65 innings of work. In the Gulf Coast League, the club's ninth and tenth round picks combined for a 7-5 record while yielding less than one hit per inning.

It remains to be seen whether or not the loss of Johnson will impact the Expos' current success story. They will receive an extra first round pick next summer, but their need for a catcher may soon be chronic.

NEW YORK METS

1989 Farm System Record
403-362 (.527)

Tidewater	IL	AAA	77	69	.527
Jackson	TL	AA	61	74	.452
St. Lucie	FSL	A	79	55	.590
Columbia	SAL	A	73	67	.521
Pittsfield	NYP	A	53	23	.697
Kingsport	APPY	Rookie	35	37	.486
Sarasota	GCL	Rookie	25	37	.403

The Mets' farm system has generally been recognized as one of the strongest in the game throughout the last decade. The sheer number of major leaguers to come up through their organization is testament enough to support that belief. However, with the arrival of Gregg Jefferies last spring, the New York's minor league affiliates were left without a standout position player prospect for the first time in many years. The Mets' scouting is no longer as good as it once was and their last three drafts have been rather weak.

In response to the situation, the Mets have begun to deal off some of their pitching prospects to acquire proven major leaguers—such as Dave West, Kevin Tapani, and Rick Aguilera for Frank Viola—and to trade excess major league position players for young pitching talent. Mets fans should look for this trend to continue over the next several years.

All is not doom and gloom in the New York farm system, however. They have an outstanding set of minor league coaches and managers, and they field a consistent winner at the Triple A level in Tidewater. The organization's prospects know what it takes to win and most are ready for the big leagues when called upon. Aside from the top prospects, one young man who could be ready very quickly is Julio Valera. This twenty-one-year-old right- hander led all Mets farmhands with 15 victories, 162 strikouts and a 2.12 ERA.

The Mets' top prospects are:

Blaine Beatty	Wally Whitehurst
Todd Hundley	Dave Proctor
Julio Machado	Terry Bross
Kevin Brown	Brian Givens
Chris Hill	Dale Plummer

Blaine Beatty
Pitcher

Blaine compiled his fourth winning campaign in as many seasons last year with Tidewater, and he could challenge for a spot on the major league staff this spring. Originally selected in the ninth round of the June 1986 draft by Baltimore, Beatty came to the Mets in the deal that sent Doug Sisk to the Orioles. In 1988, Blaine's first year in the organization, he produced a Texas League-high 16 victories, 12 complete games and 5 shutouts. For his performance, Beatty was the recipient of the Doubleday Award given by the Mets to the Most Valuable Player at each level in the farm system.

A crafty left-hander, Beatty reminds many Mets coaches of Bob Ojeda because of his ability to change speeds and hit locations with his fastball. While an 88 mph fastball is not exactly a finesse pitch, Blaine mixes it well with an outstanding curve and a good straight change-up. What sets him apart from most young hurlers, however, is the poise and composure he shows on the mound. Beatty's attitude is the same, whether he's shutting a team down or he's three runs behind. It's this makeup that will make Blaine a success in the big leagues.

height	weight	bats	throws	birthplace	birthdate
6'2"	185	L	L	Victoria, TX	4/25/64

year	team	league	g	ip	h	so	bb	gs	cg	sho	sv	w	l	era
1986	Newark	NYP	15	119	98	93	30	15	8	3	0	11	3	2.11
1987	Hagerstown	CAR	13	100	81	65	11	13	4	1	0	11	1	2.52
1987	Charlotte	SL	15	106	110	57	20	15	3	1	0	6	5	3.07
1988	Jackson	TL	30	208	191	103	34	28	12	5	0	16	8	2.46
1989	Tidewater	IL	27	185	173	90	43	27	6	3	0	12	10	3.31

Wally Whitehurst
Pitcher

Although Wally has not posted outstanding won-loss records during his four year professional career, he has the potential to be something special. This right-hander has solid mechanics and a good command of four pitches. His fastball will register at 87+ mph on the radar gun and he complements it with a tight curve, a hard slider and a straight change-up. In his career, Whitehurst has allowed only 2.34 walks and struck out an average of nearly 6 batters per 9 innings.

Originally selected by Oakland in the third round of the June 1985 draft out of the University of New Orleans, Wally came to the Mets in a three-way deal that sent Jesse Orosco to the Dodgers. He has made brief appearances for New York in each of the past two seasons and figures to get more innings in 1990. The organization likes Whitehurst's competitive spirit and composure, both of which serve him well in tight situations. While Wally may not have the best stuff of the club's young pitching prospects, he does exhibit the kind of gritty determination that is sorely lacking on the big league roster.

height	weight	bats	throws	birthplace	birthdate
6'2"	175	R	R	Shreveport, LA	4/11/64

year	team	league	g	ip	h	so	bb	gs	cg	sho	sv	w	l	era
1985	Medford	NWL	14	88	92	91	29	14	2	0	0	7	5	3.58
1985	Modesto	CAL	2	10	10	5	5	2	0	0	0	1	0	1.80
1986	Madison	MWL	8	61	42	47	16	8	5	4	0	6	1	0.59
1986	Huntsville	SL	19	105	114	54	46	19	2	0	0	9	5	4.64
1987	Huntsville	SL	28	183	192	106	42	28	5	3	0	11	10	3.98
1988	Tidewater	IL	26	165	145	113	32	26	3	1	0	10	11	3.05
1989	Tidewater	IL	21	133	123	95	32	20	3	1	0	8	7	3.25

Todd Hundley
Catcher

The son of former major league catcher Randy Hundley, Todd's stock as a prospect rose as quickly as his batting average last summer. Selected in the second round of the June 1987 draft as compensation for losing Ray Knight to free agency, Hundley showed improved contact and power with Class A Columbia. Simply by relaxing at the plate, his solid stroke began to pay the dividends the scouts projected when he signed. Todd is a switch-hitter who should open the 1990 campaign in Double A Jackson.

If any doubts exist about Hundley's offensive abilities, there is no question about his defense. He has been schooled in the finer art of catching since childhood and is widely recognized as the finest backstop in the organization. Todd is smooth and solid behind the plate, both in calling a game and blocking balls in the dirt. He has a quick release and a rifle arm, as demonstrated by his league-leading 39.2% success rate in throwing out runners at Little Falls in 1988. If he continues to produce at the plate, Todd could skip Tidewater and head straight for the major leagues next year.

height	weight	bats	throws	birthplace	birthdate
5'11"	170	B	R	Martinsville, VA	5/27/69

year	team	league	g	ab	r	h	2b	3b	hr	rbi	sb	bb	so	avg
1987	Little Falls	NYP	34	103	12	15	4	0	1	10	0	12	27	.146
1988	Little Falls	NYP	52	176	23	33	8	0	2	18	1	16	31	.188
1988	St. Lucie	FSL	1	1	0	0	0	0	0	0	0	2	1	.000
1989	Columbia	SAL	125	439	67	118	23	4	11	66	6	54	67	.269

Dave Proctor
Pitcher

Another Met prospect with family roots in the big leagues, Dave is the nephew of former pitcher Mike Torrez. This twenty-two-year-old right-hander was the organization's first round pick, and the twenty-first overall, in the June 1988 draft, and he has pitched impressively in his first two campaigns. Proctor is a raw talent who didn't even play baseball in high school. However, he is a fine natural athlete—runner-up for the Kansas Mr. Basketball Award as a senior—who learns quickly and should move through the system in a hurry.

In a poll of league managers taken by *Baseball America* last summer, Dave was rated not only the best pitching prospect but also the pitcher with the best fastball in the Florida State League. His heater runs radar guns up to 93 mph and it has explosive action into the strike zone. Proctor also throws a hard slider and tight curve, but has had some difficulty getting them over the plate. He has the stuff to be a front-line starter in the major leagues, but will need to work on his mechanics and control during his journey through the farm system.

height	weight	bats	throws	birthplace	birthdate
6'3"	190	L	R	Topeka, KS	3/17/68

year	team	league	g	ip	h	so	bb	gs	cg	sho	sv	w	l	era
1988	Little Falls	NYP	12	68	57	53	45	12	3	0	0	5	3	4.21
1989	St. Lucie	FSL	22	133	104	85	73	21	3	0	0	7	6	2.36

Julio Machado
Pitcher

Originally signed as a non-drafted free agent by Philadelphia in 1985, Julio hooked on with the Mets organization after being released by the Phillies' Double A roster last spring. Machado surprised everyone but himself by storming through three classifications to reach the major leagues by September. His stellar minor league performance included 10 saves, 5 victories and 118 strikeouts in 97 innings pitched—an average of 11 Ks per 9 innings. The Mets will give Julio a long look this spring; and he could open the season with the right-hander's setup role.

Machado is a free-wheeling pitcher with good ball movement and excellent velocity. He varies his delivery angles and speeds effectively and keeps batters off balance with a slight wild streak. Known to play head games with hitters, Julio intentionally hit the first major leaguer he faced and let it be known that he likes to eat Iguana—a story that made headlines in the New York papers. He may make headlines with his pitching in the Big Apple this year.

height	weight	bats	throws	birthplace	birthdate
5'9"	160	R	R	Zulia, Venezuela	12/1/65

year	team	league	g	ip	h	so	bb	gs	cg	sho	sv	w	l	era
1985	Spartanburg	SAL	32	81	75	71	38	3	1	0	0	4	5	4.32
1986	Spartanburg	SAL	43	79	68	81	52	5	2	1	7	2	5	3.73
1987	Clearwater	FSL	7	34	31	32	19	5	0	0	1	2	0	2.60
1987	Reading	EL	21	108	112	89	40	17	2	0	0	4	5	4.74
1988	Reading	EL	26	63	69	52	34	5	0	0	3	6	1	5.43
1988	Clearwater	FSL	13	36	34	45	14	3	0	0	5	1	4	2.95
1989	St. Lucies	FSL	4	10	5	14	3	0	0	0	2	1	0	0.00
1989	Jackson	TL	32	57	42	67	27	0	0	0	3	3	5	2.84
1989	Tidewater	IL	14	29	16	37	17	1	0	0	5	1	2	0.62
1989	New York	NL	10	11	9	14	3	0	0	0	0	0	1	3.27

Terry Bross
Pitcher

A former basketball center and part-time pitcher for St. John's University, Terry showed a great deal of improvement in his first full season as a professional last summer. Bross earned 11 saves and posted a career-best 2.79 ERA to go with an 8-2 record. He was selected by New York in the thirteenth round of the June 1987 draft and is being groomed as a power closer from the right side.

Bross is 6'9" and presents an imposing figure on the mound. His fastball reaches home plate at over 90 mph and he complements it with a fine hard slider. Inherent to his size, however, are slight mechanical difficulties. Although his control has shown improvement each year, Terry still walked nearly 1 batter per 2 innings; to be effective he must work on getting his breaking ball over the plate.

The organization is hopeful that the twenty-four-year-old Bross will progress quickly. But, with his lack of experience, the Mets will give him time to develop. 1990 should find Terry at Class AA Jackson, though an assignment at Tidewater is not out of the question.

height	weight	bats	throws	birthplace	birthdate
6'9"	230	R	R	El Paso, TX	3/30/66

year	team	league	g	ip	h	so	bb	gs	cg	sho	sv	w	l	era
1987	Little Falls	NYP	10	28	22	21	20	3	0	0	0	2	0	3.86
1988	Little Falls	NYP	20	55	43	59	38	6	0	0	1	2	1	3.09
1989	St. Lucies	FSL	35	58	39	47	26	0	0	0	11	8	2	2.79

Kevin Brown
Pitcher

Acquired by the Mets in the deal that sent Terry Blocker to Atlanta, Brown was the recipient of Class A St. Lucie's Doubleday Award for the Most Valuable Player in his first season with the organization. In 1989, only his second year with New York, Kevin reached Triple A Tidewater on the strength of a fine performance at Jackson, where he posted a 5-2 record with a 2.26 ERA, and he seems poised to make a run at the major league club within the next year.

Like Blaine Beatty, Brown is another left-handed prospect who gets by with guile and control rather than with an overpowering fastball. Kevin's mid-80s mph velocity is more than adequate when coupled with his ability to change speeds and hit locations; and he rarely hurts himself with walks—only 2.76 free passes per 9 innings pitched since joining the organization.

Kevin's future with the big leagues may depend on the status of Ojeda and Beatty. New York has far and away the most pitching talent in the majors and will probably only use one of the crafty left-handers in the rotation. Unless Brown makes the shift to middle relief, he may ply his trade elsewhere in the majors.

height	weight	bats	throws	birthplace	birthdate
6'1"	172	L	L	Oroville, CA	3/5/66

year	team	league	g	ip	h	so	bb	gs	cg	sho	sv	w	l	era
1986	Idaho Falls	PIO	12	68	65	44	41	12	1	0	0	3	6	5.03
1987	Sumter	SAL	9	56	53	45	19	9	0	0	0	7	1	1.93
1987	Durham	CAR	13	73	78	48	42	12	1	0	0	4	4	5.20
1988	St. Lucie	FSL	20	134	96	113	37	20	5	1	0	5	7	1.81
1988	Jackson	TL	5	32	24	24	11	5	1	1	0	1	2	2.20
1989	Jackson	TL	8	51	51	40	11	8	2	2	0	5	2	2.26
1989	Tidewater	IL	13	75	81	46	31	13	4	0	0	6	6	4.44

Brian Givens
Pitcher

The leading strikeout pitcher in the nation—115 in 70 innings—at Trinidad Junior College in Colorado in 1983, Givens was selected by the Mets in the tenth round of the January 1984 draft. A big, hard-throwing left-hander, Brian has shown streaks of brilliance in his six-year pro career, but he has yet to progress past the Double A level. His main problem has been a lack of consistency, though an elbow operation prevented a promotion to Class AAA last summer.

Givens throws four types of fastballs that run in, out, down, and away, depending on his grip. With this repertoire alone, he has consistently held opposing batters to averages of .215 or less. To start in the major leagues, however, he will need to improve the consistency and location of his breaking pitches. Given Brian's high level of emotion and his dominating heater, the Mets may consider moving him to the bull pen for the upcoming campaign. He was able to throw only 85 innings for Jackson last year, and may be well-suited to a closer's role.

height	weight	bats	throws	birthplace	birthdate
6'5"	220	R	L	Lompoc, CA	11/6/65

year	team	league	g	ip	h	so	bb	gs	cg	sho	sv	w	l	era
1984	Kingsport	APP	14	44	41	51	52	10	0	0	0	4	1	6.50
1985	Little Falls	NYP	11	74	54	81	43	11	3	1	0	3	4	2.93
1985	Columbia	SAL	3	21	15	25	13	3	1	0	0	1	2	2.95
1986	Columbia	SAL	27	172	147	189	100	27	2	1	0	8	7	3.77
1987	Tidewater	IL	1	4	9	3	6	1	0	0	0	0	1	24.55
1987	Lynchburg	CAR	21	112	112	96	69	21	3	0	0	6	8	4.65
1988	Jackson	TL	76	164	140	156	68	26	4	3	0	6	14	3.78
1989	St. Lucie	FSL	1	5	7	8	1	1	0	0	0	0	1	0.00
1989	Jackson	TL	13	85	76	68	55	13	2	0	0	3	5	3.39

Chris Hill
Pitcher

Only twenty-one-years-old, Chris may still be several years away from the major leagues, but he opened some eyes in the Mets' front office last summer with an 11-7 record and a 3.04 ERA at Class A Columbia. New York made Hill their forty-third selection in the June 1987 draft after he earned All-District honors with a 1.38 ERA and 166 strikeouts in 97 innings pitched during his senior year at Duncanville High School in Texas. His 1989 dominance over SAL hitters should earn Chris a spot in the Jackson Mets' rotation for the upcoming campaign.

Although slight of build at 6'0" and 160 lbs., Hill is still maturing physically and should only gain velocity on his 90 mph fastball. But even if it never increases in speed, Chris' heater would rate above-average due to its riding action and his ability to hit spots with it. The main concern for the organization's minor league pitching instructors will be improving the rotation on Hill's curve and getting him to develop a third pitch. With the number of quality starters ahead of Chris in the system, New York will look at this young left-hander as a project—one that could pay great dividends.

height	weight	bats	throws	birthplace	birthdate
6'0"	160	L	L	Dallas, TX	4/13/69

year	team	league	g	ip	h	so	bb	gs	cg	sho	sv	w	l	era
1988	Little Falls	NYP	13	79	56	66	35	13	2	1	0	5	5	3.06
1989	Columbia	SAL	29	165	140	157	78	25	2	1	0	11	7	3.04

Dale Plummer
Pitcher

Winner of the Doubleday Award at Little Falls in his first professional season, the twenty-five-year-old Plummer made great strides again in 1989. The Mets' twenty-third pick in the June 1988 draft out of the University of Maine, Dale split the season between St. Lucie and Jackson and combined for a 6-0 record and 5 saves. He is a versatile performer whose future major league role may be middle relief and spot starting.

A rangy 6'4", 190 lbs., Plummer throws mainly from a three-quarters delivery. While he can't be classified as either a power or a control pitcher, he is fairly effective in both areas—5.8 strikeouts and 2.5 walks per 9 innings pitched. Dale works with a 86-88 mph fastball, along with the usual curve and straight change as complements. Each pitch grades at least average in terms of movement and consistency, and he'll throw them any time in the count. Plummer will not be a flashy big league pitcher, but he is the type of solid day-in, day-out performer that winning teams must have.

height	weight	bats	throws	birthplace	birthdate
6'4"	190	R	R	Bath, ME	1/26/65

year	team	league	g	ip	h	so	bb	gs	cg	sho	sv	w	l	era
1988	Little Falls	NYP	25	40	27	37	7	0	0	0	10	5	1	1.33
1989	St. Lucie	FSL	10	13	20	8	7	0	0	0	3	1	0	5.93
1989	Jackson	TL	25	71	60	36	21	5	2	1	2	5	0	2.03

Draft Analysis

Top Ten Picks:
1. Alan Zinter, Catcher (University of Arizona)
2. Tom Engle, Right-hand Pitcher (Fairfield Union High School, Lancaster, OH)
3. Brook Fordyce, Catcher (St. Bernards High School, Old Lyme, CT)
4. Tim McClinton, Outfield (Downers Grove North High School, Woodridge, IL)
5. Paul Meyer, Catcher (Patrick Henry High School, Minneapolis, MN)
6. Robert Rees, Right-hand Pitcher (Lake Washington High School, Kirkland, WA)
7. Robert Huskey, Third Base (Eisenhower High School, Lawton, OK)
8. Derek Henderson, Shortstop (Tennessee State University)
9. Nathan Florell, Outfield (Sullivan High School, Chicago, IL)
10. Scot McCloughland, Right-hand Pitcher/Shortstop (Loveland High School, Loveland, CO)

Whether it was a shift in philosophy or merely the recognition of a need, the Mets chose position players with eight of their top ten round picks last summer. At the head of the list was catcher Alan Zinter. The 6'2", 190 lb. Zinter, a product of the strong Arizona college program, opened his pro career with a .265 average, 5 home runs and 44 RBIs in a season split between St. Lucie and Pittsfield. To solidify their talent behind the plate, New York also drafted catchers in the third and fifth rounds. High schooler Brook Fordyce responded with a .327 mark and 9 round-trippers in 69 games of Appalachian League play. Among the other offensive selections, the most promising campaign was turned in by third baseman Chris Butterfield. He topped the .300 plateau and showed both power and speed while playing solid defense at the "hot corner" for Pittsfield.

Even though the focus of the Mets' draft was certainly on offense; it would not be accurate to say that they ignored pitching prospects. Of the club's fifty-four selections, twenty-three were spent on young hurlers—twelve of those out of high school. While these pitchers may not represent the best that last June's draft had to offer, New York is confident in the ability of their organization to develop them. Already, one successful campaign has been garnered from right-hander Elgardo Vazquez. He went 7-2 last summer at Kingsport and issued only 24 walks in 83 innings pitched.

New York may have suffered a slight setback by failing to sign their ninth and tenth round picks, but the 1989 draft should start the flow of position players into the club's top prospect list within one to two years.

PHILADELPHIA PHILLIES

1989 Farm System Record
317-385 (.452)

Scranton	IL	AAA	64	79	.448
Reading	EL	AA	68	71	.489
Clearwater	FSL	A	57	79	.419
Spartanburg	SAL	A	62	79	.440
Batavia	NYP	A	37	39	.487
Martinsville	APPY	Rookie	29	38	.433

There was not one winning team in the entire Philadelphia organization in 1989. The combined winning percentage of the club's six minor league affiliates was the second worst in baseball, behind Boston's, and there is very little hope that 1990 will see much improvement. To compound matters, the Phillies' system is not even turning out players to help the major league club. There are immediate needs in Philadelphia for a shortstop, a third baseman and a catcher, but help is at least several years away.

The Phillies are pursuing a new strategy; building the organization through pitching. Certainly, the success of the Mets, Dodgers and Orioles makes this seem a sensible solution. However, Philadelphia must stress quality over quantity. There are many young pitchers in the farm system, but only a few top-notch prospects. Management will have the luxury of picking early in upcoming drafts and must make every selection count. The brightest spots for 1989 were the performances of Pat Combs and Jason Grimsley. Both jumped from Class AA to the major leagues by September and could open 1990 in the Phillies' rotation.

The Phillies' top prospects are:

Ron Jones	Pat Combs
Jason Grimsley	Tim Mauser
Dave Holdridge	Kim Batiste
Jim Vatcher	Chuck McElroy
Bob Scanlan	Brad Brink

Ron Jones
Outfield

The Phillies' need for another solid offensive player was evident after the departure of Mike Schmidt last season. After a fine 1988 campaign at Class AAA Maine and a solid start in the major leagues last spring, Jones looked to be that player. However, a torn tendon in his right knee suffered on April 19th put Ron out of action for the remainder of the 1989 season. If healthy, this twenty-five-year-old outfielder has the offensive potential to challenge for the N.L. Rookie of the Year Award.

Jones has the type of quick, short stroke that sends line drives to all parts of the field. Not only does Ron make good contact against either left- or right-handed pitching, but he also shows good home run potential. His 24 round-trippers and 101 RBIs in a 1988 campaign that was split between Triple A and the majors promise big things to come.

If Jones has a shortcoming, it would be his play in the outfield. He has decent speed and an average arm, but seems to suffer from a lack of concentration at times. Ron will need to give 100% consistently to reach a level of respectability in the field.

height	weight	bats	throws	birthplace	birthdate
5'10"	200	L	R	Seguin, TX	6/11/64

year	team	league	g	ab	r	h	2b	3b	hr	rbi	sb	bb	so	avg
1985	Bend	NWL	73	286	54	90	13	1	10	60	9	34	28	.315
1986	Clearwater	FSL	108	412	76	153	18	12	7	73	33	40	30	.371
1986	Portland	PCL	11	34	4	4	1	0	0	2	0	0	1	.118
1987	Maine	IL	90	316	33	78	13	4	7	32	13	38	50	.247
1988	Philadelphia	NL	33	124	15	36	6	1	8	26	0	2	14	.290
1988	Maine	IL	125	445	64	119	15	3	16	75	16	49	53	.267
1989	Philadelphia	NL	12	31	7	9	0	0	2	4	1	9	1	.290

Pat Combs
Pitcher

In his first season as a professional, Combs jumped from Class A Clearwater to Double A Reading, finishing the campaign in the major leagues. The Phillies' number-one draft pick in 1988 out of Baylor University posted winning records at each level and sported fine walks-to-strikeouts and hits-to-innings-pitched ratios. At only twenty-three-years-old, this big left-hander could earn a permanent spot in the Philadelphia starting rotation in 1990.

Pat has a deep pitching repertoire. He throws two types of fastballs—one that moves in on a right-hander and one that moves down and away—a curve, a slider, a change-up and a forkball. While this assortment was successful in college, most scouts feel he'll have to drop at least two pitches to be an effective major leaguer. Quality is far more important than quantity. Combs has good control and and a strong, reliable arm. He could be the kind of pitcher who can work well over 200 innings a year if he learns to challenge hitters more effectively and if he can get ahead in the count early. The Phillies can certainly use a quality left-handed starter.

height	weight	bats	throws	birthplace	birthdate
6'4"	200	L	R	Newport, RI	6/11/64

year	team	league	g	ip	h	so	bb	gs	cg	sho	sv	w	l	era
1989	Clearwater	FSL	6	412	35	24	11	6	0	0	0	2	1	1.30
1989	Reading	EL	19	125	104	77	40	19	4	0	0	8	7	3.38
1989	Philadelphia	NL	6	39	37	30	6	6	1	1	0	4	0	2.09

Jason Grimsley
Pitcher

Another of the young Philadelphia pitchers to debut in the major leagues last September, Grimsley was picked in the eleventh round of the June 1985 draft. Jason reached the Phillies after an 11-8 record for Reading, and he finished second in the Eastern League with his 134 strikeouts and 8 complete games. Although he has spent considerably more time in the farm system than Pat Combs, Grimsley is still only twenty-two and could have a bright future in the Senior Circuit.

The concern with Jason has always been his control. His career average stands at better than 6.27 walks per 9 innings pitched and he led the New York-Penn League with 77 bases-on-balls in 1986. Grimsley sometimes has a tendency to overthrow, though his stuff is good enough not to. He has a fastball that consistently reaches the low 90s and a tight, hard curve which rates above- average in quality. With solid mechanics and good work habits, Jason should assert himself as third or fourth in the major league starting rotation sometime soon, though he may begin the 1990 season in Triple A.

height	weight	bats	throws	birthplace	birthdate
6'3"	180	R	R	Cleveland, TX	8/7/67

year	team	league	g	ip	h	so	bb	gs	cg	sho	sv	w	l	era
1985	Bend	NWL	6	11	12	10	25	1	0	0	0	1	0	13.50
1986	Utica	NYP	14	65	63	46	77	14	3	0	0	1	0	6.40
1987	Spartanburg	SAL	23	88	59	98	54	9	3	0	0	7	4	3.16
1988	Clearwater	FSL	16	101	80	90	37	15	2	0	0	4	7	3.73
1988	Reading	EL	5	21	20	14	13	4	0	0	0	1	3	7.17
1989	Reading	EL	26	172	121	134	109	26	8	2	0	11	8	2.98
1989	Philadelphia	NL	4	18	19	7	19	4	0	0	0	1	3	5.89

Tim Mauser
Pitcher

A product of Texas Christian University and the Phillies' third round selection in the June 1988 draft, Tim has a record of 17-15 in two years of professional service. He has started each campaign at the Single A level, but a strong performance at Reading last summer suggests that Mauser will be assigned to either Double or Triple A to begin the 1990 season. He is a young man who complements his considerable talent with tremendous composure, and he could advance to the major leagues quickly.

Mauser is a fine athlete who generates good velocity—90+ mph— with his 6'0", 185 lb. frame. To complement his fastball, this young right-hander throws a hard, breaking curve and a fine split-finger pitch. Tim's ball shows good movement and he is always around the plate. While his average of 6.34 strikeouts per 9 innings pitched does not make Mauser a power pitching prospect, he can get the strikeout when he needs one and likes pressure situations. With the club's need for starting pitching, Philadelphia fans may get a chance to see Tim this September.

height	weight	bats	throws	birthplace	birthdate
6'0"	185	R	R	Fort Worth, TX	10/4/66

year	team	league	g	ip	h	so	bb	gs	cg	sho	sv	w	l	era
1988	Spartanburg	SAL	4	23	15	18	5	3	0	0	0	2	1	1.96
1988	Reading	EL	5	28	27	17	6	5	0	0	0	3	2	3.49
1989	Clearwater	FSL	16	107	105	73	40	16	5	0	0	6	7	2.69
1989	Reading	EL	11	72	62	54	33	11	4	2	0	7	4	3.63

Dave Holdridge
Pitcher

Holdridge was acquired by the Phillies in the trade that sent catcher Lance Parrish to California in October of 1988. He was originally selected by the Angels in the first round of the June 1987 supplemental draft. Although Dave's two-year record of 13-22 is certainly less than impressive, the fact that he has performed for poor teams in each campaign (1988 Quad Cities 60-79 and 1989 Clearwater 57-79) leaves the Phillies optimistic about his future. He should begin the 1990 season in Double A Reading.

This young right-hander's calling card is a 92 mph fastball that sails away from right-handed hitters. He complements his heater with a hard slider and a tight curve, both of which rate above-average. While Holdridge has posted two decent walks-to-innings-pitched ratios, he does need to work on his control. In an effort to limit walks, he sometimes has a tendency to throw the ball right down the middle of the plate. As a result, Dave has given up an average of more than one hit per inning to Class A batters. This summer will be a pivotal one in Holdridge's career and the organization will be watching him closely.

height	weight	bats	throws	birthplace	birthdate
6'3"	190	R	R	Wayne, MI	2/5/68

year	team	league	g	ip	h	so	bb	gs	cg	sho	sv	w	l	era
1988	Quad Cities	MWL	28	154	151	110	79	28	0	0	0	6	12	3.87
1989	Clearwater	FSL	24	132	147	77	77	24	3	0	0	7	10	5.71

Kim Batiste
Shortstop

Though Dickie Thon stepped in last summer to fill the perennial void at shortstop for Philadelphia, the club is still intent on developing a young player to field that position throughout the 1990s. Kim Batiste may be that player. He was selected by the Phillies in the third round of the June 1987 free agent draft and showed some improvement at the plate in the Florida State League last year.

Kim has some power in his 6'0", 175 lbs. frame, though he couldn't be classified as a home run threat. He has the swing to hit .270 or better, with 50 RBIs, if he remains disciplined enough to make consistent contact. Of primary interest to the Phillies was the fact that Batiste reduced his strikeout total from 99 to 13 in the space of a year. That should indicate a Double A assignment this season.

There is little doubt that this young man can play defense. He has excellent first step quickness and range, soft hands and a strong throwing arm. Kim's sometimes erratic play in the field is more attributable to his young age of twenty-one than to any lack of ability. Given another two years in the minors, he should be ready to take over in Philadelphia.

height	weight	bats	throws	birthplace	birthdate
6'0"	175	R	R	New Orleans, LA	unknown

year	team	league	g	ab	r	h	2b	3b	hr	rbi	sb	bb	so	avg
1987	Utica	NYP	46	150	15	26	8	1	2	10	4	7	65	.173
1988	Spartanburg	SAL	122	430	51	107	19	6	6	52	16	14	99	.249
1989	Clearwater	FSL	114	385	36	90	12	4	3	33	13	17	67	.234

Jim Vatcher
Second Base/Outfield

A twentieth round draft pick of the Phillies in 1987, Jim has put together two consecutive All-Star campaigns in the club's farm system. He was selected as one of the Florida State League's top performers last summer before receiving a call to Class AA Reading; and, in 1987, he was both a South Atlantic League All-Star and Philadelphia's Minor League Player of the Year. Hitting at .306 over those two years, and .299 lifetime, Vatcher has almost certainly earned an assignment to Triple A Scranton/Wilkes-Barre for the 1990 season and could see his first major league action this September.

Jim is a fine athlete with good speed and an excellent work ethic. At 5'9", 165 lbs., he will not be noted for his home run exploits, but he does make solid contact with the ball and has a line drive stroke. Last year, nearly 30% of his hits went for extra bases. Defensively, Vatcher does a credible job either at second base or in the outfield. He has good range, sure hands and an arm that will play from either center or left. While Vatcher may have a difficult time cracking the Phillies' starting lineup anytime soon, this twenty-four-year-old could challenge for a job in the majors next spring.

height	weight	bats	throws	birthplace	birthdate
5'9"	165	R	R	Santa Monica, CA	5/27/66

year	team	league	g	ab	r	ho	2b	3b	hr	rbi	sb	bb	so	avg
1987	Utica	NYP	67	249	44	67	15	2	3	21	10	28	31	.269
1988	Spartanburg	SAL	137	496	90	150	32	2	12	72	26	89	73	.302
1989	Clearwater	FSL	92	349	51	105	30	5	4	46	7	41	49	.301
1989	Reading	EL	48	171	27	56	11	3	4	32	2	26	29	.327

Chuck McElroy
Pitcher

McElroy moved from the starting rotation to the bull pen last spring, and from Scranton to Philadelphia last autumn. Despite a 14-4 record at Spartanburg in 1987, Chuck's career record as a starter stood at 27-22 before the change was made and the organization felt he had both the makeup and arm to attain greater success as a reliever. He has a history of losing the velocity on his fastball after several innings, but shows good composure and control on the mound despite his youth.

This wiry left-hander performed well enough with the big club to earn a spot on the staff for 1990. He can run his fastball up to 90+ mph on the radar gun and has a sharp-breaking curve that consistently finds the strike zone. While his stuff is not overpowering, McElroy has averaged nearly 7 strikeouts per 9 innings and could fit in nicely as a setup man in Philadelphia. He will not be considered for the southpaw's closing role until he demonstrates a greater level of consistency over a full season.

height	weight	bats	throws	birthplace	birthdate
6'0"	165	L	L	Galveston, TX	5/27/66

year	team	league	g	ip	h	so	bb	gs	cg	sho	sv	w	l	era
1986	Utica	NYP	14	95	85	91	28	14	5	1	0	4	6	2.95
1987	Spartanburg	SAL	24	130	117	115	49	21	5	2	0	14	4	3.11
1988	Reading	EL	28	160	173	92	70	26	4	2	0	9	12	4.50
1989	Reading	EL	32	47	39	39	14	0	0	0	12	3	1	2.68
1989	Scranton	IL	14	15	13	12	11	0	0	0	3	1	2	2.93
1989	Philadelphia	NL	11	10	12	8	4	0	0	0	0	0	0	1.74

Bob Scanlan
Pitcher

The jury is still out on Bob's future in the big leagues. After Scanlan's 5-18 campaign at Triple A Maine in 1988, the Phillies sent him back to Class AA Reading last spring alternating him between the rotation and the bull pen. His main problem has been a lack of consistency, which stems from mechanical difficulties with his delivery—a common situation with very tall pitchers. If he can fix on a steady motion, Bob may be a true force in Philadelphia.

Scanlan's fine work habits will increase his chances of reaching the major leagues. There is no question that he has the velocity and movement on his pitches to get any hitter out if he gets the ball over the plate. Everything he throws—including a 90 mph fastball and a hard slider—has a heavy sinking action that, more often than not, keeps the ball on the ground. Although not a strikeout pitcher, Bob is not afraid to challenge hitters or work the inside part of the plate. The organization will probably try Scanlan full-time in the bull pen this summer at Triple A Scranton/Wilkes-Barre and they may give him a look in the majors before the year is out.

height	weight	bats	throws	birthplace	birthdate
6'7"	200	R	R	Los Angeles, CA	8/9/66

year	team	league	g	ip	h	so	bb	gs	cg	sho	sv	w	l	era
1985	Spartanburg	SAL	26	152	160	108	53	25	4	0	0	8	12	4.14
1986	Clearwater	FSL	24	126	147	51	45	22	5	0	0	8	12	4.15
1987	Reading	EL	27	164	187	91	55	26	3	1	0	15	5	5.10
1988	Maine	IL	28	161	181	79	50	27	4	1	0	5	18	5.59
1989	Reading	EL	31	118	124	63	58	17	4	1	0	6	10	5.78

Brad Brink
Pitcher

Recurring difficulties with his rotator cuff forced Brad out of action for the second straight season last May. An All-American and three-time All-PAC 10 performer at the University of Southern California, Brink has appeared in only 54 minor league games since signing as the Phillies' first round draft choice in 1986. The organization hopes that arthroscopic surgery performed last summer will be the beginning of this young right-hander's road to recovery—and the big leagues.

When healthy, Brink is a fine competitor with three outstanding pitches. In addition to a sailing fastball that reaches the upper-80 mph range, he throws a tight curve and a baffling straight change-up. He mixes his pitches very well and knows how to work the strike zone. The only question open on Brad will be the condition of his arm. A full recovery could mean a quick ticket to Philadelphia, while anything less could mean a lifetime of minor league work.

height	weight	bats	throws	birthplace	birthdate
6'2"	195	R	R	Roseville, CA	1/20/65

year	team	league	g	ip	h	so	bb	gs	cg	sho	sv	w	l	era
1986	Reading	EL	5	24	21	8	20	4	0	0	0	0	4	3.80
1987	Clearwater	FSL	17	94	99	64	39	17	2	1	0	4	7	3.82
1987	Reading	EL	12	72	76	50	23	11	1	1	0	3	2	5.00
1988	Maine	IL	17	86	100	58	21	17	3	1	0	5	5	4.29
1989	Scranton	IL	3	11	11	3	6	3	0	0	0	0	1	4.09

Draft Analysis

Top Ten Picks:
1. Jeff Jackson, Outfield (Simeon High School, Chicago, IL)
2. Chris Roberts, Left-hand Pitcher (Middleburgh High School, Middleburgh, FL)
3. Lamar Foster, Third Base (Bibb County High School, Brent, AL)
4. Julio Vargas, Catcher (Santa Ana High School, Santa Ana, CA)
5. Steve Parris, Right-hand Pitcher (College of St. Francis)
6. Miah Bradbury, Catcher (Loyola Marymount University)
7. Corey Thomas, Outfield (Don Lugo High School, Chino, CA)
8. Darrell Goedhart, Right-hand Pitcher (Mt. San Jacinto Junior College)
9. Paul Carson, Outfield (Woodinville High School, Woodinville, WA)
10. Cary Williams, Outfield (University of Alabama)

The woes of the Phillies may be best described by last June's free agent draft. While the club did get outfielder Jeff Jackson, the Gatorade Circle of Champions high school player of the year, two other top ten choices went unsigned—Chris Roberts and Miah Bradbury; and, with help needed at virtually every position, Philadelphia was unable to concentrate their choices in any one area. Wisely, however, the Phillies chose thirty-seven players with their fifty-one draft picks in the hopes of getting support in the major leagues quickly.

Among the bright spots in the Philadelphia draft were Jackson and outfielder Cary Williams. The first round pick has been described as an Eric Davis clone. Though he had difficulty making consistent contact in his first pro campaign, Jeff did show the good speed and power-potential club officials expected. Williams, on the other hand, exceeded expectations. He reached Class AA Reading by the end of the summer on the strength of a strong season at Clearwater.

Philadelphia fans will need to be patient in the years to come. The 1989 draft may produce several prospects, but at least two more classes of draftees will be needed to rebuild the system.

PITTSBURGH PIRATES

1989 Farm System Record
368-403 (.477)

Buffalo	AA	AAA	80	62	.563
Harrisburg	EL	AA	63	76	.453
Salem	CAR	A	63	75	.457
Augusta	SAL	A	77	67	.535
Welland	NYP	A	32	44	.421
Princeton	APPY	Rookie	32	37	.464
Bradenton	GCL	Rookie	21	42	.333

Hopes ran high for the Bucs when they headed into the 1989 season. The club was coming off a surprising 1988 campaign and there were plenty of prospects in the pipeline. Or were there? When Pittsburgh got off to a bad start last year, much of the blame was placed on departed GM Syd Thrift. The argument went that Thrift had left nothing but an empty shell in the minors and he was signing on with the Yankees for personal gain before the facade was uncovered. In reality, Pirate management could not stomach the high cost of rebuilding. Syd revitalized Pittsburgh's scouting and player development systems, but with little support, was unable to finish the job. A true evaluation of his effectiveness can not be made for several years.

There were only two winning teams among Pittsburgh's seven minor league affiliates in 1989. At the Triple A level, Buffalo enjoyed another record year at the gate (over one million in attendance), but was unable to provide the depth and quality of players the Bucs needed when a rash of injuries struck in April and May. Manager Jim Leyland was particularly disappointed in the pitchers called up from the farm. Oddly enough though, pitching may be the strength of the system. In addition to the fine relief prospects profiled in this section, Pittsburgh has a developing starter in Randy Tomlin (14 wins and a 2.79 ERA at Class AA Harrisburg). Pirate fans should still have hope.

The Pirates' top prospects are:

Moises Alou	Jeff King
Stan Belinda	Willie Smith
Keith Richardson	Wes Chamberlain
Jeff Cook	Mike York
Rick Reed	Tom Prince

Moises Alou
Outfield

This twenty-three-year-old outfielder is the son of former major league star Felipe Alou, and was selected by the Pirates in the first round of the January 1986 draft. Moises first played organized ball at Canada Junior College in Redwood City, California, just a few short years ago, but he has made outstanding progress in his short tenure with the Pittsburgh organization. He is a fine natural athlete with a long, lean build, good strength and impressive speed.

Alou began to show some home run pop to go with his line drive power last year. In a season split between Single A Salem and Double A Harrisburg, Moises more than doubled his previous career-high in homers with 17, and 35% of his hits went for extra bases. A very patient hitter, he uses the whole field effectively and should average near .300 in the major leagues.

Defensively, Moises may already be as good as or better than Andy Van Slyke in center field. He has excellent instincts, good range and an above-average throwing arm. Alou will most likely begin the 1990 campaign at Class AAA Buffalo.

height	weight	bats	throws	birthplace	birthdate
6'3"	175	R	R	Atlanta, GA	7/3/66

year	team	league	g	ab	r	h	2b	3b	hr	rbi	sb	bb	so	avg
1986	Watertown	NYP	69	254	30	60	9	8	6	35	14	22	72	.236
1987	Watertown	NYP	39	117	20	25	6	2	4	18	6	16	36	.214
1988	Augusta	SAL	105	358	58	112	23	5	7	62	24	51	84	.313
1989	Harrisburg	EL	54	205	36	60	5	2	3	19	8	17	38	.293
1989	Salem	CAR	86	321	50	97	29	2	14	53	12	35	69	.302

Jeff King
Third Base

Despite a low batting average with Pittsburgh last year, Jeff did show the ability to come through in the clutch, and better than half of his hits went for extra bases. King was Pittsburgh's first round selection in the June 1986 free agent draft, and he has put up some good numbers in the minor leagues. His major league production should improve as he settles in as a Pirate regular in 1990.

Once considered an outstanding power hitting prospect, Jeff has failed to live up to expectations. However, he has the stroke to average 20 home runs per season. With his natural strength, King would benefit from trying to make solid contact rather than swinging for the fences—an attitude that could raise his average to around .275. Jeff's main attraction to Pittsburgh is his ability to play third base. The club needs Bobby Bonilla's bat in the lineup, but can't afford the errors he makes at third base. King's quickness, sure hands and strong arm should play well on the artificial surface at Three Rivers and allow Bonilla to move to first.

height	weight	bats	throws	birthplace	birthdate
6'1"	180	R	R	Marion, IN	12/26/64

year	team	league	g	ab	r	h	2b	3b	hr	rbi	sb	bb	so	avg
1986	Prince William	CAR	37	132	18	31	4	1	6	20	1	19	34	.235
1987	Salem	CAR	90	310	68	86	9	1	26	71	5	61	88	.277
1987	Harrisburg	EL	26	100	12	24	7	0	2	25	0	4	27	.240
1988	Harrisburg	EL	117	411	49	105	21	1	14	66	5	46	87	.255
1989	Buffalo	AA	51	169	26	43	5	2	6	29	7	13	22	.254

Stan Belinda
Pitcher

A tenth round draft pick in 1986, Stan reached the major leagues for the first time last September. Belinda made "The Show" on the strength of solid performances at Harrisburg and Buffalo, netting 3 victories and 22 saves, and his 0.95 ERA at Class AAA was the best in the American Association for pitchers with five or more appearances. The fact that Bill Landrum earned the right-handed closer's role in Pittsburgh last summer may mean a minor league assignment for Stan this spring, but he should see some big league action before the year is out.

Belinda throws three pitches—fastball, slider and change-up—from two different deliveries. He can reach 90 mph with his three-quarter fastball or sacrifice 5 mph for a sinking sidearm version. By mixing his pitches well and challenging batters, Stan can get a strikeout when he needs one and he isn't afraid to work inside. He has the ideal makeup for a closer and, at only twenty-three, he should be in the Pittsburgh bull pen for many years to come.

height	weight	bats	throws	birthplace	birthdate
6'3"	185	R	R	Huntingdon, PA	8/6/66

year	team	league	g	ip	h	so	bb	gs	cg	sho	sv	w	l	era
1986	Bradenton	GCL	17	20	23	17	2	0	0	0	7	3	2	2.66
1987	Florence	SAL	50	82	61	75	28	0	0	0	16	6	4	2.30
1988	Salem	CAR	53	72	54	63	32	0	0	0	14	6	4	2.76
1989	Buffalo	AA	19	28	13	28	13	0	0	0	9	2	2	0.95
1989	Harrisburg	EL	32	38	32	33	25	0	0	0	13	1	4	2.33
1989	Pittsburgh	NL	8	10	13	10	2	0	0	0	0	0	1	6.10

Willie Smith
Pitcher

Signed out of Savannah High School as a non-drafted free agent in 1986, Willie is a big, hard-throwing right-hander with a future in the Pirates' bull pen. Although used by the organization in a long relief and a spot starter's role on occasion, Smith has the size and competitive nature to be an intimidating closer along the lines of Goose Gossage or Lee Smith. He will most likely begin the 1990 campaign at Class AA Harrisburg, but a solid effort in spring training could earn Smith a Triple A job instead.

With a sailing fastball that consistently reaches 96-98 mph and a heavy 90 mph slider, Willie doesn't bother with offspeed pitches, and shouldn't. He is capable of dominating hitters at any level and has a career average of nearly 8 strikeouts per 9 innings pitched. Some fine tuning of his mechanics could add a few feet to Smith's fastball, and even more strikeouts to his totals.

The contrast in styles between Willie and fellow bull pen prospect Stan Belinda will give Pittsburgh solid relief pitching through the '90s. Smith should reach the major leagues by next year.

height	weight	bats	throws	birthplace	birthdate
6'5"	225	R	R	Savannah, GA	1/27/67

year	team	league	g	ip	h	so	bb	gs	cg	sho	sv	w	l	era
1987	Pirates	GCL	10	19	12	27	11	1	0	0	4	2	1	1.40
1988	Augusta	SAL	30	48	35	48	29	1	0	0	6	1	4	2.98
1989	Harrisburg	EL	12	18	11	21	10	0	0	0	0	3	0	2.45
1989	Salem	CAR	23	64	46	58	40	9	0	0	4	4	5	2.94

Keith Richardson
Pitcher

The Pirates' second round selection in the June 1988 draft out of Georgia Southern University, Keith has made tremendous progress in the organization's farm system in two years as a professional. His composite 21-12 record has earned Richardson no less than three promotions to end the 1989 campaign at Class AA Harrisburg. Although he stumbled somewhat in his first season of Eastern League action, Keith's work ethic and capacity to learn quickly should produce a solid outing in 1990.

Richardson has excellent command of both a 90 mph fastball and a tight curve. He has registered an average of 7.10 strikeouts per 9 innings pitched while walking only 2.4 batters a game. Keith is very poised and collected on the mound and has enough movement on his pitches to challenge batters effectively. Ideally, Pittsburgh would like to give their young right-hander another two years in the minors. However, the dearth of pitching at the major league level could force Keith into the rotation next year.

height	weight	bats	throws	birthplace	birthdate
6'5"	210	R	R	Statesboro, GA	1/24/67

year	team	league	g	ip	h	so	bb	gs	cg	sho	sv	w	l	era
1988	Watertown	NYP	8	45	29	35	8	6	0	0	0	6	1	1.21
1988	Augusta	SAL	4	29	18	17	4	4	1	0	0	3	1	0.31
1989	Harrisburg	EL	21	117	121	96	39	21	3	1	0	8	10	4.59
1989	Salem	CAR	5	32	30	26	10	5	2	0	0	4	0	0.84

Wes Chamberlain
Outfield

The Pirates' organization is very impressed with this young outfielder. A fourth round selection in the June 1987 free agent draft, Chamberlain's average and power figures have improved every year. In 1989, his 144 hits and 87 RBIs led the Eastern League. Wes also finished second in home runs and batting average, as he was named league MVP. Though a season at Triple A Buffalo is most likely in order for this twenty-four-year-old, it's conceivable he could make the jump to Pittsburgh sometime this summer.

Offensively, Chamberlain's stats prove that he can hit. What's more impressive, however, is the blend of strength and discipline he shows at the plate. Wes hits to all fields, rarely strikes out and will take a walk when necessary. Defensively, Chamberlain has good speed and covers plenty of ground playing either center or right field. It would be a shame, though, to play an arm like his—very strong and accurate—anywhere but in right. Pirate insiders are excited about Wes' arrival in the Steel City—fans should be, too.

height	weight	bats	throws	birthplace	birthdate
6'2"	210	R	R	Chicago, IL	4/13/66

year	team	league	g	ab	r	h	2b	3b	hr	rbi	sb	bb	so	avg
1987	Watertown	NYP	66	258	50	67	13	4	5	35	22	25	48	.260
1988	Augusta	SAL	27	107	22	36	7	2	1	17	1	11	11	.336
1988	Salem	CAR	92	365	66	100	15	1	11	50	14	38	59	.274
1989	Harrisburg	EL	129	471	65	144	26	3	21	87	11	32	82	.306

Jeff Cook
Outfield

A fine all-around athlete in high school, Jeff got a late start in baseball because there was no team at Paseo High in Kansas City, Missouri. Drafted in the tenth round in 1985 out of Phillips University in Enid, Oklahoma, Cook has been impressive in the Pirates' farm system during his four years as a pro. Jeff has twice gone over the .300 mark in batting, averaged more than 40 steals per season, and has consistently ranked among league leaders in assists from the outfield. He'll most likely open the 1990 campaign at Class AAA Buffalo, but could see some major league action before the year is out.

Jeff is a switch-hitter with a quick bat and line drive power from both sides of the plate. He rarely strikes out and his speed could make him a dangerous top-of-the-order-type batter. Defensively, Cook has good range and an excellent arm in the outfield. He is capable of playing any of the three positions, but seems best suited for right. Even at age twenty-six, Jeff is still considered a prospect. He should be given the opportunity to earn a major league job next year.

height	weight	bats	throws	birthplace	birthdate
6'0"	185	B	R	Kansas City, MO	12/17/63

year	team	league	g	ab	r	h	2b	3b	hr	rbi	sb	bb	so	avg
1985	Bradenton	GCL	46	167	32	44	1	1	1	13	19	14	25	.263
1986	Prince William	CAR	128	511	86	154	16	5	2	29	43	54	77	.301
1987	Harrisburg	EL	53	193	26	44	6	0	0	4	11	9	26	.228
1987	Salem	CAR	69	298	48	101	9	4	1	26	39	26	30	.339
1988	Harrisburg	EL	127	490	55	126	9	2	1	29	45	45	57	.257
1989	Harrisburg	EL	18	63	11	18	1	1	0	3	7	9	11	.286
1989	Buffalo	AA	97	315	35	78	7	5	0	20	21	25	41	.248

Mike York
Pitcher

Originally selected by the Yankees in the fortieth round of the June 1982 free agent draft, Mike is now twenty-five years old and with his fourth organization. He was released by the Yankees, the White Sox and the Tigers for alcohol related problems, but seems to have straightened himself out over the past two years and could reach the big leagues with Pittsburgh. There has never been any question of York's ability. In the four seasons in which he's started 20 or more games, Mike's record is a stellar 47-18. The Pirates will be paying close attention as he works his first full season at Triple A this year.

York has an above-average fastball and one of the best curves in the organization. He is very consistent and knows how to work a game. Although he can't be considered a power pitcher, Mike can get a strikeout when he needs one, and he's averaged better than 8 Ks per 9 innings pitched over the last three seasons. Despite his past problems, York is currently pitching well and would be a welcome addition to the Pirate staff.

height	weight	bats	throws	birthplace	birthdate
6'1"	185	R	R	Oak Park, IL	9/6/64

year	team	league	g	ip	h	so	bb	gs	cg	sho	sv	w	l	era
1985	Bristol	APP	21	38	24	31	34	0	0	0	2	9	2	2.37
1986	Lakeland	FSL	16	41	49	29	43	0	0	0	1	1	3	6.42
1986	Gastonia	SAL	22	34	26	27	27	0	0	0	9	2	2	3.44
1987	Florence	SAL	28	166	129	169	88	28	3	2	0	17	6	3.26
1988	Salem	CAR	13	84	65	77	52	13	2	1	0	9	2	2.68
1988	Harrisburg	EL	13	82	92	61	45	13	2	0	0	0	5	3.72
1989	Buffalo	AA	8	41	48	28	25	8	0	0	0	1	3	5.93
1989	Harrisburg	EL	18	121	105	106	40	18	3	2	0	11	5	2.31

Rick has been cited as a Pittsburgh prospect for most of his four professional seasons with the organization. However, this former twenty-sixth round pick from 1986 has failed to meet expectations in his two brief major league stints. His 29-19 lifetime minor league record has been accompanied by two sub-2.00 ERAs and an excellent walks-to-strikeouts ratio, but he was touched for more than one hit per inning in Pittsburgh last summer.

Reed is a classic control pitcher. He doesn't have much velocity, but can hit spots with his sinking fastball, tight curve and straight change-up. A poised performer on the mound, he is adept at changing speeds and moving the ball in and out. Rick does not have the stuff to challenge hitters in the middle of the strike zone and has trouble working when he's behind in the count—although he rarely is. He has proven himself in Triple A and deserves a true shot at the major league rotation. If Reed doesn't fit in with the Pirates' plans, he may be offered in a trade over the winter.

Rick Reed
Pitcher

height	weight	bats	throws						birthplace				birthdate	
6'1"	205	R	R						Huntington, WV				8/16/64	

year	team	league	g	ip	h	so	bb	gs	cg	sho	sv	w	l	era
1986	Pirates	GCL	8	24	20	15	6	3	0	0	0	0	2	3.75
1986	Macon	SAL	1	1	1	0	0	1	0	0	0	0	0	2.84
1987	Macon	SAL	46	94	80	92	29	0	0	0	7	8	4	2.50
1988	Salem	CAR	15	72	56	73	17	8	4	1	0	6	2	2.74
1988	Harrisburg	EL	2	16	11	17	2	2	0	0	0	1	0	1.13
1988	Buffalo	AA	10	77	62	50	12	9	3	2	0	5	2	1.64
1988	Pirates	NL	2	12	10	6	2	2	0	0	0	1	0	3.00
1989	Buffalo	AA	20	125	130	75	28	20	3	0	0	9	8	3.72

Another longtime Pittsburgh prospect, Tom has played in the major leagues briefly these past two seasons, but he's spent most of his time in Triple A Buffalo. This solidly built catcher was selected by the Pirates in the fourth round of the secondary phase in the January 1984 draft; he has shown good offensive and defensive potential in the minor leagues. He earned All-Star honors in the Eastern League (1987) and in the American Association (1988), and has reached double figures in home runs three times.

Prince has above-average power to left field, but has been working on using the whole field to raise his average. He will not be an offensive force in the big leagues, but could be a fine situation or platoon hitter. Behind the plate, however, Tom is an excellent receiver. He calls a great game, sets a good target and blocks balls in the dirt well. His arm is among the best in minor league baseball and he gets rid of the ball quickly. With the scarcity of young catchers in the game, Tom should land a major league job in Pittsburgh, or elsewhere, within two years.

Tom Prince
Catcher

height	weight	bats	throws						birthplace				birthdate	
5'11"	180	R	R						Kankakee, IL				8/13/64	

year	team	league	g	ab	r	h	2b	3b	hr	rbi	sb	bb	so	avg
1985	Macon	SAL	124	360	60	75	20	1	10	42	13	96	92	.208
1986	Prince William	CAR	121	395	59	100	34	1	10	47	3	50	74	.253
1987	Harrisburg	EL	113	365	41	112	23	2	6	54	6	51	46	.307
1987	Pirates	NL	4	9	1	2	1	0	1	2	0	0	2	.222
1988	Buffalo	AA	86	304	35	79	16	0	14	42	3	23	53	.260
1989	Buffalo	AA	65	183	21	37	8	1	6	33	2	22	30	.202

Draft Analysis

Top Ten Picks:

1. Willie Greene, Shortstop (Jones County High School, Gray, GA)
2a. Rich Aude, Third Base (Chatsworth High School, Chatsworth, CA)
2b. John Hope, Right-hand Pitcher (Stranahan High School, Ft. Lauderdale, FL)
3. Rob Bailey, Outfield (Fullerton Junior College)
4. Patrick Hicks, Catcher (Overland High School, Aurora, CO)
5. Michael Brown, First Base (Vacaville High School, Vacaville, CA)
6. Kevin Rychel, Left-hand Pitcher (Midland High School, Midland, TX)
7. Tim Williams, Outfield (Springboro High School, Springboro, OH)
8. Ricardo Ufret, Shortstop (Aquinas Junior College)
9. Joe Ronca, Outfield (Tate High School, Cantonment, FL)
10. David Bird, Left-hand Pitcher (Chapman College)

Pittsburgh is a self-professed "best available athlete" organization when it comes to the draft. And their 1989 first round pick fits that mold perfectly. At 5'11' and 160 lbs., Willie Greene has the speed, reflexes and instincts to advance rapidly at a position in the Pirate organization. In 62 games with the club's rookie league affiliates in the Gulf Coast and Appalachian circuits, Greene hit .306 with 7 home runs and 8 stolen bases. Behind him, however, Pittsburgh draftees did not fair as well.

Among the top position player choices, second round pick Rich Aude led the way with a .216 average in the Gulf Coast League. Aude's teammate Joe Ronca had the most home runs with one. On the mound, Hope, Rychel and Bird each suffered losing seasons, though the tenth round pick did notch 75 strikeouts in 65 innings with Welland. Overall, while team officials were pleased with their selections, it will take several more drafts to restock a farm system filled with aging prospects.

For the record, Pittsburgh made forty-nine picks in last June's draft. Nineteen were pitchers and ten were catchers, infielders and outfielders. Twenty-seven picks came from the college ranks.

HOUSTON ASTROS

1989 Farm System Record
318-372 (.454)

Tucson	PCL	AAA	56	86	.394
Columbus	SL	AA	71	72	.497
Osceola	FSL	A	72	65	.526
Asheville	SAL	A	68	70	.493
Auburn	NYP	A	35	42	.455
Sarasota	GCL	Rookie	16	47	.254

Houston promoted two regulars to their major league roster last year—Craig Biggio and Ken Caminiti. They equaled the total of significant contributions the Astros received from the farm system in the previous five years. The young talent the club has had in recent years either failed to develop major league potential or has been struck down by injury. 1990 will be a telling season in regards to the current crop of prospects. Of paramount importance to the club are the recoveries of outfielder Cameron Drew and four of their young pitching prospects.

Houston does have the top power-hitting prospect in the game in Eric Anthony, and they have plenty of speed and defense in the system. Among the club's developing prospects, Astro fans should watch Andy Mota and Andujar Cedeno. These young men hit .319 and .300 respectively and drove in a combined 162 runs in Class A ball last summer. Houston is in desperate need of more power in their lineup and may be quick to send the call for either or both of them in the near future.

The Astros' top prospects are:

Eric Anthony	Cameron Drew
Brian Meyer	Karl Rhodes
Scott Servais	Fred Costello
Ryan Bowen	Luis Gonzalez
Mike Simms	Darryl Kile

The most prolific home run hitter in minor league baseball over the past two seasons, Anthony may be the answer to Houston's long-time need for a left-handed power hitter. His long, smooth swing and quick wrists have produced one round-tripper for every 16 professional at bats and over 40% of Eric's hits go for extra bases. With these kinds of credentials, it's easy to see why this former thirty-fourth round pick from the 1986 June draft earned a promotion to the major leagues last August.

If Anthony doesn't begin the 1990 campaign in Houston, it will be because the organization wants him to sharpen his raw defensive skills in Triple A Tucson first. He has the speed and the arm to play either right or left field. He needs to concentrate on getting a better jump on the ball and throwing to the proper cutoff man, however, if he wants to earn a permanent spot in the

Eric Anthony
Outfield

Astro lineup. As with many power hitters, Eric has a tendency to strikeout, but the club is willing to trade his high number of strikeouts for the runs he's sure to produce.

height	weight	bats	throws	birthplace	birthdate
6'2"	195	L	L	San Diego, CA	11/8/67

year	team	league	g	ab	r	h	2b	3b	hr	rbi	sb	bb	so	avg
1986	Astros	GCL	13	12	2	3	0	0	0	0	1	5	5	.250
1987	Astros	GCL	60	216	38	57	11	6	10	46	2	26	58	.264
1988	Asheville	SAL	115	439	73	120	36	1	29	89	10	40	101	.273
1989	Columbus	SL	107	403	67	121	16	2	28	79	14	35	127	.300
1989	Tuscon	PCL	12	46	10	10	3	0	3	11	0	6	11	.217
1989	Houston	NL	25	61	7	11	2	0	4	7	0	9	16	.180

A left knee injury suffered sliding into second base on June 16, 1988, and subsequent surgery, have kept Cameron on the shelf for nearly one-and-a-half seasons. However, this former number-one draft pick from 1985 may have more natural ability than any player in the Astro farm system, and certainly must be rated among their top prospects. An imposing batter at 6'5", Cameron has a long, solid swing with some power. His frequent line drives to the gaps have produced 405 hits in two-and-a-half professional campaigns—a .312 life-time average—and fully one-third of those hits have gone for extra bases.

If Drew's knee recovers fully, he has the speed to play any of the outfield positions. But, with Gerald Young firmly entrenched in center, Houston may use Cameron's strong, accurate arm in right and move an aging Kevin Bass to left field. After a full year off to

Cameron Drew
Outfield

recuperate, and at twenty-six years of age, Drew is ready for a major league assignment. Look for Cameron to have a big year, if he remains healthy.

height	weight	bats	throws	birthplace	birthdate
6'5"	215	L	R	Boston, MA	2/12/64

year	team	league	g	ab	r	h	2b	3b	hr	rbi	sb	bb	so	avg
1986	Asheville	SAL	124	439	77	143	26	4	26	0	8	36	59	.326
1987	Columbus	SL	133	490	66	136	26	1	17	70	8	25	81	.277
1988	Tuscon	PCL	97	354	50	126	22	7	4	70	18	23	35	.356
1988	Houston	NL	7	16	1	3	0	1	0	1	0	0	1	.187
1989	Did Not Play													

Brian Meyer
Pitcher

Although Meyer may not step directly into the right-handed closer's role because of the presence of Dave Smith, he will definitely earn a spot on the Astros' pitching staff this spring. Selected by Houston in the sixteenth round of the June 1986 free agent draft out of Rollins College in Florida, this twenty-seven-year-old has averaged better than 18 saves in four professional campaigns and has twice posted sub-2.00 ERAs.

Brian seems well-suited to bull pen work. He is a hard-nosed performer with outstanding control who, by his own admission, thrives on pressure. Meyer works with an excellent sharp slider and a deceptive fastball that reaches the upper 80s. More recently, he has been mixing in a split-finger pitch. The manner in which Brian challenges batters and comes up with the big out when he needs one, will keep this young man in the major leagues for many years to come,

height	weight	bats	throws	birthplace	birthdate
6'1"	190	R	R	Camden, NJ	1/29/63

year	team	league	g	ip	h	so	bb	gs	cg	sho	sv	w	l	era
1986	Auburn	NYP	32	57	44	66	10	0	0	0	8	5	2	1.43
1987	Osceola	FSL	52	77	58	58	23	0	0	0	25	8	9	1.99
1988	Columbus	SL	62	83	61	68	36	0	0	0	25	4	3	2.27
1988	Houston	NL	8	12	9	10	4	0	0	0	0	0	0	1.46
1989	Tuscon	PCL	58	80	81	56	33	0	0	0	15	5	4	2.80

Karl Rhodes
Outfield

An All-State performer and the Greater Cincinnati Player of the Year when he led Western Hills High School to the Ohio State Championship in 1986, Karl was selected by Houston in the third round of that summer's free agent draft. He is a fundamentally sound outfielder with good speed and an excellent attitude. However, at only twenty-one-years-old, Rhodes will probably see at least two more seasons' action at the minor league level due to the crowd in Houston's major league outfield.

Offensively, Karl is a disciplined hitter who uses the whole field. He doesn't have much power and will have difficulty catching up with the hard inside fastball, but his slap-and-go style should play well on the Astrodome's artificial surface. Rhodes' 6.7 speed in the 60-yard dash is good enough to steal 20 or more bases and allows him to cover plenty of ground in the field, though an average throwing arm may dictate a future in left.

height	weight	bats	throws	birthplace	birthdate
5'11"	170	L	L	Cincinnati, OH	8/21/68

year	team	league	g	ab	r	h	2b	3b	hr	rbi	sb	bb	so	avg
1986	Astros	GCL	62	222	36	65	10	3	0	22	14	32	33	.293
1987	Asheville	SAL	129	413	62	104	16	4	3	50	43	77	82	.252
1988	Osceola	FSL	132	452	69	128	4	2	1	34	65	81	58	.283
1989	Columbus	SL	143	520	81	134	25	5	4	63	18	93	105	.258

Scott Servais
Catcher

Although 1989 was Scott's first season as a professional, this young catcher gained enough experience at Creighton University, and as a member of the U.S. Gold Medal Olympic team, to move up quickly in the Houston farm system. Servais, a third round selection in the June 1988 free agent draft, earned a promotion to Class AA Columbus after a strong start in the Florida State League last year and he could open the 1990 campaign at Triple A Tucson.

Scott is a fine defensive backstop with an exceptionally strong, accurate arm. He is quick and agile behind the plate and knows how to call a game. The only question in the minds of Astro management is Servais' ability to develop offensively. He has not shown the power one would expect from his 6'2", 195 lb. frame and had difficulty making contact at the Double A level last year. While defense is of paramount importance for a catcher, Scott's bat may make it difficult for him to pass Craig Biggio on the Astros' depth chart.

height	weight	bats	throws	birthplace	birthdate
6'2"	195	R	R	La Crosse, WI	6/4/67

year	team	league	g	ab	r	h	2b	3b	hr	rbi	sb	bb	so	avg
1989	Osceola	FSL	46	153	16	41	9	0	2	23	0	16	35	.268
1989	Columbus	SL	63	199	20	47	5	0	1	22	0	19	42	.236

Fred Costello
Pitcher

Selected as a starter in the fourth round of the June 1986 free agent draft, Fred's consecutive losing campaigns in the Gulf Coast League precipitated a move to the bull pen in 1988. Although he averaged just better than 5 innings per start, Costello is the type of pitcher who can throw hard for several innings day after day. He has a good mix of pitches for a short reliever—90 mph fastball, slider, sinker and offspeed split-finger—and seems to like pressure situations.

When Fred has good command, he can be dominating. During one stretch of 20.1 innings in April of 1988, he posted a 0.89 ERA, and then held opponents scoreless for an entire month later that season. However, Costello will have a difficult time securing the stopper's role with the Astros. With right-handers Dave Smith and Brian Meyer in front of him, Fred will probably spend the 1990 campaign in Tucson. His first shot at the major leagues may come in middle relief.

height	weight	bats	throws	birthplace	birthdate
6'4"	190	R	R	Clearlake, CA	12/1/66

year	team	league	g	ip	h	so	bb	gs	cg	sho	sv	w	l	era
1986	Astros	GCL	14	66	74	51	26	12	1	1	0	4	5	4.75
1987	Astros	GCL	13	73	74	45	28	12	0	0	0	5	7	3.22
1988	Asheville	SAL	51	76	76	65	31	0	0	0	11	6	7	3.55
1989	Columbus	SL	30	54	39	39	21	0	0	0	3	4	5	3.33

Ryan Bowen
Pitcher

Houston's number-one selection in the June 1986 draft, Ryan has compiled a 21-11 record in slightly more than two years' work as a pro. He's an intelligent pitcher with an excellent attitude, sound mechanics and the desire to win. At twenty-two, Bowen won't be pushed by the Astro organization into the major leagues too quickly, but he's successfully made the transition to a higher level of ball each year and could be ready as soon as 1992.

In the minors, Ryan has worked with a five-pitch repertoire—an 88-90 mph fastball, a tight curve, a slider, a forkball and a straight change-up. While each pitch is at least average and good enough to get Class AA hitters out, three of them may have to be perfected in order for Ryan to succeed in Houston. The other area Bowen must work on is his walks-to-strikeouts ratio.

Although he has good control, Ryan gets too fine at times and forgets to challenge hitters. His ball moves well enough to come in to batters without getting hurt.

height	weight	bats	throws	birthplace	birthdate
6'0"	185	R	R	Hanford, CA	2/10/68

year	team	league	g	ip	h	so	bb	gs	cg	sho	sv	w	l	era
1987	Asheville	SAL	26	160	143	126	78	26	6	2	0	12	5	4.04
1988	Osceola	FSL	4	14	12	12	10	4	0	0	0	1	0	3.95
1989	Columbus	SL	27	139	123	136	116	27	1	1	0	8	6	4.25

Luis Gonzalez
Third Base

It's risky at best to predict the future prospects of a twenty-two-year-old after only 559 at bats, but Luis Gonzalez has the makings of a fine major league hitter. A fourth round pick in the June 1988 draft, this young infielder holds a .286 lifetime average as a professional, along with 13 home runs, 11 triples and 33 doubles. He makes good contact consistently with a pure left-handed stroke, shows excellent knowledge of the strike zone and uses the whole field. With one of the lowest team averages in the National League, Houston could use Luis' bat in the lineup as soon as possible.

The question with Gonzalez is where to put him in the field. He has shown good hands at both first and third base, possesses a strong arm and works hard on his defense. However, Luis does not have the glove to replace Ken Caminiti or the power to oust Glenn Davis. He is too big to play either of the middle infield positions and has no experience in the outfield. The fact that he was used primarily as a designated hitter at Class AA Columbus last year could suggest a possible trade.

height	weight	bats	throws	birthplace	birthdate
6'2"	180	L	R	Tampa, FL	9/3/67

year	team	league	g	ab	r	h	2b	3b	hr	rbi	sb	bb	so	avg
1988	Auburn	NYP	39	157	32	49	10	3	5	27	2	12	19	.312
1988	Asheville	SAL	31	115	13	29	7	1	2	14	2	12	17	.252
1989	Osceola	FSL	86	287	46	82	16	7	6	38	2	37	49	.286

Mike Simms
First Base

Mike's 39 home runs at Class A Asheville in 1987 stand as a South Atlantic League record and were the most hit by any minor leaguer that year. In three-and-a-half professional campaigns, Simms' exceptional strength has accounted for 79 round trippers and 291 RBIs. Like most power hitters, though, his high slugging average has come at the expense of too many strikeouts and too few singles. And, his lifetime average of .258 does not compare favorably with the .293 mark held by Glenn Davis—the man whose job Simms is after—at a similar stage.

Defensively, the rangy Brooklyn native moves wells around first base. He has soft hands and a good arm. If there has been a problem with Mike's play in the field, it's been a lack of concentration. Some scouts feel that he thinks too much about hitting home runs to focus on the other aspects of the game. Simms certainly has the talent to reach the major leagues, but will need at least two more years in the farm system to sharpen his skills.

height	weight	bats	throws	birthplace	birthdate
6'4"	185	R	R	Brooklyn, NY	11/29/65

year	team	league	g	ab	r	h	2b	3b	hr	rbi	sb	bb	so	avg
1986	Sarasota	GCL	54	181	33	47	14	1	4	37	2	22	48	.260
1987	Asheville	SAL	133	469	93	128	19	0	39	100	7	73	167	.273
1988	Osceola	FSL	123	428	63	104	19	1	16	73	9	76	130	.243
1989	Columbus	SL	109	378	64	97	21	3	20	81	12	66	110	.257

Darryl Kile
Pitcher

The Astros' thirtieth round selection in the June 1987 free agent draft, Darryl has progressed more rapidly than the organization ever could have expected. Just two years out of Chaffey Junior College in California, this young right-hander reached the Triple A level with Tucson last season after a dominant stint in the Southern League. While with the Columbus Mudcats, Kile went 11-6 with a 2.58 ERA and allowed just 74 hits in 126 innings of work.

An imposing figure on the mound at 6'5", Darryl is a classic power pitcher with a 93 mph fastball and big curve. What makes him more effective than other hard throwers, however, is the fact that he knows the velocity and movement are hard for hitters to handle, so he challenges them. Such confidence is a necessary element of success for starting pitchers and the Houston organization will try to preserve it by giving Kile a full season at Tucson in 1990. If he is able to survive a hitters' league like the PCL, Darryl should get a shot at the major league club next year.

height	weight	bats	throws	birthplace	birthdate
6'5"	185	R	R	Garden Grove, CA	12/2/68

year	team	league	g	ip	h	so	bb	gs	cg	sho	sv	w	l	era
1988	Sarasota	GCL	12	60	48	54	33	12	0	0	0	5	3	3.17
1989	Columbus	SL	20	125	74	108	68	20	6	2	0	11	6	2.58
1989	Tuscon	PCL	6	25	33	18	13	6	1	1	0	2	1	5.96

Draft Analysis

Top Ten Picks:

1a. Jeff Juden, Right-hand Pitcher (Salem High School, Salem, MA)
1b. Todd Jones, Right-hand Pitcher (Jacksonville State University)
2a. Brian Hunter, Outfield (Fort Vancouver High School, Vancouver, WA)
2b. Jermaine Swinton, Outfield (Fort Hamilton High School, Brooklyn, NY)
3. Shane Reynolds, Right-hand Pitcher (University of Texas)
4. Tyrone Scott, Left-hand Pitcher (Leuzinger High School, Palmdale, CA)
5. John Stanczak, First Base (LaSalle High School, Philadelphia, PA)
6. Scott Markarewicz, Catcher (Michigan State University)
7. Gershon Dallas, Outfield (Hillsborough Community College)
8. Craig Curtis, Outfield (North Kansas City High School, Kansas City, MO)
9. Cole Hyson, Right-hand Pitcher (University of Arkansas)
10. Mark Hampton, Right-hand Pitcher (Southwest Junior College)

Houston was both surprised and pleased to find pitcher Jeff Juden still available when their turn came to select a player in the first round (twelfth pick). Juden had been a standout performer in high school where, in four years, he posted a 25-3 record, a 0.42 ERA and struck in 388 batters in 204 innings. Although Jeff's professional debut in the Gulf Coast League failed to measure up to his previous standards (1-4, 3.40 and 49 Ks in 49.2 innings), Houston still liked what they saw.

Even if Juden doesn't develop as expected, however, the Astros' 1989 draft may still be seen as a success. The team had four picks in the first two rounds and selected an incredible eighty-nine players in all—an increase of twenty-five from 1988. They found power in first baseman Howard Prager (.335 with 8 HRs and 58 RBIs in 73 games at Auburn), speed in outfielder Craig Curtis (.323 with 28 stolen bases in 51 games at Sarasota) and grace on the mound in Donne Wall (6-0, 1.85 at Auburn). The number of fine performances turned in by Astro draftees is impressive. If even a handful of these players advance through the system, June 1989 may prove to be a significant factor in big league success.

ATLANTA BRAVES

1989 Farm System Record
461-437 (.513)

Richmond	IL	AAA	81	65	.555
Greenville	SL	AA	70	69	.504
Durham	CAR	A	84	54	.609
Sumter	SAL	A	60	80	.429
Burlington	MWL	A	60	77	.438
Pulaski	APPY	Rookie	42	26	.618
Idaho Falls	PIO	Rookie	27	40	.403
Bradenton	GCL	Rookie	37	26	.587

Despite the Braves' record as the worst in baseball these past several years, the future looks very bright. The club has, arguably, the deepest and best pitching talent in all of baseball and the makings of some fine young position players. Atlanta's philosophy under General Manager Bobby Cox has been to expand the base of talent. The Braves have more minor league affiliates than any other team and consistently draft the most players each June, which gives Cox the luxury of evaluating talent quickly and weeding out the dead wood.

Success at the minor league level in 1989 bears out the fact that Atlanta is on the upswing. Five of their eight affiliates posted winning records, and two won pennants. Fine performances were turned in at each level in the system; and a late-season trade for catcher Francisco Cabrera could be the answer to the major league club's problems at that position.

In addition to the top prospects detailed in this section, Brave fans should keep an eye on pitchers Gary Eave and Lee Upshaw (both 13-game winners) and long-time prospect Dave Justice. Any or all three could see playing time in Atlanta this season.

The Braves' top prospects are:

Steve Avery	Mark Lemke
Kent Mercker	Tommy Greene
Dennis Burlingame	Barry Jones
Dennis Hood	David Nied
Jimmy Kremers	Brian Deak

Steve Avery
Pitcher

The Braves' top prospect at the tender age of twenty, Avery may well have more potential than any left-hander in all of minor league baseball. He was Atlanta's first round draft choice, and the third overall, in 1988, after a stellar career at J.F.K. High School in Taylor, Michigan, and has compiled a 19-8 record in his two professional seasons. Steve's rapid progression through the farm system saw him reach Double A Greenville last summer after only 23 previous starts. Although he'll be given a chance to make the major league team this spring, Avery will more likely begin 1990 in Richmond.

On the mound, Steve already looks like a veteran. With outstanding control of three excellent pitches—90+ mph fastball, big curve and straight change-up—he changes speeds effectively and moves the ball around in the strike zone at will. His delivery is as smooth and sound as any in the Braves' organization. Together with Atlanta starters John Smoltz, Tom Glavine and Derek Lilliquist, Avery should round out one of the finest young pitching staffs in baseball by 1991.

height	weight	bats	throws	birthplace	birthdate
6'4"	185	L	L	Trenton, MI	4/14/70

year	team	league	g	ip	h	so	bb	gs	cg	sho	sv	w	l	era
1988	Pulaski	APP	10	66	38	80	19	10	3	2	0	7	1	1.50
1989	Durham	CAR	13	86	59	90	20	13	3	1	0	6	4	1.45
1989	Greenville	SL	13	84	68	75	34	13	1	0	0	6	3	2.72

Mark Lemke
Second Base

If not for the acquisition of Jeff Treadway last spring, Mark would have been the Braves' starting second baseman in 1989. As Atlanta's twenty-seventh round selection in the 1983 draft, he has been an All-Star in five of his seven professional seasons, was the winner of the Hank Aaron Award as the organization's top offensive minor league player in 1988 and earned the MVP Award in last year's Triple A All-Star Game in Columbus, Ohio. Lemke's list of honors is surpassed only by his hard work, hustle and desire to win.

Offensively, Mark is a scrappy switch-hitter with some power from both sides. He usually finds a way to get on base and is a difficult man to strike out. He supplements decent speed with outstanding base running instincts and technique, giving him the ability to steal 20 bases a year. In the field, Lemke is as steady as they come. He has enough range to make all the necessary plays at second and turns the double play extremely well. He is the kind of tough competitor every winning ball club needs and should open the 1990 campaign with a major league job.

height	weight	bats	throws	birthplace	birthdate
5'9"	167	B	R	Utica, NY	8/13/65

year	team	league	g	ab	r	h	2b	3b	hr	rbi	sb	bb	so	avg
1986	Sumter	SAL	126	448	99	122	24	2	18	66	11	87	31	.272
1987	Durham	CAR	127	489	76	143	28	3	20	68	10	54	45	.291
1988	Greenville	SL	143	567	81	153	29	4	16	80	18	52	92	.270
1988	Atlanta	NL	16	58	8	13	4	0	0	2	0	4	5	.224
1989	Richmond	IL	146	518	69	143	22	7	5	61	4	66	45	.276
1989	Atlanta	NL	14	55	4	10	2	1	2	10	0	5	7	.182

Kent Mercker
Pitcher

A three-time winner of the Central Ohio Player of the Year Award at Dublin High School, Kent was the Braves' first round selection in the June 1986 free agent draft, and fifth overall. In 1988, his first full professional season, he continued his success with an 11-4 mark at Class A Durham, which earned him a Carolina League All-Star selection and the Phil Niekro Award as the organization's outstanding minor league hurler. Although control problems and a 9-12 record in 1989 may keep Mercker in Triple A Richmond this year, he is a pitcher whose tremendous talent and fine, live arm should make a splash in the big leagues before too long.

When Kent was drafted, he was known mostly for his fastball, but since turning pro, he has developed an above-average curve and straight change-up. He mixes his pitches well and shows the ability to hit the corners at times. The Braves like the fact that Mercker can strike men out—an average of better than one K per inning—and pitch out of jams. However, questions remain about his stamina and ability to hold men on base. The young left-hander completed an average of only 6.26 innings per start last year and will be watched closely this season.

height	weight	bats	throws		birthplace		birthdate
6'2"	195	L	L		Dublin, OH		2/1/68

year	team	league	g	ip	h	so	bb	gs	cg	sho	sv	w	l	era
1986	Bradenton	GCL	9	47	37	42	16	8	0	0	0	4	3	2.47
1987	Durham	CAR	3	12	11	14	6	3	0	0	0	0	1	5.40
1988	Durham	CAR	19	128	102	159	47	19	5	0	0	11	4	2.68
1988	Greenville	SL	9	48	36	60	26	9	0	0	0	3	1	3.35
1989	Richmond	IL	27	168	107	144	95	27	4	0	0	9	12	3.20
1989	Atlanta	NL	2	4	8	4	6	1	0	0	0	0	0	12.46

Tommy Greene
Pitcher

Another young hard thrower in the Atlanta system, Tommy was the club's number-one choice in the June 1985 draft. At 6'5" he's intimidating on the mound and demands respect when working the inside of the plate with his 91 mph fastball. Greene also knows how to pitch and can be extremely tough when his big curve finds the strike zone—his career average of 7.2 strikeouts per 9 innings and two 3-shutout seasons are a testament to that.

Considered the jewel in the organization's future big league staff after posting consecutive 11-win campaigns in his first two seasons—the first of which earned Greene the Brave's Minor League Pitcher of the Year Award—his prospects have dimmed somewhat with two disappointing outings at Class AAA Richmond. However, unlike most teams, Atlanta has a surplus of left-handed prospects and will need solid right arms in the rotation. At twenty-two years old, Tommy may still have a bright future with the Braves, but 1990 will be a pivotal season in his career.

height	weight	bats	throws		birthplace		birthdate
6'5"	225	R	R		Lumberton, NC		4/6/67

year	team	league	g	ip	h	so	bb	gs	cg	sho	sv	w	l	era
1985	Pulaski	APP	12	51	49	32	27	12	1	1	0	2	5	7.64
1986	Sumter	SAL	28	175	162	169	82	28	5	3	0	11	7	4.69
1987	Greenville	SL	23	142	103	101	66	23	4	2	0	11	8	3.29
1988	Richmond	IL	29	177	169	130	70	29	4	3	0	7	17	4.77
1989	Richmond	IL	26	152	136	125	50	26	2	1	0	9	12	3.61
1989	Atlanta	NL	4	26	22	17	6	4	1	1	0	1	2	4.10

Dennis Burlingame
Pitcher

Although injuries limited Burlingame to only 11 starts in 1989, he pitched well enough in those appearances to earn a Carolina League All-Star selection. Along with an unblemished 4-0 record, Dennis posted an amazing 0.50 ERA and issued only 5 walks in 54 innings. His dominance over Class A hitters would surely have earned Burlingame a promotion to Triple A Richmond for the upcoming campaign. However, last year's lack of work and his youth—he's only twenty—will probably find Dennis in Greenville in 1990.

Atlanta can pursue several avenues with their former number-five pick in 1987. He has been used exclusively as a starter thus far, but with his outstanding control, a 90+ mph fastball and a tough mentality, Dennis could be a fine reliever. If Burlingame is to be a starter, though, the club must also decide whether to utilize his power pitch and tight curve or to have him concentrate on fine-tuning a baffling knuckleball. Whichever route the Braves take with Dennis, he should be a big league performer within two years.

height	weight	bats	throws		birthplace				birthdate		
6'4"	200	R	R		Woodbury, NJ				6/17/69		

year	team	league	g	ip	h	so	bb	gs	cg	sho	sv	w	l	era
1988	Sumter	SAL	24	163	132	89	43	24	8	4	0	9	11	2.55
1989	Durham	CAR	11	54	28	42	5	11	2	2	0	4	0	0.50

Barry Jones
Outfield

An All-State performer in both baseball and football at Jackson High School in Alabama, Barry signed with Atlanta as an undrafted free agent in 1984. Although his performances over three seasons in the lower levels of the club's farm system were less than noteworthy, Jones has opened some eyes with solid campaigns at Durham in 1987, Greenville in 1988 and Richmond in 1989. His recent surge has included a Southern League All-Star selection and team-pacing numbers in almost every offensive category. He has an outside chance to earn a spot on the major league roster this spring.

Jones has both good speed and a strong throwing arm. He can play any of the outfield positions, but may find his big league opportunity in right—the position from which he led all Carolina League outfielders with 16 assists in 1987. Offensively, Barry can steal a base, but he is more attractive because of the power he exhibits. His quick left-handed swing has produced 42 home runs over the last three years and could be even more effective in the friendly confines of Fulton County Stadium.

height	weight	bats	throws	birthplace	birthdate
6'2"	198	L	R	Jackson, AL	2/14/65

year	team	league	g	ab	r	h	2b	3b	hr	rbi	sb	bb	so	avg
1986	Sumter	SAL	98	288	60	78	11	0	6	51	17	56	41	.270
1986	Durham	CAR	10	27	2	4	1	0	0	3	0	2	3	.148
1987	Durham	CAR	117	424	72	120	23	4	15	52	23	49	55	.282
1988	Greenville	SL	101	384	56	109	18	8	16	55	11	24	55	.284
1988	Richmond	IL	35	126	12	35	7	0	3	10	4	6	12	.277
1989	Richmond	IL	125	429	49	113	16	5	8	55	12	38	57	.263

Dennis Hood
Outfield

Speed runs in Dennis Hood's family. This twenty-three-year-old outfielder is the cousin of St. Louis Cardinal star Willie McGee and is perhaps the fastest player in the Atlanta organization. A twelfth round pick in the June 1984 free agent draft, he has stolen 30 or more bases in each of the last four seasons, with a high of 43 at Class A Sumter in 1986. After two straight campaigns with Greenville, Hood will get a chance to play at the Triple A level for the first time in 1990.

On offense, Dennis is more than just a base stealer. He has good power to the alleys and can take the inside pitch over the fence. His main problem has been a lack of patience at the plate. In order to reach his major league potential, Hood must cut down on his strikeouts and learn to take more walks. Defensively, he's ready for the big time now. In addition to covering incredible amounts of territory with his long strides, Dennis has excellent instincts on fly balls and a solid, accurate arm. On-base percentage will determine the future of this young talent.

height	weight	bats	throws	birthplace	birthdate
6'2"	180	R	R	Pasadena, CA	7/3/66

year	team	league	g	ab	r	h	2b	3b	hr	rbi	sb	bb	so	avg
1984	Bradenton	GCL	49	155	16	31	7	0	1	18	4	15	40	.200
1985	Bradenton	GCL	59	204	19	49	14	0	1	17	7	21	59	.240
1986	Sumter	SAL	135	562	104	142	25	3	7	42	43	62	146	.253
1987	Durham	CAR	121	438	73	118	19	4	13	62	32	51	114	.269
1988	Greenville	SL	141	525	85	135	15	8	14	47	30	52	139	.257
1989	Greenville	SL	136	464	68	117	20	5	11	44	32	48	124	.252

David Nied
Pitcher

While he may not be as advanced in the art of pitching as some of the other Braves' prospects, this young right-hander's aggressive nature and live arm allow him to be rated as a player on the rise. A fourteenth round draft pick in 1987, Nied has compiled a 22-17 record in two professional seasons at the Class A level. The result of a sneaky-quick fastball and a tight-breaking curve, David's average of 7.25 strikeouts per 9 innings is complemented by the fact that he issues less than 3 walks per game. He establishes the inside part of the plate early in the game and challenges hitters well.

In order to progress to higher levels, Nied must develop an additional pitch. While his fastball and curve may be above-average, a successful starter must have at least three pitches. Even at Class A, David has been touched for better than one hit per inning. A good attitude and sound mechanics should make coaching Nied an easy task, but the organization will be watching his progress closely at Greenville this summer. His current repertoire could mean a future in the Braves' bull pen.

height	weight	bats	throws	birthplace	birthdate
6'2"	175	R	R	Dallas, TX	12/22/68

year	team	league	g	ip	h	so	bb	gs	cg	sho	sv	w	l	era
1988	Sumter	SAL	27	165	156	133	53	27	3	1	0	12	9	3.76
1989	Burlington	MWL	13	80	78	73	23	12	2	1	0	5	6	3.83
1989	Durham	CAR	12	58	74	38	23	12	0	0	0	5	2	6.63

A two-time MVP at the University of Arkansas, Jimmy was Atlanta's second round selection in the June 1987 free agent draft. Although he played three different positions for the Razorbacks in college, the Braves are only interested in developing Kremers as a catcher on the professional level. Thus far, their instincts seem to be good, for the 6'3" Jimmy moves well behind the plate and has an excellent arm. His mechanics and game calling abilities are still slightly raw, but he's improving with every game.

Offensively, Kremers shows good hitting technique. Keeping his head behind the ball and front shoulder in, the young backstop hits solid line drives and plenty of home runs. Over one-and-a-half seasons in the farm system Jimmy has collected 56 extra base hits and knocked in 90 runs. With aging veterans in front of him, Kremers has an excellent opportunity to reach the major leagues quickly. The Braves will try him at Class AAA Richmond to begin the 1990 campaign, but he may get the call to Atlanta before the season ends.

Jimmy Kremers
Catcher/First Base/ Outfield

height	weight	bats	throws	birthplace	birthdate
6'3"	185	R	R	Little Rock, AR	10/8/65

year	team	league	g	ab	r	h	2b	3b	hr	rbi	sb	bb	so	avg
1988	Sumter	SAL	72	255	30	68	12	3	5	42	1	39	53	.266
1989	Greenville	SL	121	388	41	91	19	1	16	58	5	34	95	.235

Right behind Kremers at catcher on the Braves' depth chart is power-hitting Brian Deak. As the organization's third round selection in the January phase of the 1986 draft, Deak began his professional career by winning Player of the Year honors in the Appalachian League with a .325 average and 12 home runs for Pulaski. Overall, this twenty-two-year-old has belted 68 round-trippers in four pro campaigns—an average of one home run for every 16.5 at bats.

Brian has the potential to be much more than a one-dimensional offensive player. He has decent speed for a catcher and can steal a base or leg out a triple on occasion. Like most young power hitters, however, he needs to cut down on his strikeouts. Deak has the strength to hit the ball out of the park without taking a big cut, but doesn't seem to realize it. While his hitting should improve with seasoning, his defense is the bigger concern. Brian has a strong arm and blocks the plate well, but needs to take charge of a game and smooth out his mechanics. Both the Braves, and Kremers, will be watching his progress at Greenville closely this year.

Brian Deak
Catcher

height	weight	bats	throws	birthplace	birthdate
6'0"	185	R	R	Harrisburg, PA	10/25/67

year	team	league	g	ab	r	h	2b	3b	hr	rbi	sb	bb	so	avg
1986	Pulaski	APP	62	198	45	64	15	2	12	43	12	49	57	.325
1987	Sumter	SAL	92	252	50	51	6	0	15	49	7	68	89	.202
1988	Burlington	MWL	119	345	58	85	19	1	20	59	3	79	130	.246
1989	Durham	CAR	113	327	44	77	10	0	21	64	3	66	111	.235

Draft Analysis

Top Ten Picks:

1. Tyler Houston, Catcher (Valley High School, Las Vegas, NV)
2a. Tab Brown, Right-hand Pitcher (St. Xavier High School, Louisville, KY)
2b. Brian Boltz, Left-hand Pitcher (Catawba College)
3. Kevin Castleberry, Second Base (University of Oklahoma)
4. George Virgilio, Second Base (Elizabeth High School, Elizabeth, NJ)
5. Ryan Klesko, Left-hand Pitcher (Westminster High School, Westminster, CA)
6. Mike Mordecai, Shortstop (University of South Alabama)
7. Stuart McMillan, Outfield (Withrow High School, Cincinnati, OH)
8. Troy Hughes, Outfield (Mt. Vernon High School, Mt. Vernon, IL)
9. Nathan Fults, Outfield/Catcher (Franklin County High School, Decherd, TN)
10. David Williams, Right-hand Pitcher (Westark Community College, Westark, AR)

Atlanta addressed a persistent problem area when they selected catcher Tyler Houston in the first round last year (second pick overall). The highly touted high-school product from Las Vegas opened his professional career with a .244 average in 50 games at Idaho Falls and reported directly to the Instructional League at season's end. Along with Houston, the Braves took three middle infielders and three outfielders in the first ten rounds. The top producer among these selections was shortstop Mike Mordecai. He reached Class AA Greenville late in the year despite a .253 mark at Burlington. 1989 was supposed to be a draft focused on the offensive talent in the Braves' system.

Once again, however, the organization turned to pitching prospects. Both second round choices were spent on young hurlers, as were the fifth and tenth round picks. Of these four pitchers, only Brian Boltz threw during the summer (3-3, 3.04 in the Carolina League). Tab Brown and David Williams drew Instructional League assignments and Ryan Klesko was sidelined with tendonitis. Overall, Atlanta used twenty-nine of its sixty-two draft choices on pitchers.

As with any draft, it will take several years to evaluate the Braves' success in the June 1989 affair. The fact that the organization took steps to shore up several shortcomings in their lineup, and managed to sign each of their high-round draftees, are positive signs in and of themselves.

LOS ANGELES DODGERS

1989 Farm System Record
414-347 (.544)

Albuquerque	PCL	AAA	80	62	.563
San Antonio	TL	AA ·	49	87	.360
Bakersfield	CAL	A	82	60	.577
Vero Beach	FSL	A	69	66	.511
Salem	NWL	A	41	35	.539
Great Falls	PIO	Rookie	53	14	.791
Sarasota	GCL	Rookie	40	23	.635

In recent years, the Dodgers have been building their major league roster through trades and free agent signings rather than from within the system. This is an uncharacteristic tact for a team with a traditionally strong player development program, but it should end in the near future. Los Angeles has some of the best prospects in the game. The depth of talent in the system is improving each year and a strong presence in the Dominican Republic should perpetuate the trend.

The Dodgers' Triple A affiliate in Albuquerque fielded another strong team in 1989, but the talent base was even more evident at the Class A level. Four of the top five home run and RBI totals in the farm system came from Class A Bakersfield, as did three of the top five pitching performances. By the mid 1990s, Dodgers' fans will be rooting for a major league team anchored by a fine young pitching staff and two slick middle infielders.

In addition to the top prospects detailed in this section, Los Angeles has some promising talent in the form of first baseman Brian Traxler (.323 with 12 HRs and 73 RBIs at Class AA/AAA) and pitcher Jeff Hartsock (12-5 with a 2.63 ERA and 146 Ks at Bakersfield).

The Dodgers' top prospects are:

Ramon Martinez	Jose Offerman
John Wetteland	Chris Nichting
Dave Hansen	Braulio Castillo
Eric Karros	Jose Vizcaino
Dan Opperman	Mike Huff

Ramon Martinez
Pitcher

Only twenty-two years old, Ramon is both the youngest, and the best, of the Dodgers' many pitching prospects. After bursting on the professional scene with a 16-5 record at Class A Vero Beach in the Florida State League in 1987, this hard-throwing right-hander has gone on to dominate minor league hitters at higher levels as well. His career mark in the farm system stands at a stellar 47-22. Although Martinez' performance in his brief stints at the major league level over the past two seasons has not been quite as impressive, he should be ready to step into the Los Angeles rotation this year.

Ramon works with three fine pitches. His fastball is consistently clocked in the low 90s and his sharp curve can freeze even major league batters. However, Martinez' best pitch is an outstanding change-up—he disguises it well and can throw it for strikes. The perfection of this repertoire has led to better than 8 strikeouts per 9 innings pitched over the last three seasons and should make Ramon a big winner for the Dodgers.

height	weight	bats	throws	birthplace	birthdate
6'2"	190	R	R	Santo Domingo, Dom. Rep.	3/22/68

year	team	league	g	ip	h	so	bb	gs	cg	sho	sv	w	l	era
1985	Bradenton		23	59	57	42	23	6	0	0	1	4	1	2.59
1986	Bakersfield	CAL	20	106	119	78	63	20	2	1	0	4	8	4.75
1987	Vero Beach	FSL	25	170	128	148	78	25	6	1	0	16	5	2.17
1988	San Antonio	TL	14	95	79	89	34	14	2	1	0	8	4	2.46
1988	Albuquerque	PCL	10	59	43	40	32	10	1	1	0	5	2	2.76
1988	Los Angeles	NL	9	36	27	23	22	6	0	0	0	1	3	3.79
1989	Albuquerque	PCL	18	113	92	127	50	18	2	1	0	10	2	2.79
1989	Los Angeles	NL	15	99	79	89	41	15	2	2	0	6	4	3.19

Jose Offerman
Shortstop

Another product of the shortstop factory in San Pedro de Macoris, Offerman has been described as the top prospect in all of baseball by some scouts. In addition to his amazing defensive skills, Jose's offensive potential is virtually unlimited. In two professional campaigns, this switch-hitting Dominican has posted a combined .309 average and stolen 126 bases.

Offerman projects as a fine leadoff hitter. He combines line drive power to the alleys with good bunting ability and blazing speed. A catalyst along the lines of Vince Coleman, Jose has also shown the capability to hit an occasional home run. As a shortstop, he has few, if any, weaknesses. His excellent range, soft hands and strong arm have convinced Dodger insiders that he could play in the big leagues now. At only twenty-one-years-old, however, Offerman will not be rushed. 1990 will see him open at San Antonio, with a promotion to Albuquerque promised for a solid performance.

height	weight	bats	throws	birthplace	birthdate
6'0"	150	B	R	San Pedro de Macoris, Dom. Rep.	11/8/68

year	team	league	g	ab	r	h	2b	3b	hr	rbi	sb	bb	so	avg
1988	Great Falls	PIO	60	251	75	84	11	5	2	28	57	38	42	.335
1989	Bakersfield	CAL	62	245	53	75	9	4	2	22	37	35	48	.306
1989	San Antonio	TL	68	278	47	80	6	3	2	22	32	40	39	.288

The Dodgers' second round selection in the June 1985 draft, John went to the Tigers at the 1987 winter meetings as a non-roster draftee. However, he failed to make the Detroit pitching staff, and returned to the Los Angeles organization that spring. Since that time, Wetteland has been among the brightest prospects in the organization—posting 27 minor league victories in 62 starts. He reached the major leagues one year ahead of schedule in 1989, and pitched very well in limited duty as a middle reliever and spot starter.

John is a tough competitor who endlessly studies opposing batters, and he knows what to do on the mound. His sharp-breaking curve is recognized as the finest in the Dodger organization and it's complemented by an 88-90 mph fastball. Wetteland's problems arise when he can't find the plate with the curve. Moreover, his fastball shows little movement and can be an easy target when batters know it's on the way. Although his control has improved markedly, John would benefit from developing an extra pitch—either a change-up or hard slider. Los Angeles fans can expect to see this young right-hander in the rotation to open the 1990 campaign.

John Wetteland
Pitcher

height	weight	bats	throws	birthplace	birthdate
6'1"	195	R	R	San Mateo, CA	8/22/66

year	team	league	g	ip	h	so	bb	gs	cg	sho	sv	w	l	era
1985	Great Falls	NWL	11	21	17	23	15	2	0	0	0	1	1	3.92
1986	Bakersfield	CAL	15	67	71	38	46	12	4	0	0	0	7	5.78
1986	Great Falls	NWL	12	69	70	59	40	12	1	0	0	4	3	5.45
1987	Vero Beach	FSL	27	176	150	144	92	27	7	2	0	12	7	3.13
1988	San Antonio	TL	25	162	141	140	77	25	3	1	0	10	8	3.88
1989	Albuquerque	PCL	10	69	61	73	20	10	1	0	0	5	3	3.65
1989	Los Angeles	NL	31	103	81	96	34	12	0	0	1	5	8	3.77

Chris suffered through a rough 1989 campaign with a terrible Class AA San Antonio team in the Texas League. His numbers looked bad across the board and made the Dodgers wonder if Nichting was the same pitcher who dominated the Florida State League one year earlier. The fact remains, however, that this former Pan American team member and number-three draft choice in 1987 has an abundance of talent and should bounce back with a solid season at Triple A Albuquerque in 1990.

Nichting's repertoire includes three solid big league pitches. His fastball is consistently clocked in the 92 mph range and shows excellent movement into the strike zone. To complement his heater, Chris throws a tight curve and good straight change-up. International and college experience have taught Nichting to challenge batters and get ahead in the count. In two professional seasons, he has averaged nearly one strikeout per inning pitched.

Playing for the perennially strong Albuquerque club should improve Chris' attitude and statistics this summer. The organization will be watching him closely in the hopes that their young right-hander will be ready for the big leagues in 1991.

Chris Nichting
Pitcher

height	weight	bats	throws	birthplace	birthdate
6'1"	205	R	R	Cincinnati, OH	5/13/66

year	team	league	g	ip	h	so	bb	gs	cg	sho	sv	w	l	era
1988	Vero Beach	FSL	21	138	90	151	51	19	5	1	1	11	4	2.09
1989	San Antonio	TL	26	154	160	136	101	26	2	0	0	4	14	5.03

Dave Hansen
Third Base

The Dodgers' second round selection in the June 1986 draft, Dave moved through Class AA without difficulty last summer to end the season in Triple A Albuquerque. As his numbers continue to improve with progression through the farm system, Hansen may soon pass Tracy Woodson on the Los Angeles depth chart at third base. At only twenty-one-years-old, Dave will surely open the 1990 campaign in the minor leagues, but could see major league action before the year is out.

At the plate, Hansen makes consistent contact with a solid left-handed stroke. His line drive power has produced better than 20 doubles in each of the last three seasons—despite only average speed—and scouts feel that Dave's home run figures will increase as he matures. In addition to his run-producing potential on offense, Hansen will bring steady defense to the Dodgers as well. He has the first-step quickness, sure hands and strong throwing arm required of a third baseman and he works hard in the field.

height	weight	bats	throws	birthplace	birthdate
6'0"	180	L	R	Long Beach, CA	11/24/68

year	team	league	g	ab	r	h	2b	3b	hr	rbi	sb	bb	so	avg
1986	Great Falls	PIO	61	204	39	61	7	3	1	36	9	27	28	.299
1987	Bakersfield	CAL	132	432	68	113	22	1	3	38	4	65	61	.262
1988	Vero Beach	FSL	135	512	68	149	28	6	7	81	2	56	46	.291
1989	San Antonio	TL	121	464	72	138	21	4	6	52	3	50	44	.297
1989	Albuquerque	PCL	6	30	6	8	1	0	2	10	0	2	3	.267

Braulio Castillo
Outfield

Signed by Los Angeles as a free agent in October of 1985, twenty-one-year-old Braulio Castillo lived up to his advance billing at Class A Bakersfield last year. In addition to raising his average 18 points over the previous season, the young outfielder doubled his home run and RBI output. Coming off two consecutive All-Star campaigns, Castillo will likely open the 1990 season at San Antonio in the Texas League.

Braulio excels in all of the four areas necessary to be a star. He can hit for both average and power, and has outstanding speed and a strong throwing arm. Offensively, his potential is limitless. Extremely quick hands allow Castillo to adjust to pitches well and he makes consistent contact with the ball. He has good base-running technique to go with his speed and should steal as many as 30 bases per season in the big leagues. Defensively, Braulio covers plenty of ground in the outfield and seems comfortable with any of the three positions. He is the type of player who could advance quickly in the Dodger farm system.

height	weight	bats	throws	birthplace	birthdate
6'0"	160	R	R	Elias Pina, Dom. Rep.	5/13/68

year	team	league	g	ab	r	h	2b	3b	hr	rbi	sb	bb	so	avg
1987	Dodgers	GCL	49	140	21	28	4	2	1	19	7	16	41	.200
1988	Salem	NWL	73	306	51	86	20	5	8	41	16	22	72	.280
1989	Bakersfield	CAL	126	494	83	147	28	8	18	82	31	42	132	.298

Eric Karros
First Base

The fact that Karros is limited to first base in the field could be the only factor that keeps him in the farm system for two more years. An All-American and two-time All-PAC 10 performer at UCLA, Eric is steady and sure-handed with the glove, but hardly ready to replace Eddie Murray in the Dodger lineup. His potential with the bat made him Los Angeles' sixth round d pick in 1988, and he's posted outstanding numbers in two professional campaigns.

Karros has a quick, compact stroke and makes more consistent contact that most young power hitters—as his .323 lifetime average will attest. With a solid 6'4", 205 lb. frame, he hits hard line drives to all parts of the field and has enough speed to have legged-out a California League high of 40 doubles in 1989. If his performance thus far is any indication of what's to come, Eric should be a fine big league run-producer. Over 30% of his 263 hits have gone for extra bases.

1990 should find Karros at Class AA San Antonio. The organization will be interested to see how Eric can handle the numerous breaking balls he's bound to see. Another successful campaign could find him getting a long look next spring.

height	weight	bats	throws	birthplace	birthdate
6'4"	205	R	R	Hackensack, NJ	11/4/67

year	team	league	g	ab	r	h	2b	3b	hr	rbi	sb	bb	so	avg
1988	Great Falls	PIO	66	268	68	98	12	1	12	55	8	32	35	.366
1989	Bakersfield	CAL	142	545	86	165	40	1	15	86	18	63	99	.303

Jose Vizcaino
Shortstop

As the Dodgers' "other" Dominican-born shortstop, Jose would have the inside track on a major league job with almost any other organization. Unfortunately for him, the Dodgers' Jose Offerman may get a shot at the position first. But, Vizcaino has an impressive resume in the minor leagues. In addition to a .282 lifetime average, he has finished at or near the top of his league in several defensive categories and was selected to play in the 1988 California League All-Star game. His call up last September indicates that Jose will be given a shot to make the Dodgers this spring—probably as a reserve infielder.

Vizcaino is a pesky switch-hitter with decent speed. He has occasional power to the gaps and can steal a base, but won't hit many home runs. Jose's game is his defense. With a rangy 6'1", 155 lb. frame and exceptional quickness, he can make all the plays. His arm is strong enough to throw out runners from the hole and few shortstops turn the double play as well as Vizcaino. If there isn't room for Jose with Los Angeles, look for him to earn a job elsewhere within one year.

height	weight	bats	throws	birthplace	birthdate
6'1"	150	B	R	Palenque de San Cristobal, Dom. Rep.	3/26/68

year	team	league	g	ab	r	h	2b	3b	hr	rbi	sb	bb	so	avg
1987	Sarasota	GCL	49	150	26	38	5	1	0	12	8	22	24	.252
1988	Bakersfield	CAL	122	434	77	126	11	4	0	38	13	50	54	.289
1989	Albuquerque	PCL	129	434	60	123	10	4	1	44	16	33	41	.283
1989	Los Angeles	NL	7	10	2	2	0	0	0	0	0	0	1	.200

Dan Opperman
Pitcher

The near-certain success predicted for Dan when he was selected in the first round of the June 1987 draft has yet to come. After missing two complete seasons with elbow problems and two operations, the young right-hander suffered through a winless professional debut with Class A Vero Beach in 1989. Though his ERA was a respectable 3.54, Opperman failed to exhibit the over-powering fastball and pinpoint control which character-ized his brilliant high school career.

When healthy, Dan throws a rising 92 mph fastball, big curve and good straight change-up. There are no flaws in his delivery and he really knows how to pitch. Opperman's 1989 campaign leaves his future very much in doubt. The Dodgers will probably move him to Class A Bakersfield to monitor the situation more closely, but Dan's chances of moving up quickly in the system have been put on hold. Many number-one draft choices never reach the major leagues, but a talent like Opperman will be given plenty of time to develop.

height	weight	bats	throws	birthplace	birthdate
6'2"	175	R	R	Las Vegas, NV	11/13/68

year	team	league	g	ip	h	so	bb	gs	cg	sho	sv	w	l	era
1989	Vero Beach	FSL	19	61	51	35	23	19	0	0	0	0	7	3.54

Mike Huff
Outfielder

A product of Northwestern University, Mike was a sixteenth round pick in the June 1985 draft. Like many other Dodger outfielders, Mike's game is characterized by speed and solid defense. Despite missing most of the 1987 campaign with knee problems, he has aver-aged better than 24 stolen bases in five professional seasons and still covers plenty of ground in the field. Huff's excellent performance at Albuquerque last year should give him an outside shot at making the major league team this spring.

Although not known for his power, Mike did hit 10 home runs through the thin New Mexican air in 1989. More indicative of his strengths were the 29 doubles and 7 triples he collected. Huff hits line drives to the alleys and can stretch many of them for extra bases. He is a good contact man who could do well in the leadoff role or at the bottom of the order, and should be a fine role player along the lines of Jose Gonzalez.

height	weight	bats	throws	birthplace	birthdate
6'1"	180	R	R	Honolulu, HI	8/11/63

year	team	league	g	ab	r	h	2b	3b	hr	rbi	sb	bb	so	avg
1985	Great Falls	NWL	70	247	70	78	6	6	0	35	28	56	44	.316
1986	Vero Beach	FSL	113	362	73	106	6	8	2	32	28	67	67	.293
1987	San Antonio	TL	31	135	23	42	5	1	3	18	2	9	21	.311
1988	San Antonio	TL	102	395	68	120	18	10	2	40	33	37	55	.304
1989	Albuquerque	PCL	115	471	75	150	29	7	10	78	32	38	55	.318
1989	Los Angeles	NL	12	25	4	5	1	0	1	2	0	3	6	.200

Draft Analysis

Top Ten Picks:

1a. Kiki Jones, Right-hand Pitcher (Hillsborough High School, Tampa, FL)

1b. Tom Goodwin, Outfield (Fresno State University)

1c. Jamie McAndrew, Right-hand Pitcher (University of Florida)

2a. Bill Lott, Outfield (Petal High School, Hattiesburg, MS)

2b. Steve Payne, Left-hand Pitcher (Clark Central High School, Athens, GA)

3. Phil Nevin, Shortstop (El Dorado High School, Placentia, CA)

4. Javier Delahoya, Right-hand Pitcher (Grant High School, Van Nuys, CA)

5. John Deutsch, First Base (Montclaire State University)

6. Tim Barker, Shortstop (Virginia Commonwealth University)

7. Bryan Baar, Catcher (Western Michigan University)

8. Jason Brosnan, Left-hand Pitcher (Fresno State University)

9. Barry Parisotto, Right-hand Pitcher (Gonzaga University)

10. Kevin Jordan, Second Base (Canada Junior College)

Los Angeles had five picks in the first two rounds of last June's draft and used them to their full advantage. The combined peformances of the three first round picks at Great Falls looked more like the numbers of Hall of Famers than those of professional rookies. Pitchers Kiki Jones and Jamie McAndrew went 8-0 and 11-0 respectively. Both had ERAs of 1.65 or better, and both struck out more than one batter per inning. Outfielder Tom Goodwin more than doubled the total of his nearest rival with 60 stolen bases in only 63 games, and hit .308 with 2 homers and 33 RBIs as well.

Despite these, and other fine performances, Los Angeles' draft was tainted somewhat by the fact that the club failed to sign three of their picks from the first ten rounds—Steve Payne, Phil Nevin and Kevin Jordan. The loss of left-hander Payne was probably the most difficult given the club's need for hard-throwing southpaws.

In all, however, the Dodgers had a typically solid draft. The organization signed young men with power and speed, fortified their catching ranks with eight picks and added depth to an already strong base of pitching talent. Los Angeles earned high marks for June 1989.

SAN FRANCISCO GIANTS

1989 Farm System Record
338-364 (.481)

Phoenix	PCL	AAA	67	76	.469
Shreveport	TL	AA	75	61	.551
San Jose	CAL	A	81	61	.570
Clinton	MWL	A	55	84	.396
Everett	NWL	A	31	44	.413
Pocatello	PIO	Rookie	29	38	.433

The 1989 National League champion San Francisco Giants received some much needed help from their farm system last summer. Young Matt Williams stepped into the lineup to provide protection for slugger Kevin Mitchell, and catcher Kirt Manwaring was solid defensively in spelling Terry Kennedy behind the plate. Although there are few power hitting prospects behind Williams, San Francisco has plenty of speed and defense waiting in the minor leagues. This talent can only serve to solidify the Giants' position as a baseball power in the 1990s.

This organization has an excellent record of developing and keeping their prospects. It's conceivable that by the middle of the decade, San Francisco could field a team made up solely of home-grown players. The organization is also cognizant of saving their young pitchers' arms. Major league manager Roger Craig, a split-finger fastball guru, will not allow his minor league hurlers to throw the forkball until they reach the Triple A level.

In addition to the players profiled, Giants' fans should watch the progress of Double A players Rich Aldrete (.321 and 56 RBIs) and Dee Dixon (.282 with 42 stolen bases). Along with Class A pitchers Kevin Rogers (13-8, 2.25) and Steve Lienhard (12-3, 1.79), they could move up quickly.

The Giants' top prospects are:

Matt Williams	Andres Santana
Eric Gunderson	Mike Remlinger
Royce Clayton	Kirt Manwaring
Trevor Wilson	Ted Wood
Tony Perezchica	Jamie Cooper

A former number-one pick in 1986 out of the University of Nevada at Las Vegas, Williams was one of the most feared sluggers in minor league baseball for three years, but he was a bust in the big leagues. However, in his one half-season of major league work last summer, he finally came of age. His frequent home runs gave Kevin Mitchell protection in the order and Matt was integral part of the Giants' successful pennant push. Williams is a lock to open the 1990 campaign with a regular job at third base.

Matt generates outstanding bat speed with a short, quick-wristed swing. Williams' trouble has come with hitting the outside pitch because he tries to pull the ball too often, but he feasts on any offering from the middle of the strike zone in. Although he has played three infield positions professionally, Matt is best suited to the "Hot Corner." There he can use his quick reactions, powerful upper body and strong arm at maximum potential. Williams will be a solid, if unspectacular, fielder and an effective power hitter for many major league seasons to come.

Matt Williams
Infield

height	weight	bats	throws	birthplace	birthdate
6'2"	205	R	R	Bishop, LA	11/28/65

year	team	league	g	ab	r	h	2b	3b	hr	rbi	sb	bb	so	avg
1986	Everett	NWL	4	17	3	4	0	1	1	10	0	1	4	.235
1986	Clinton	MWL	68	250	32	60	14	3	7	29	3	23	62	.240
1987	Phoenix	PCL	56	211	36	61	15	2	6	37	6	19	53	.289
1987	San Francisco	NL	84	245	28	46	9	2	8	21	4	16	68	.188
1988	Phoenix	PCL	82	306	45	83	19	1	12	51	6	13	56	.271
1988	San Francisco	NL	52	156	17	32	6	1	8	19	0	8	41	.205
1989	Phoenix	PCL	76	284	61	91	20	2	26	61	9	32	51	.320
1989	San Francisco	NL	84	292	31	59	18	1	18	50	1	14	72	.202

Signed as a free agent in 1987, Santana may be the brightest defensive prospect in all of baseball. A native of San Pedro de Macoris, his range and acrobatic skills have drawn favorable comparisons to Ozzie Smith. The only area of fielding in which Andres needs improvement is his throwing accuracy. He has a tendency to get rid of the ball too quickly but will be schooled in the art of setting his feet properly before reaching the major league level.

Andres' progress was slowed in 1989 by a broken ankle suffered early in the season. However, his brief performance at Class A San Jose showed that he was capable of hitting on that level and his performance should earn him a spot in Double A ball for the upcoming campaign. Santana projects as a top-of-the-order hitter with his slap-and-go style and switch-hitting capabilities. With his exceptional speed, a walk or infield hit is as good as a double. Andres' two full seasons of play have garnered two stolen base titles and his ratio of successful attempts should continue to climb as he refines his technique. He should reach San Francisco by 1992.

Andres Santana
Shortstop

height	weight	bats	throws	birthplace	birthdate
5'11"	150	B	R	San Pedro de Macoris, Dom. Rep.	3/19/68

year	team	league	g	ab	r	h	2b	3b	hr	rbi	sb	bb	so	avg
1987	Pocatello	PIO	67	256	51	67	2	3	0	9	45	36	37	.262
1988	Clinton	MWL	118	450	77	126	4	1	0	24	88	42	83	.280
1988	Shreveport	TL	11	36	3	6	0	0	0	3	3	4	9	.167
1989	San Jose	CAL	18	69	14	18	3	0	0	3	10	8	16	.261

Eric Gunderson
Pitcher

Gunderson was San Francisco's second round pick in the June 1987 draft, and he asserted himself as a top prospect with a fine split-season at Shreveport and Phoenix last summer. In three years as a professional, this Portland State University product has posted a composite 31-16 record and issued an average of only 3 walks per 9 innings pitched. Eric should spend the 1990 season in Triple A Phoenix.

Gunderson is a crafty left-hander with good control and a deceptive delivery. He works with a standard fastball, curve and change-up repertoire—all of which rate above-average—and his ball shows good movement. Although Eric doesn't throw hard, he always challenges hitters and is adept at pitching inside. There has been speculation that Gunderson may be well-suited to a short relief role. However, as his strikeout ratio continues to drop as he advances through the farm system, it appears that Eric might be groomed as a starter. At twenty-four, Eric could earn a shot at the Giants' rotation in 1991 if he has a solid campaign in the Pacific Coast League this summer.

height	weight	bats	throws	birthplace	birthdate
6'0"	175	R	L	Vancouver, WA	3/29/66

year	team	league	g	ip	h	so	bb	gs	cg	sho	sv	w	l	era
1987	Everett	NWL	15	99	80	99	34	15	5	3	0	8	3	2.46
1988	San Jose	CAL	20	149	131	151	52	20	5	4	0	12	5	2.65
1988	Shreveport	TL	7	37	45	28	13	6	0	0	0	1	2	5.15
1989	Shreveport	TL	11	72	68	61	23	11	2	1	0	8	2	2.72
1989	Phoenix	PCL	14	85	93	56	36	14	2	1	0	2	4	5.04

Mike Remlinger
Pitcher

The only thing holding Mike out of the big leagues at this point is his control. Since being drafted in the first round in 1987 out of Dartmouth University, Remlinger has issued an average of more than 7 walks per 9 innings pitched—a figure far too high to be successful with the Giants. The organization hopes that the stability of working one full season with Phoenix this year will allow the young left-hander to settle down.

On the positive side, Mike has an outstanding arm and can throw a darting fastball at speeds of better than 90 mph. The combination of his fastball, straight change-up and overhand curve has dominated minor league hitters to the point where Remlinger has registered 10.13 strikeouts and allowed only 6.75 hits per 9 innings pitched. He is an intense competitor who has shown excellent poise despite the control problems; and he has the ability to be a number-one or -two starter at the major league level within two years.

height	weight	bats	throws	birthplace	birthdate
6'0"	195	L	L	Middletown, NY	3/23/66

year	team	league	g	ip	h	so	bb	gs	cg	sho	sv	w	l	era
1987	Everett	NWL	2	5	1	11	5	1	0	0	0	0	0	3.60
1987	Clinton	MWL	6	30	21	43	14	5	0	0	0	2	1	3.30
1987	Shreveport	TL	6	34	14	51	22	6	0	0	0	4	2	2.36
1988	Shreveport	TL	3	13	7	18	4	3	0	0	0	1	0	0.69
1989	Shreveport	TL	16	90	68	92	73	16	0	0	0	4	6	2.98
1989	Phoenix	PCL	11	43	51	28	52	10	0	0	0	1	6	9.21

The Giants' number-one pick in 1988 out of St. Bernard High School in California, Royce is a twenty year old with tremendous talent and good power potential. Scouts feel that his quick, strong swing could yield as many as 20 home runs per season and, combined with his speed and intensity, could make Clayton a solid run-producer. Although his 1989 campaign with Class A Clinton and Class A San Jose was less than spectacular, Royce did collect 16 doubles and 38 stolen bases—figures that should increase as he gains physical maturity.

Though Clayton was a shortstop throughout his high school and professional careers, he may have difficulty securing that position with San Francisco due to the presence of both Jose Uribe and Andres Santana. He has the quickness and sure hands to play a middle infield position effectively. However, his speed, strong throwing arm and offensive abilities may dictate

Royce Clayton
Shortstop

a future in the outfield. Royce's youth and 1989 numbers will probably find him in San Jose to open the upcoming season. He has the ability to skip one level in the farm system if the organization sees fit though, and could reach the major leagues by 1992.

height	weight	bats	throws	birthplace	birthdate
6'0"	175	R	R	Inglewood, CA	1/2/70

year	team	league	g	ab	r	h	2b	3b	hr	rbi	sb	bb	so	avg
1988	Everett	NWL	60	212	35	55	4	0	3	30	10	27	54	.259
1989	Clinton	MWL	104	385	39	91	13	3	0	24	28	39	101	.236
1989	San Jose	CAL	28	92	5	11	2	0	0	4	10	13	27	.120

A former second round draft pick in 1986 and veteran of four professional campaigns, Manwaring has played at the major league level only briefly in each of the last three seasons. However, his solid defensive performance in 1989 and the aging of catchers Terry Kennedy and Bob Brenly should make Kirt the Giants' starter for the first time this year.

Offensively, Manwaring does not swing the big bat as often as is expected for major league receivers. He has shown the ability to hit for a decent average and make consistent contact, but only about one in every five of his hits goes for extra bases. Although Kirt will never be a home run hitter, the Giants do feel that he will develop into a good RBI man.

Kirt Manwaring
Catcher

This twenty-four-year-old makes up for his lacks at the plate behind it. Manwaring is by far the top defensive catcher in the system. He is quick and agile with a fine, accurate arm and he knows how to call a game. With his solid build and hard work-ethic, Kirt should be a mainstay in the San Francisco lineup for many years.

height	weight	bats	throws	birthplace	birthdate
5'11"	185	R	R	Elmira, NY	7/15/65

year	team	league	g	ab	r	h	2b	3b	hr	rbi	sb	bb	so	avg
1986	Clinton	MWL	49	147	18	36	7	1	2	16	1	14	26	.245
1987	Shreveport	TL	98	307	27	82	13	2	2	22	1	19	33	.267
1987	San Francisco	NL	6	7	0	1	0	0	0	0	0	0	1	.143
1988	Phoenix	PCL	81	273	29	77	12	2	2	35	3	14	32	.282
1988	San Francisco	NL	40	116	12	29	7	0	1	15	0	2	21	.250
1989	San Francisco	NL	85	200	44	42	4	2	0	18	2	11	28	.210

Trevor Wilson
Pitcher

Trevor's future role with the Giants has yet to be determined. He has been used primarily as a starter since being drafted in the eighth round of the June 1985 draft, but he worked out of the bull pen in 7 of his 11 big league appearances last summer. San Francisco may feel that Wilson will have difficulty maintaining major league velocity on his pitches over 7 innings. If so, he has the type of repertoire and composure that could serve him well as a stopper.

A twenty-three-year-old left-hander, Trevor challenges hitters with a 90 mph fastball, tight curve and offspeed split-finger pitch. All three rate above-average and he can throw them for strikes. Wilson has had difficulty with his control, but only at higher levels in the system and in the late innings of a game, when he tends to overthrow. Given the chance to pitch one or two innings at a time, Trevor could be very effective. He should open the 1990 season with the big league club.

height	weight	bats	throws	birthplace	birthdate
6'0"	175	L	L	Torrance, CA	6/7/66

year	team	league	g	ip	h	so	bb	gs	cg	sho	sv	w	l	era
1985	Everett	NWL	17	55	67	50	26	7	0	0	3	2	4	4.23
1986	Clinton	MWL	34	131	126	85	64	21	0	0	2	6	11	4.27
1987	Clinton	MWL	26	161	130	146	77	26	3	2	0	10	6	2.01
1988	Shreveport	TL	12	73	55	53	23	11	0	0	0	5	4	1.86
1988	Phoenix	PCL	11	52	49	49	33	9	0	0	0	2	3	5.05
1988	San Francisco	NL	4	22	25	15	8	4	0	0	0	0	2	4.09
1989	Phoenix	PCL	23	115	109	77	76	20	2	0	0	7	7	3.12
1989	San Francisco	NL	14	39	28	22	24	4	0	0	0	2	3	4.35

Ted Wood
Outfield

A starting right fielder for the 1988 U.S. Olympic team, and a .400 hitter, Ted was San Francisco's second selection, a supplemental first round pick, in the June 1988 draft. He is a fine all-around athlete with excellent baseball instincts who could move up in the system quickly. Wood spent his first professional campaign at Class AA Shreveport last summer and hit .258 with 43 RBIs. He should open with Triple A Phoenix this year.

Wood has a solid left-handed stroke and makes consistent contact. He'll hit the ball where it's pitched, and although he doesn't have tremendous home run power, Ted can take the inside pitch over the fence at times. He is a heady runner who will take the extra base when possible and steal a base when necessary. In the field, Ted shows the same awareness and hustle. He gets a good break on the ball and rarely misses a cutoff man with his accurate arm. Average speed is the only factor that may keep Wood out of center field. He'll be tried there in the minor leagues, but should end up in right with the Giants.

height	weight	bats	throws	birthplace	birthdate
6'2"	178	L	L	Chagrin Falls, OH	1/4/67

year	team	league	g	ab	r	h	2b	3b	hr	rbi	sb	bb	so	avg
1989	Shreveport	TL	114	349	44	90	13	1	0	43	9	51	72	.258

Tony Perezchica
Second Base/Shortstop

Two consecutive .300 seasons in the farm system caught the attention of San Francisco management in 1988. However, Tony failed to impress in a brief stint with the big league club that autumn and was sent back to Class AAA Phoenix for 1989. The obstacle for Perezchica is that he plays the same position as Robbie Thompson and may never be given an opportunity to start with the Giants.

Tony has good strength for a player his size and can drive the ball a long way when he makes solid contact. His above-average speed translates into plenty of extra base hits and he can steal some bases. For Perezchica's offensive game to measure up to his solid defense, however, he will need to cut down on his strikeouts. He can be overpowered by the inside fastball and chases too many pitches out of the strike zone.

If Tony remains in the Giants' organization, his future may be as a utility infielder, though the presence of solid major league regulars and bright prospects at second base and shortstop may indicate an upcoming trade.

height	weight	bats	throws	birthplace	birthdate
5'10"	160	R	R	Mexicali, Mexico	4/20/66

year	team	league	g	ab	r	h	2b	3b	hr	rbi	sb	bb	so	avg
1984	Everett	NWL	33	119	10	23	6	1	0	10	0	6	24	.193
1985	Clinton	MWL	127	452	54	109	21	8	4	40	23	28	77	.241
1986	Fresno	CAL	126	452	65	126	30	8	9	54	17	35	91	.279
1987	Shreveport	TL	89	332	44	106	24	1	11	47	3	19	74	.319
1988	Phoenix	PCL	134	517	79	158	18	10	9	64	10	44	125	.306
1988	San Francisco	NL	7	8	1	1	0	0	0	1	0	2	1	.125
1989	Phoenix	PCL	94	307	40	71	11	3	8	33	5	15	65	.231

Jamie Cooper
Outfield

Selected by the Giants in the sixth round of the June 1987 free agent draft, twenty-three-year-old Jamie Cooper is one of the fastest players in the organization. He has been timed at 6.2 seconds in the 60-yard dash and has stolen 149 bases in two-and-a-half seasons as a professional. Now that he's put in two consecutive Class A campaigns, Cooper should open the 1990 season at Shreveport in the Texas League.

A product of Dallas Baptist University, Jamie was a switch-hitter when he signed with San Francisco. He began batting exclusively from the right side in 1988 and raised his average 80 points to earn All-Star status in the Midwest League. Although Cooper has line drive power and the speed to leg-out plenty of doubles and triples, he must make more consistent contact to advance in the farm system.

Defensively, this young Texan has few peers. He can play very shallow in center field due to outstanding instincts on balls hit over his head; moreover, he has a strong, accurate arm and covers tremendous amounts of territory. His production with the bat will determine how quickly Cooper reaches the major leagues.

height	weight	bats	throws	birthplace	birthdate
6'2"	185	R	R	DeKalb, TX	5/31/66

year	team	league	g	ab	r	h	2b	3b	hr	rbi	sb	bb	so	avg
1987	Everett	NWL	59	203	32	44	5	1	0	13	26	16	64	.217
1988	Clinton	MWL	125	502	74	149	28	2	5	50	63	19	128	.297
1989	San Jose	CAL	105	418	60	107	21	3	1	36	60	21	104	.256

Draft Analysis

Top Ten Picks:

1. Steve Hosey, Outfield (Fresno State University)
2. Clay Bellinger, Shortstop (Rollins College)
3. Jason McFarlin, Outfield (Pensacola High School, Pensacola, FL)
4. Mike Grahovac, Catcher/First Base (Chapman College)
5. Brian Dour, Right-hand Pitcher (Bradley University)
6. Renaldo Bullock, Outfield (Proviso West High School, Bellewood, IL)
7. Matt Watson, Right-hand Pitcher (Cal State Fullerton)
8. Frank Carey, Second Base (Stanford University)
9. Rafael Novoa, Left-hand Pitcher (Villanova University)
10. Ricky Ward, Shortstop (Chemeketa Junior College)

Apparently satisfied with the state of the pitching talent in their system, San Francisco went after position players with seven of ten picks to open the draft, and twenty-six of fifty picks overall. All but seven of the club's draftees are products of college programs and many could develop quickly.

The cream of the Giants' crop is outfielder Steve Hosey. Not really known for his power in college, Hosey belted 13 homers and knocked in 59 runs in 73 games with Everett last summer. Though less productive with the bat, rookie league teammate and second round pick Clay Bellinger sparkled at shortstop in his first pro campaign. He may put some pressure on incumbent prospect Andres Santana in the near future.

Of the three pitchers taken in the first ten rounds, only Rafael Novoa had an impressive season. His 5-5 record and 2.97 ERA with Clinton and Everett was complemented by 81 strikeouts in 78 innings of work. Brian Dour was 3-6, while Matt Watson went unsigned.

With a solid, and relatively young major league lineup, it was a surprise to see San Francisco pick so many college players. A logjam for prospects could occur at the Triple A level in the next few years.

SAN DIEGO PADRES

1989 Farm System Record
394-430 (.478)

Las Vegas	PCL	AAA	74	69	.517
Wichita	TL	AA	73	63	.537
Riverside	CAL	A	64	78	.451
Charleston (SC)	SAL	A	72	68	.514
Waterloo	MWL	A	47	89	.346
Spokane	NWL	A	41	34	.547
Scottsdale	ARIZ	Rookie	23	29	.442

The rebuilding process that started in the Padres' farm system five years ago should begin to pay big dividends this season. In addition to the top catching prospect in the game—Sandy Alomar—San Diego has a number of power pitchers, middle infielders and strong, fast outfielders ready to compete for big league jobs. All this talent is courtesy of a bolstered scouting and player development program instituted by "Trader Jack" McKeon. The Padres have been particularly effective in signing Puerto Rican players.

At first glance, San Diego's farm system seems to be a bit top heavy. Six of the club's top ten prospects played at Las Vegas last year, as did the three top hitters in the organization (aside from Tony Gwynn). Actually, the Padres have had three consecutive strong drafts and have plenty of prospects waiting in the wings. Aside from watching those players detailed in this section, keep an eye on pitchers Pedro Martinez (14-8 with a 1.97 ERA at Class A Charleston) and Rafael Valdez (15-5, 2.19 at AA Wichita), as well as outfielder Jerald Clark. Clark, a long-time prospect, blossomed in the Pacific Coast League last summer, batting .313 with 22 HRs and 83 RBIs. He was also one of three Las Vegas players to earn league All-Star honors.

The Padres' top prospects are:

Sandy Alomar, Jr.	Andy Benes
Thomas Howard	Shawn Abner
Roger Smithberg	Darren Reichle
Luis Lopez	Dave Hollins
Carlos Baerga	Omar Olivares

Sandy Alomar, Jr.
Catcher

Though Alomar has yet to play a full season in the major leagues, many scouts feel he is one of the finest catchers in the game. Unfortunately for Sandy, he plays in the same organization as Benito Santiago. Signed as a free agent by the Padres in 1983, this son of former big leaguer Sandy Alomar, Sr. has been named the Class AAA Pacific Coast League MVP in each of the past two seasons. At twenty-three years old, he has begun to show the offensive punch expected of a backstop and is ready for a big league assignment this year.

Defensively, there has never been any doubt about Sandy's ability. He's a big, strong player and his soft hands and excellent agility make him a polished receiver. No one blocks balls in the dirt better than Alomar, and his arm is strong and accurate. On offense, he is a line-drive hitter who makes consistently solid contact. Though home runs will not come frequently for Sandy, he has outstanding speed for a catcher and hits plenty of doubles and triples.

The Padres can no longer wait to make a decision about their catching situation. Either Santiago or Alomar must be traded this year. If Sandy is not starting in San Diego this spring, look for him in either Atlanta or New York.

height	weight	bats	throws	birthplace	birthdate
6'2"	200	B	R	Salinas, PR	6/18/66

year	team	league	g	ab	r	h	2b	3b	hr	rbi	sb	bb	so	avg
1984	Spokane	NWL	59	219	13	47	5	0	0	21	3	13	20	.215
1985	Charleston	SAL	100	352	38	73	7	0	3	43	3	31	30	.207
1986	Beaumont	TL	100	396	37	83	15	1	4	27	2	15	36	.240
1987	Wichita	TL	103	536	88	171	41	4	12	68	1	21	37	.319
1988	Las Vegas	PCL	93	337	59	100	9	5	16	71	1	28	35	.297
1988	San Diego	NL	1	1	0	0	0	0	0	0	0	0	1	.000
1989	Las Vegas	PCL	131	523	88	160	33	8	13	101	3	42	58	.306
1989	San Diego	NL	7	19	1	4	1	0	1	6	0	3	3	.211

Andy Benes
Pitcher

After being awarded an NCAA strikeout title at the University of Evansville and a Gold Medal performance with the U.S. Olympic team in 1988, Andy reached the major leagues in his first professional season last year. The Padres number-one selection in the June 1988 draft, Benes dominated Texas League batters in his stint with Wichita—an 8-4 record with 118 strikeouts in 108 innings pitched—and moved through Triple A Las Vegas with only 5 starts. Though his first few big league outings were rough, Andy settled into the rotation and showed good poise and talent through September.

Benes' big pitch is a heavy 94 mph fastball. He was able to throw it by most minor leaguers, but learned quickly that he needs to keep the heater down in the strike zone to be successful in San Diego. As complements, Andy throws an excellent slider, tight curve and an occasional change-up. With sound mechanics and control, he can get by with two pitches, but he should be a real treat to watch as his offspeed pitches develop. Benes' 1989 performance should earn him a starting job in the big leagues this spring and promises only good things to come.

height	weight	bats	throws	birthplace	birthdate
6'6"	235	R	R	Evansville, IN	8/20/67

year	team	league	g	ip	h	so	bb	gs	cg	sho	sv	w	l	era
1989	Wichita	TL	16	108	79	115	39	16	5	3	0	8	4	2.16
1989	Las Vegas	PCL	5	26	41	29	12	5	0	0	0	2	1	8.10
1989	San Diego	NL	10	67	51	66	31	10	0	0	0	6	3	3.51

Thomas Howard
Outfield

Now in his fifth year out of Ball State University, Howard was the Padres' first round selection in the June 1986 free agent draft. A well-rounded athlete with speed, strength and good baseball instincts, Thomas was a football quarterback in college as well as a standout outfielder. Though a nagging right shoulder injury has kept him from playing even one full minor league season since his outstanding 1987 campaign in Wichita, Tom's part-time production and hard work ethic bode well for the future.

Offensively, the switch-hitting Howard is a free swinger with line drive power from the right side of the plate and home run power from the left. However, from either side, he has a very quick bat and makes solid contact. With speed enough to steal 25-30 bases per season, Thomas picks up quite a few extra-base hits and scores a lot of runs from his slot near the top of the order. On defense, he can play any of the three outfield positions, but has an arm best suited to left.

At twenty-five, Thomas looks to be ready for the major leagues. However, the San Diego outfield situation is getting crowded, and Howard will need a good spring training to make the big club.

height	weight	bats		throws				birthplace				birthdate		
6'0"	198	B		R				Middletown, OH				12/11/64		
year	team	league	g	ab	r	h	2b	3b	hr	rbi	sb	bb	so	avg
1986	Spokane	NWL	13	55	16	23	3	3	2	17	2	3	9	.418
1986	Reno	CAL	61	223	35	57	7	3	10	39	10	34	39	.256
1987	Wichita	TL	113	401	72	133	27	4	14	60	26	36	72	.332
1988	Las Vegas	PCL	44	167	29	42	9	1	0	15	3	12	31	.251
1988	Wichita	TL	29	103	15	31	9	2	0	16	6	13	14	.301
1989	Las Vegas	PCL	80	303	45	91	18	3	3	31	22	30	56	.300

Shawn Abner
Outfield

Though it's been six years since Shawn came out of Mechanicsburg High School in Pennsylvania as the number-one draft pick in the minors, he's still only twenty-three years old and may yet have a bright future in the major leagues. A two-time All-Star, and the Carolina League MVP while playing in the Mets' farm system, he was acquired by the Padres in the deal that sent Kevin McReynolds to New York. Abner has struggled in his brief appearances with San Diego, but may get a shot at a full-time position this year.

At his best, Shawn is a line drive hitter with power to all fields. He has the strength and stroke to hit 20+ home runs per year, but may have to cut down his swing somewhat to make more consistent contact. Though not a threat to steal, Abner runs the bases well and has the speed to cover plenty of ground in the outfield. He gets an excellent jump on the ball and has a good enough arm to play in right.

Abner's tenure as a professional has not been easy. He has been mishandled in both the Met and Padre organizations and needs the proper attention to reach his potential. Although it's been said before, 1990 could be Shawn's year.

height	weight	bats		throws				birthplace				birthdate		
6'1"	190	R		R				Hamilton, OH				6/17/66		
year	team	league	g	ab	r	h	2b	3b	hr	rbi	sb	bb	so	avg
1984	Kingsport	APP	46	183	32	50	8	0	10	35	9	10	24	.273
1984	Little Falls	NYP	18	68	7	18	2	0	1	5	3	5	16	.265
1985	Lynchburg	CAR	139	542	71	163	30	11	16	89	8	28	77	.301
1986	Jackson	TL	134	511	80	136	29	8	14	76	8	23	76	.266
1987	Las Vegas	PCL	105	406	60	121	14	11	11	85	11	26	68	.298
1987	San Diego	NL	16	47	5	13	3	1	2	7	1	2	8	.277
1988	San Diego	NL	37	83	6	15	3	0	2	5	0	4	19	.181
1988	Las Vegas	PCL	63	252	35	64	16	2	4	34	0	11	39	.254
1989	Las Vegas	PCL	56	223	31	60	11	2	8	31	3	17	53	.269
1989	San Diego	NL	57	102	13	18	4	0	2	14	1	5	20	.176

Roger Smithberg
Pitcher

After starting only 15 games at Class A Riverside in the California League in 1988, Smithberg spent his first minor league campaign at Triple A Las Vegas last summer. The former Bradley University star owned a 6-2 record and a 3.21 ERA after 10 starts, but he may have suffered for his low-inning count of years past as he dropped 6 of his last 7 decisions to end the season with an even mark. With Andy Benes joining the Padres' staff this spring, Roger will most likely get another year in the Pacific Coast League.

Smithberg was San Diego's second round selection in the June 1987 draft, and the organization's confidence in the young right-hander was underscored by the fact that he skipped Double A ball completely. Roger has a sturdy 6'3" frame and an unusual repertoire—his top pitches are a heavy sinker and a split-finger fastball that breaks late and sharply. Though his regular fastball is still showing improvement in both velocity and movement, Roger's control cannot get much better. He is able to hit spots consistently and has no fear of working the inside portion of the plate. Smithberg should post better numbers at Las Vegas this year than last.

height	weight	bats	throws	birthplace	birthdate
6'3"	195	R	R	Elgin, IL	3/21/66

year	team	league	g	ip	h	so	bb	gs	cg	sho	sv	w	l	era
1988	Riverside	CAL	15	103	90	72	32	15	5	0	0	9	2	3.31
1989	Las Vegas	PCL	22	137	159	58	35	22	4	0	0	7	7	4.47

Darrin Reichle
Pitcher

In May of 1988, Darrin threw two no-hitters for Class A Charleston, South Carolina of the South Atlantic League. In April of 1989, he threw the first six innings of another no-hit game for Riverside of the California League. These outings, as well as a career average of better than one strikeout per inning, leave no doubt that Reichle has the ability to dominate hitters. He throws as hard as any pitcher in the organization and has a baffling array of offerings. As it is with so many young pitchers, however, the question with Darrin has been his control.

Selected by San Diego in the fourth round of the June 1987 free agent draft, Reichle seems to have sound mechanics. He feels that his problems finding the strike zone are due to a lack of concentration, but coaches decided to limit Darrin to three pitches—fastball, curve and change-up—to correct the trouble. Whatever the case, steps must be taken to reduce a 1989 average of 5.7 walks per 9 innings. The organization will give Reichle a shot at Double A this spring. But his success will be measured in balls and strikes rather than wins and losses.

height	weight	bats	throws	birthplace	birthdate
6'5"	215	R	R	Melbourne, FL	2/24/66

year	team	league	g	ip	h	so	bb	gs	cg	sho	sv	w	l	era
1987	Reno	CAL	4	12	24	6	16	3	0	0	0	0	3	13.86
1987	Spokane	NWL	11	55	45	47	40	10	0	0	0	4	1	2.96
1988	Charleston, SC	SAL	20	108	62	115	61	20	3	3	0	10	3	2.84
1989	Riverside	CAL	26	149	121	158	100	26	3	1	0	10	10	4.15

Luis Lopez
Shortstop

A native of Cidra, Puerto Rico, Luis signed with San Diego as a free agent on September 9, 1987. After two years as a professional, he is still young, only nineteen, and could be the Padres' shortstop of the future. He opened his tenure with the organization as a .304 hitter at Class A Spokane in 1988, but his average fell over 80 points last year. His 1989 production is more indicative of a player with Lopez' age and stature. However, scouts feel that Luis could develop some power as he matures.

Lopez' solid swing from both sides of the plate is only part of his package. He has the speed and base running instincts to steal upwards of 50 bases per year, as well as the quickness, range, hands and strong arm to excel in the field. With an aging Gary Templeton in the major leagues and limited shortstop competition within the San Diego system, Luis could advance quickly. The Padres did not hesitate to start a twenty-year-old Roberto Alomar at second base in 1988 and may have few reservations about promoting Lopez if his offense picks up this season at Wichita.

height	weight	bats	throws	birthplace	birthdate
5'11"	165	B	R	Cidra, PR	9/4/70

year	team	league	g	ab	r	h	2b	3b	hr	rbi	sb	bb	so	avg
1988	Spokane	NWL	70	312	50	95	13	1	0	35	14	18	59	.304
1989	Charleston, SC	SAL	127	460	50	102	15	1	1	29	12	17	85	.222

Dave Hollins
Third Base

The third switch-hitter among the Padres' top prospects, Dave was a sixth round selection in the June 1987 free agent draft. In three professional seasons, Hollins has compiled a composite .294 average and over 100 of his 369 hits have gone for extra bases. He has the potential to be a complete player and, like Luis Lopez, could move up quickly through the system considering the third base situation in San Diego.

Hollins does not have outstanding power, but on occasion can clear the fences from the right side of the plate. Mainly, he relies on good bat speed to hit line drives to all fields. His speed is good enough to stretch some singles into doubles and to steal 15-20 bases per season. If Dave lacks the potency usually associated with big league third basemen, he'll make up for it on his defense. He has first-step quickness and good range to his left; sure hands and his throwing arm are rated among the best in the game. If Hollins catches the ball, even the fastest base runners are sure outs.

Though this twenty-four-year-old may start the 1990 season in Las Vegas, if he posts numbers resembling his past three campaigns, the call may come from San Diego.

height	weight	bats	throws	birthplace	birthdate
6'1"	195	B	R	Buffalo, NY	5/25/66

year	team	league	g	ab	r	h	2b	3b	hr	rbi	sb	bb	so	avg
1987	Spokane	NWL	75	278	52	86	14	4	2	44	20	53	35	.309
1988	Riverside	CAL	139	517	90	157	32	1	9	92	13	82	67	.304
1989	Wichita	T	131	459	69	126	30	4	9	79	8	63	86	.275

Carlos Baerga
Infield

At only twenty-one years of age, Carlos is already a veteran both of four professional campaigns in the Padres' organization and of three winters in the Puerto Rican League. He has topped the .270 mark in batting at each stop in the San Diego system and consistently ranks among his team's leaders in hits, runs and RBIs. Though his age might keep Carlos in Las Vegas for the 1990 season, he should be ready for a major league assignment at any time.

Baerga's main asset to the Padres may be his versatility. He is a switch-hitter with quickness, a good glove and strong throwing arm; also, he's capable of playing well at second base, third base or shortstop. In these respects, Carlos reminds Padre coaches of former utility man Tim Flannery. However, Baerga packs more offensive punch than his predecessor and is definitely more fleet of foot. At 5'11" and only 165 lbs., this young infielder relies on quick, strong wrists and excellent timing to generate power. While his home run totals of the last two years may be deceiving due to the extra carry a ball gets in some PCL and Texas League parks, Carlos does have good power to the alleys and makes consistent contact with the ball.

height	weight	bats	throws	birthplace	birthdate
5'11"	165	B	R	Caguas, PR	11/4/68

year	team	league	g	ab	r	h	2b	3b	hr	rbi	sb	bb	so	avg
1986	Charleston	SAL	111	378	57	102	14	4	7	41	6	26	60	.270
1987	Charleston	SAL	134	515	83	157	23	9	7	50	26	38	107	.305
1988	Wichita	TL	122	444	67	121	28	1	12	65	4	31	83	.273
1989	Las Vegas	PCL	132	520	63	143	28	2	10	74	6	30	98	.275

Omar Olivares
Pitcher

Another young right-handed pitcher the Padres are watching closely is Omar Olivares. Signed as a free agent in 1986, Olivares completed his third professional season last summer with a composite 32-31 record. By far, his best campaign came in 1988. While splitting time with Charleston and Riverside, Omar won 16 games—including 3 by shutout—and walked only 52 batters in over 200 innings. He is an outstanding athlete, capable of moving up in the system rapidly. 1990 should see Omar in the rotation at Triple A Las Vegas.

Olivares throws the standard mix of pitches—fastball, curve and change-up—but consistently puts the ball over the plate in good locations. His velocity is increasing by the year and the improvement of his fastball will make Omar's offspeed pitches that much better. Olivares will never be a big strikeout pitcher; he nibbles at the corners and changes speeds in search of weakly hit balls instead. However, his effectiveness should increase with the umpiring consistency at the big league level.

height	weight	bats	throws	birthplace	birthdate
6'1"	183	R	R	Mayaguez, PR	7/6/67

year	team	league	g	ip	h	so	bb	gs	cg	sho	sv	w	l	era
1987	Charleston, SC	SAL	31	170	182	86	57	24	5	0	0	4	14	4.60
1988	Charleston, SC	SAL	24	185	166	94	43	24	10	3	0	13	6	2.23
1988	Riverside	CAL	4	23	18	16	9	3	1	0	0	3	0	1.16
1989	Wichita	TL	26	185	175	79	61	26	6	1	0	12	11	3.39

Draft Analysis

Top Ten Picks:
1. No Selection
2. Kenny Felder, Outfield (Niceville High School, Niceville, FL)
3. Scott Bream, Shortstop (Millard South High School, Omaha, NE)
4. Russell Garside, Left-hand Pitcher (Douglas High School, Garnerville, NV)
5. Dave Stanton, First Base (Cal State Fullerton)
6. Darrell Sherman, Outfield (Long Beach State University)
7. Rick Davis, Right-hand Pitcher (Cal State Dominguez Hills)
8. Billy Johnson, Right-hand Pitcher (South Georgia Junior College)
9. Ray McDavid, Outfield (Clairemont High School, San Diego, CA)
10. Lee Henderson, Catcher (West Covina High School, West Covina, CA)

The Padres organization cannot be overly pleased with their results from the early rounds of last June's draft. The club had no selection in the first round, as a result of signing class 'A' free agent Bruce Hurst, and second round pick Kenny Felder did not sign. The news was no better for young shortstop Scott Bream who hit only .175 in 28 games with the rookie league affiliate in Arizona. However, beginning with the fourth round, San Diego seems to have hit paydirt.

First baseman David Stanton led the offensive draftees with a .362 average, 17 home runs and 72 RBIs in 70 games at Spokane, while outfielder Darrell Sherman posted a .318 mark and 58 stolen bases over the same schedule. On the mound, seventh round choice Rick Davis went 9-2 with a 1.35 ERA in the Northwest League. He dominated opposing batters, allowing only 71 hits and striking out 106 in 93 innings of work.

In all, San Diego drafted forty-two players. There was no startling concentration of picks at any one position; however, it's interesting to note that with two of the game's finest catchers in the system, Padre officials still signed six new backstops.

CINCINNATI REDS

1989 Farm System Record
353-337 (.512)

Nashville	AA	AAA	74	72	.507
Chattanooga	SL	AA	58	81	.417
Cedar Rapids	MWL	A	80	57	.584
Greensboro	SAL	A	78	60	.565
Billings	PIO	Rookie	26	41	.388
Plant City	GCL	Rookie	37	26	.587

Cincinnati has always had one of the stronger farm systems in the game. The organization consistently produces major league talent and it boasted a Rookie of the Year winner in Chris Sabo as recently as 1988. However, while there are still some solid prospects in the upper reaches of the system, the future for the Reds' player development program does not look bright. The dearth of talent in the Reds' system at the Rookie and Class A levels is a direct result of cost-cutting measures taken by club owner Marge Schott. The lack of support shown for her scouting staff has resulted in mass resignations of instructors, administrators and the scouts themselves. It will take several years, and a change of philosophy, for the organization to put the pieces back together again.

In 1989, Cincinnati's big league club got solid contributions from several farm products. Rolando Roomes and Joe Oliver showed excellent promise in their maiden campaigns, and a twenty-one-year-old Scott Scudder stepped into the Reds' rotation. Before the talent well runs dry in several years, these young performers should be joined by a power-hitting first baseman, several middle infielders and some excellent pitching. After that, Cincinnati will be building through trades.

The Reds' top prospects are:

Jack Armstrong	Scott Scudder
Reggie Jefferson	Chris Hammond
Butch Henry	Joe Oliver
Brian Lane	Eddie Taubensee
Freddie Benavides	Keith Brown

An All-Big Eight performer in his senior year at the University of Oklahoma after a 9-3 campaign, Jack was the Reds' first round selection in the June 1987 draft. In three professional seasons, this young, twenty-four-year-old right-hander has made great strides in refining his outstanding natural ability with hard work on his delivery and control. He has the size, durability and pitches to be a top-notch major league starter for years to come and could earn a spot in the Cincinnati rotation this season.

Armstrong once struck out 22 batters in a 9-inning high school game, and can intimidate even big league batters with his overhand delivery and 6'5" frame. His fastball reaches 90 mph consistently and his tight curve showed good progress in 1989. He's not afraid to challenge hitters and pitches effectively on the inside part of the plate.

Jack Armstrong
Pitcher

After posting two consecutive ERAs of 3.00 or better at Class AAA Nashville, Jack has little left to prove on the minor league level. Reds' fans expect Armstrong to perform much better than he did in previous stints—he should win more than 10 games.

height	weight	bats	throws	birthplace	birthdate
6'5"	220	R	R	Neptune, NJ	3/7/65

year	team	league	g	ip	h	so	bb	gs	cg	sho	sv	w	l	era
1987	Billings	PIO	5	20	16	29	12	4	0	0	0	2	1	2.66
1987	Vermont	EL	5	36	24	39	23	5	2	1	0	1	2	3.03
1988	Nashville	AA	17	120	84	116	38	17	4	1	0	5	5	3.00
1988	Cincinnati	NL	14	65	63	45	38	13	0	0	0	4	7	5.79
1989	Nashville	AA	25	182	144	152	58	24	12	6	0	13	9	2.91
1989	Cincinnati	NL	9	43	40	23	21	8	0	0	0	2	3	4.64

Scott successfully made the jump from Class AA to the major leagues in 1989 and pitched respectably in his rookie campaign. Used exclusively as a starter in the minor leagues, Scudder was shifted to the bull pen by Cincinnati due to the lack of staying power he exhibited as a farmhand—less than 6 innings per start. At only twenty-two years of age, however, this young right-hander still has a future in the big league rotation.

There has never been any question about Scott's ability. He was a first round draft choice in 1986 and has been singled out as one his league's top pitchers at each stop in the system. He throws a lively 90+ mph fastball to go with an outstanding overhand curve and excellent straight change-up. Although Scudder is still learning the finer points of pitching—changing speeds and moving the ball around in the strike zone—he has shown the ability to dominate hitters and rack up plenty

Scott Scudder
Pitcher

of strikeouts.

1990 will probably see Scott get more starts than last year, but he will still be used primarily in middle relief. As he matures over the next few years, however, Scudder could earn a starter's role in Cincinnati.

height	weight	bats	throws	birthplace	birthdate
6'2"	170	R	R	Paris, TX	2/14/68

year	team	league	g	ip	h	so	bb	gs	cg	sho	sv	w	l	era
1986	Billings	PIO	12	53	42	38	36	8	0	0	0	1	3	4.78
1987	Cedar Rapids	MWL	26	154	130	128	76	26	0	0	0	7	12	4.10
1988	Cedar Rapids	MWL	16	102	61	126	41	15	1	1	0	7	3	2.02
1988	Chattanooga	SL	11	70	53	52	30	11	0	0	0	7	0	2.96
1989	Nashville	AA	12	80	54	64	48	12	3	3	0	6	2	2.68
1989	Cincinnati	NL	23	100	91	66	61	17	0	0	0	4	9	4.49

Reggie Jefferson
First Base

In future years, Cincinnati's 1989 acquisition of first baseman Todd Benzinger may prove to have been simply a stopgap measure in waiting for the arrival of prospect Reggie Jefferson. The organization's confidence in this young power hitter was underscored by another excellent season at Class AA Chattanooga last year. Reggie pounded out 17 home runs, 80 RBIs and 19 doubles, en route to a .287 average.

A former number-three draft pick in 1986, the twenty-one-year-old Jefferson has progressed quickly in the farm system and should open the 1990 campaign with Nashville. His considerable talents include quick power strokes from either side of the plate, soft sure hands and good range in the field. Defensively, Reggie could step into the Reds' lineup now. The organization won't make the mistake of pushing Jefferson too quickly, however. A natural left-handed hitter, he still needs to work on making contact from the right side and could also learn to wait on breaking pitches better. Nevertheless, Reggie should reach the big leagues by 1991.

height	weight	bats	throws	birthplace	birthdate
6'3"	195	B	L	Tallahassee, FL	9/25/68

year	team	league	g	ab	r	h	2b	3b	hr	rbi	sb	bb	so	avg
1986	Reds	GCL	59	208	28	54	4	5	3	33	10	24	40	.260
1987	Cedar Rapids	MWL	15	54	9	12	5	0	3	11	1	1	12	.222
1987	Billings	PIO	8	21	10	8	1	0	1	9	1	4	2	.381
1988	Cedar Rapids	MWL	135	517	76	149	26	2	18	89	2	40	89	.288
1989	Chattanooga	SL	135	487	66	140	19	3	17	80	2	43	73	.287

Chris Hammond
Pitcher

Selected in the sixth round of the June 1986 free agent draft, Hammond has an outside chance to make the Reds' major league roster in 1990. The twenty-four-year-old left-hander has progressed nicely over the past two seasons, posting two winning records and a fine 1.72 ERA at Chattanooga in 1988. That year, Chris' 16 regular-season victories—tops among Class AA pitchers—led the Lookouts to a Southern League Championship and earned him a spot on the circuit's All-Star team.

Although Chris is not blessed with a tremendous fastball, his pitches show good movement and he knows how to get batters out. His complement pitches include a sharp-breaking curve and an outstanding change-up. The latter compares favorably to the best in the game and he'll throw it at any time during the count. With this repertoire, Hammond can be categorized as a finesse pitcher along the lines of a John Tudor or Bob Ojeda. However, he has also shown the ability to strike men out—over 7 Ks per 9 innings pitched. His talent and composure should make Chris a fine addition to the Reds' staff.

height	weight	bats	throws	birthplace	birthdate
6'1"	185	L	L	Atlanta, GA	1/21/66

year	team	league	g	ip	h	so	bb	gs	cg	sho	sv	w	l	era
1986	Reds	GCL	7	42	27	53	17	7	1	0	0	3	2	2.81
1986	Tampa	FSL	5	22	25	5	17	5	0	0	0	0	2	3.32
1987	Tampa	FSL	25	170	174	126	60	24	6	0	0	11	11	3.55
1988	Chattanooga	SL	26	183	127	127	77	26	4	2	0	16	5	1.72
1989	Nashville	AA	24	157	144	142	96	24	3	1	0	11	7	3.38

Butch Henry
Pitcher

Another left-handed starter pushing his way up through the Reds' farm system, Butch has the makings of a big league pitcher at only twenty-one years of age. Cincinnati took a chance drafting Henry in the fifteenth round of the 1987 draft because he had scholarship offers from no less than 10 colleges—including the University of Texas—but the organization was able to sign him with a hefty bonus. Despite an injury that kept him sidelined for much of the 1989 campaign, Butch's strong arm and mound presence should earn him major league status within two years.

Henry works with four pitches and has spectacular control. His fastball reaches the upper 80s, but looks faster because of an excellent straight change-up; while the use of two breaking pitches—slider and curve—rounds out Butch's baffling repertoire. When he's hitting the corners, this left-hander can be nearly unhittable. If not for last year's setback, Henry would probably open the 1990 campaign at Triple A Nashville. It will be no surprise, however, if he joins the Sounds after a brief tune-up in Chattanooga.

height	weight	bats	throws	birthplace	birthdate
6'0"	180	L	L	El Paso, TX	10/7/68

year	team	league	g	ip	h	so	bb	gs	cg	sho	sv	w	l	era
1987	Billings	PIO	9	35	37	38	12	5	0	0	1	4	0	4.68
1988	Cedar Rapids	MWL	27	187	144	163	56	27	1	1	0	16	2	2.26
1989	Chattanooga	SL	7	26	22	19	12	7	0	0	0	1	3	3.42

Joe Oliver
Catcher

After a productive start in Class AAA Nashville to begin the 1989 season, Joe was called up to the Reds and made his mark on National League pitchers. Several of Oliver's multi-hit games keyed Cincinnati victories and his excellent work with the organization's young staff—many of whom are former minor league teammates—provided a boost for the club near the end of the campaign. 1990 should find Joe with a spot on the major league roster.

A former third round draft choice in 1983, Oliver has toiled in the Reds' farm system for seven seasons—including three straight at the Double A level. His problems have always been at the plate. He has a powerful build and a long, solid swing, but sometimes exhibits a lack of concentration by chasing pitches out of the strike zone. When Joe does make contact, he shows the power to hit 10-15 homers per season. This twenty-four-year-old is impressive defensively; he moves well behind the plate, has a strong, accurate arm and calls a good game. Oliver's future as a big league backstop will depend on how well he hits his second time through the Senior Circuit.

height	weight	bats	throws	birthplace	birthdate
6'3"	205	R	R	Memphis, TN	7/24/65

year	team	league	g	ab	r	h	2b	3b	hr	rbi	sb	bb	so	avg
1986	Vermont	EL	84	282	32	78	18	1	6	41	2	21	47	.277
1987	Vermont	EL	66	236	31	72	13	2	10	60	0	17	30	.305
1988	Nashville	AA	73	220	19	45	7	2	4	24	0	18	39	.204
1988	Chattanooga	SL	28	105	9	26	6	0	3	12	0	5	19	.247
1989	Nashville	AA	71	233	22	68	13	0	6	31	0	13	35	.292
1989	Cincinnati	NL	49	151	13	41	8	0	3	23	9	6	28	.272

Brian Lane
Third Base

Acquired in the third round of the June 1987 free agent draft, Brian has exhibited the offensive production expected of a big league third baseman in his three seasons as a professional. Still filling out his 6'3" frame, and only twenty years old, Lane dramatically increased his home run and RBI output at Class AA Chattanooga last year, and should find himself in Nashville to open the 1990 campaign.

The attribute that most often catches the eye of scouts is Lane's arm. It may be as strong as former Gold Glover Aurelio Rodriguez's. Aside from that, he is only slightly better than average in terms of quickness, range and hands-on defense. Offensively, Brian has a quick bat and loves to turn on the inside fastball. He'll need to learn the art of hitting the ball where it's pitched in order to bring up his average, and could use some work on his handling of breaking pitches. With a young Chris Sabo ahead of him, the Reds will give Lane some time to develop in the minors, but he could get a late-season look this year.

height	weight	bats	throws	birthplace	birthdate
6'3"	190	R	R	Waco, TX	6/15/69

year	team	league	g	ab	r	h	2b	3b	hr	rbi	sb	bb	so	avg
1987	Billings	PIO	56	175	20	35	6	1	3	16	2	18	73	.200
1988	Greensboro	SAL	115	451	55	127	17	3	3	52	9	32	69	.282
1989	Chattanooga	SL	130	466	60	118	19	4	12	90	6	46	95	.254

Eddie Taubensee
Catcher

Cincinnati thought enough of this young left-handed hitting catcher to protect him on the 1988 winter roster, but Eddie's stock has dropped somewhat after a disappointing 1989 campaign. Selected in the sixth round of the June 1986 draft, Eddie failed to reach the .200 mark at either Class A Cedar Rapids or Double A Chattanooga. The fact that he is a big, strong twenty-one year old with some power, at a position where the Reds sorely need help, however, keeps Taubensee among the organization's top prospects.

Eddie is a raw talent and still at least three years away from the big leagues. The Reds like his home run potential—22 in two full seasons—but there are holes in his long swing. Difficulty handling breaking pitches will probably mean a Class A assignment to begin the 1990 campaign. Behind the plate, Taubensee shows the tools to be a fine receiver. He blocks the ball well and has an exceptionally strong arm. He'll need to work on perfecting his release to be more consistent, but should get plenty of time to develop in the club's farm system.

height	weight	bats	throws	birthplace	birthdate
6'3"	200	L	R	Beeville, TX	10/31/68

year	team	league	g	ab	r	h	2b	3b	hr	rbi	sb	bb	so	avg
1986	Sarasota	GCL	35	107	8	21	3	0	1	11	0	11	33	.196
1987	Billings	PIO	56	162	24	43	7	0	5	27	2	25	47	.264
1988	Greensboro	SAL	103	330	36	85	16	1	10	40	8	44	92	.258
1988	Chattanooga	SL	5	12	2	2	0	0	1	1	0	3	4	.167
1989	Cedar Rapids	MWL	59	196	25	39	5	0	8	22	4	25	55	.199
1989	Chattanooga	SL	45	127	11	24	2	0	3	13	0	11	28	.197

Freddie Benavides
Shortstop

A product of Texas Christian University, Freddie was selected by the Reds in the second round of the June 1987 free agent draft. He's a lanky 6'2" shortstop with outstanding range, soft hands and a strong arm. But he has had difficulty with professional pitching in over two years in the farm system. Now twenty-four years old, Benavides will get a chance to prove himself on the Triple A level in 1990.

Offensively, Freddie needs to make more contact. His lack of power is inconsistent with the number of times he strikes out. He's got the speed to steal 20 or more bases, but he must learn the slap-and-go hitting style to make it in the major leagues. Even with his outstanding defensive skills, Benavides will have difficulty unseating the hard-hitting Barry Larkin at shortstop for the Reds. With slightly better offensive production, however, he could develop into an excellent utility infielder.

height	weight	bats	throws	birthplace	birthdate
6'2"	175	R	R	Laredo, TX	4/7/66

year	team	league	g	ab	r	h	2b	3b	hr	rbi	sb	bb	so	avg
1987	Cedar Rapids	MWL	5	15	2	2	1	0	0	0	0	0	7	.133
1988	Cedar Rapids	MWL	88	314	38	70	9	2	1	32	17	35	75	.223
1989	Chattanooga	SL	88	284	25	71	14	3	0	27	1	22	46	.250
1989	Nashville	AA	31	94	9	16	4	0	1	12	0	6	24	.170

Keith Brown
Pitcher

Undrafted out of high school and junior college because scouts felt he didn't throw hard enough, Keith was finally selected in the twenty-first round of the June 1986 draft. His performance in four years as a professional has shown that this young right-hander knows how to pitch. Among Brown's credits thus far are three winning campaigns and an ERA title—1987 Midwest League. Although last year's numbers at Nashville were not impressive, Keith should still have a shot to make the Reds' staff in 1990.

Keith has an unusual repertoire of pitches. He throws a sinking 85 mph fastball, a tight curve and an outstanding forkball. Despite the lack of velocity, Brown's pitches show excellent movement and hitters have difficulty making solid contact against him. This twenty-six-year-old doesn't seem bothered when pitching with runners on base or when he's behind in the count. With plenty of poise and good control, Keith may soon find himself pitching in long relief at the major league level. Cincinnati may have too many good starters for him to crack the rotation.

height	weight	bats	throws	birthplace	birthdate
6'4"	225	B	R	Flagstaff, AZ	2/14/64

year	team	league	g	ip	h	so	bb	gs	cg	sho	sv	w	l	era
1986	Reds	GCL	7	47	29	26	5	7	1	0	0	4	1	0.95
1986	Billings	PIO	4	21	18	14	7	3	0	0	0	2	0	2.11
1986	Vermont	EL	4	14	12	11	8	2	1	0	0	1	1	5.14
1987	Cedar Rapids	MWL	17	124	91	86	27	17	3	1	0	13	4	1.59
1988	Chattanooga	SL	10	70	47	34	20	10	2	0	0	9	1	1.42
1988	Nashville	AA	12	85	72	43	28	12	3	1	0	6	3	1.90
1988	Cincinnati	NL	4	16	14	6	4	3	0	0	0	2	1	2.76
1989	Nashville	AA	29	161	171	85	51	27	4	2	0	8	13	4.80

Draft Analysis

Top Ten Picks:
1. Scott Bryant, Outfield (University of Texas)
2. Aaron Goins, Outfield (Owasso High School, Owasso, OK)
3. Ross Powell, Left-hand Pitcher (University of Michigan)
4. Paul Jackson, Outfield (Oldham County High School, LaGrange, KY)
5. Danny Cox, Catcher (University of Oklahoma)
6. Tim Pugh, Right-hand Pitcher (Oklahoma State University)
7. Bert Inman, Right-hand Pitcher (Westwood High School, Austin, TX)
8. Charles Wyatt, Right-hand pitcher (Pflugerville High School, Manor, TX)
9. Rafael Diaz, Left-hand pitcher (Bayamon, P.R.)
10. Rick Allen, Third Base (Loyola Marymount University)

The number of players taken by Cincinnati in the June 1989 draft dropped for the third year in a row. Last June, the club selected fifty-five young men in the hopes of developing some help for the major league team. Among them were twenty-three pitchers, twelve outfielders, seven catchers, six middle infielders, four third basemen and three first basemen. University and college programs were the breeding grounds for thirty of the Reds' draftees.

Support for the painstaking process of scouting and drafting young talent has been in question in Cincinnati. There has been a tremendous turnover in personnel and in budget considerations for the task in recent years. On the surface, it appears that the Reds came up with few of the top prospects available. To make matters worse, they were unable to sign either Paul Jackson or Bert Inman—the fourth and seventh picks respectively.

What the club did get, however, was a proven talent—Scott Bryant. In 49 games at Class A Cedar Rapids last summer, the former Longhorn pounded out 9 home runs and collected 39 RBIs. He could advance quickly, as could pitcher Ross Powell. Powell opened his professional career with a 7-4 mark in the Midwest League. As for the rest of the picks, it will be wait and see.

THE TOP PROSPECTS

RIGHT-HANDED STARTERS

1. Ramon Martinez—Los Angeles Dodgers
2. Andy Benes—San Diego Padres
3. John Ericks—St. Louis Cardinals

There are a tremendous number of fine right-handed pitchers in the minor leagues, but these three share one attribute which sets them apart—a dominating fastball. Martinez, Benes and Ericks all averaged more than one strikeout per inning pitched last season, and all three should only improve with experience and the refinement of their breaking pitches.

At twenty-two, Dodger pitcher Ramon Martinez tops the list because of his excellent change-up. He was able to advance to the major leagues successfully last summer and should open the 1990 campaign with a full-time job in the rotation.

Padre hurler Andy Benes slipped somewhat in a brief stint at Triple A Las Vegas, but rebounded to win six decisions in ten appearances with San Diego. A new, improved Benes should emerge in 1990 after spending the winter learning an overhand curve.

John Ericks did not spend any time in the major leagues last season. Rather, he busied himself disposing of batters in the South Atlantic League. This former first round pick may still be two years away from the show, but his incredible poise and 98 mph heater should bring continued success.

Rounding out the top prospects at this position are a host of pitchers on the verge of stardom. Jack Armstrong of the Reds, Mike Harkey of the Cubs and Alex Sanchez of the Blue Jays should each get shots at the majors this summer; while Johnny Ard of the Twins and Ben McDonald of the Orioles may not appear until 1991.

LEFT-HANDED STARTERS

1. Steve Avery—Atlanta Braves

2. Pat Combs—Philadelphia Phillies

3. Kent Mercker—Atlanta Braves

Left-handed starters are among the most prized possessions in all of baseball, and the Atlanta Braves have two of the most promising in the game. There is little question that the most talented lefty in the minors is Steve Avery. He has excellent velocity, outstanding command of four pitches and tremendous poise. His two stops in the Braves' system last summer produced a 12-7 record and a 2.11 ERA. Best of all, Avery allowed only 127 hits, struck out 165 batters and walked only 54 in 171 innings of work. He could challenge for a spot in the major league rotation this spring.

Pat Combs will be a welcome addition to the Phillies' ailing staff this year. As a first year pro, he was 17-8 (4-0 with the Phillies) with a 2.47 ERA. Combs is Avery's equal in terms of poise and command, but does not have the same dominating quality. Still, this former Olympian is only twenty-three years old and should give Philadelphia plenty of quality innings.

Somewhere on the wilder side of Combs and Avery lies Kent Mercker. In any other organization, he would be the number-one prospect, hands down. However, despite his blazing fastball and intimidating mound presence, at least three left-handed Braves have better control. That aside, he should get a shot this spring.

Other lefties worthy of mention are Dave Otto of the Athletics, Mike Remlinger of the Giants and Steve Searcy of the Tigers. Each is coming off sub-par campaigns, but all have the talent to pitch effectively in the majors.

RELIEF PITCHERS

1. Aguedo Vasquez—Kansas City Royals

2. Kevin Wickander—Cleveland Indians

3. Stan Belinda—Pittsburgh Pirates

While big, strong, blow-you-away receivers were the rage in the major leagues for many years, the new breed of stopper seems to be a more cerebral, polished product. A case in point is the current crop of prospects working their way up through the minors. Each of the top three talents feature a variety of pitches and deliveries. Each knows how to change speed and hit spots. Admittedly, Aguedo Vasquez does throw harder than the other two, but he's tops on the list because Kansas City has no other closers in the system. Wickander is stuck behind Doug Jones and faces a challenge from young Steve Olin; while Belinda will be fighting the pressure from fellow prospect Willie Smith.

In Vasquez, the Royals have a proven product. The organization knows he is resilient enough to pitch nearly every day and likes the pressure situations. The "Terminator" has notched 44 saves in two years of professional service.

Wickander and Belinda are also fairly new to the relief scene. Cleveland didn't move Kevin to the bull pen until 1988, but his results were good enough to warrant him a look last September. With a deceptive delivery, good control and a live cut fastball, he could stick with the Indians this spring. Belinda's meteoric rise through the Pirate system last year was thought to be too fast by some club insiders, and he will probably begin the 1990 season in Triple A Buffalo.

CATCHERS

1. Sandy Alomar—San Diego Padres

2. Todd Zeile—St. Louis Cardinals

3. Phil Clark—Detroit Tigers

It has been argued that there is little catching talent in the minor leagues. The promotions of Damon Berryhill, Craig Biggio and Bob Geren last year began to dispel this notion, and the current crop of minor league catchers should put it to rest for good. Alomar and Zeile represent two of the most highly-touted players in the game and Phil Clark is not far behind.

In ranking these players, Alomar gets the nod for his superior defensive abilities. He is fundamentally sound, calls a great game and has one of the strongest arms in the business. Sandy also began to show increased power last summer, closing the gap with Zeile. The only unknown with Alomar is where he will be playing this year.

The Cardinals know where Todd will be—behind the plate at Busch Stadium. The 1989 American Association MVP is reknowned for both his power and clutch-hitting abilities. He will give the Redbirds another offensive dimension and challenge for the National League Rookie of the Year Award.

Eventually, Phil Clark may put up better numbers than either of the aforementioned players. After all, he will be performing in the friendly confines of Tiger Stadium. Clark is still a year or two behind either in terms of defense, but still ranks higher than other catching prospects such as Derek Parks of the Twins, Todd Hundley of the Mets or Rich Wilkins of the Cubs.

FIRST BASEMEN

1. Reggie Jefferson—Cincinnati Reds
2. Tino Martinez—Seattle Mariners
3. Bob Hamelin—Kansas City Royals

Any of these three players would be a great asset to any organization. Martinez combines a fluid swing with solid defensive abilities and Hamelin may have as much power potential as any player in the minor leagues—though his ferocious swing may lead to continued back problems. Both are certainly well-known for their fine amateur careers. But, neither can match Reggie Jefferson for all-around skills. At twenty-one years of age, Jefferson is the youngest of the group. He has a pure home run stroke and the glove to step right into the Reds' lineup. Reggie also has the advantage of playing behind Todd Benzinger, rather than George Brett or Alvin Davis.

Behind the three top prospects at this position, there is a new wave of talent ready to make a mark. Toronto's John Olerud is a veteran of only six professional contests, but fine offensive and defensive skills could vault him into a major league job this year. Tiger prospect Rico Brogna is a bit more raw, but, while it may take him longer to reach the big leagues, he may have a greater impact.

Finally, two 1989 draftees should be noted. The White Sox' Frank Thomas is a huge, 6'5", 250 lb. young man with awesome power and surprising agility. He hit .296 as a first-year professional, while committing only 9 errors in 72 games. In the Eastern League, Boston's first-rounder Maurice Vaughn hit 8 home runs in a very unforgiving park. His value should increase if the Bosox lose Nick Esasky to free agency.

SECOND BASEMEN

1. Ty Griffin—Chicago Cubs

2. Lance Blankenship—Oakland Athletics

3. Mark Lemke—Atlanta Braves

It is not known whether Ty Griffin will play second or third base when he arrives in the major leagues. However, for the time being, he performs on the right side of the infield and his performance there ranks him at the top of this list. Griffin is the youngest and, by far, the best offensive player of the group; an extra-base-hit threat with speed at a position where scrappy play and hustle usually dominate.

Defensively, there is little difference between Griffin, Blankenship and Lemke. All three have the sure hands and strong throwing arms needed for their position; though Lance may be the best at turning the double play. While Griffin may not be the first of the three to reach the major leagues —both others made appearances last year and could make the big clubs this spring—he should make the biggest impact when he arrives.

Of the remaining prospects at second, Chip Hale appears to be the best. He is a proven contact hitter with slightly better-than-average defensive abilities and a major league job awaiting him this spring. Geronimo Pena of the Cardinals is a rapidly improving talent who may garner headlines this summer and, if the Dodgers decide to move Jose Vizcaino in order to make room for Jose Offerman, he will also merit top standing.

SHORTSTOPS

1. Jose Offerman—Los Angeles Dodgers

2. Delino DeShields—Montreal Expos

3. Mark Lewis—Cleveland Indians

Perhaps no position is as laden with talent as shortstop. Gone are the lanky glove men who dominated here for years, and multi-faceted young players like Jose Offerman are on the rise. The Dodger farmhand has outstanding defensive abilities, surprising power and blazing speed. In his two years as a professional, Offerman has 126 steals and an average well over .300. Jose is not alone, however. Expos' prospect Delino DeShields may be the finest athlete in the game next to Bo Jackson. Just three years after passing on a possible college basketball career at Villanova, DeShields has made steady improvement in his climb toward the major leagues. Only a slight defensive edge keeps Offerman at the top of the list.

Mark Lewis, while not in the athletic league of his cohorts, has the look of a solid, steady performer. This Cleveland prospect does everything well and he's only nineteen years old. His power potential, range and youth rank Lewis ahead of other fine prospects like Juan Bell of the Orioles, Travis Fryman of the Tigers and Andres Santana of the Giants.

Although he may not end up at shortstop, Gary Sheffield must be considered one of the top prospects at this position as well. Despite a rough rookie campaign in Milwaukee, Sheffield is one of the premier young offensive talents in the game.

THIRD BASEMEN

1. Matt Williams—San Francisco Giants

2. Robin Ventura—Chicago White Sox

3. Scott Cooper—Boston Red Sox

At a position where power is expected, but defense is king, Matt Williams reigns supreme as the top prospect. His well-documented problems with major league pitching became a thing of the past when Williams emerged from Triple A to pound 18 home runs in 84 games with the Giants last summer. Almost overlooked, however, was Matt's outstanding play in the field. Power hitters aren't supposed to have soft, sure hands, but this one definitely does.

Also on the rise is White Sox prospect Robin Ventura. Several of his 25 doubles from 1989 may turn into homers as Ventura matures physically, but the sweet swing and sharp eye which made him a college standout will be Robin's ticket to the big leagues. He is an outstanding contact hitter with enough defensive ability to crack Chicago's lineup this spring.

Heading the list of other third basemen is Scott Cooper. When the Red Sox resigned Wade Boggs, Cooper may have suffered a slight let-down, but he is still an excellent defender with good power potential. Scott's play in the field is what keeps him ahead of Hensley "Bam Bam" Meulens—a Yankee prospect with a tremendous home run swing.

Fans should also watch the progress of Scott Hemond of Oakland and Scott Livingston of Detroit. Both are hard-nosed players with fine all-around skills.

LEFT FIELDERS

1. Greg Vaughn—Milwaukee Brewers

2. Joey Belle—Cleveland Indians

3. Felix Jose—Oakland Athletics

Powerful young outfielders reside in left field. Vaughn and Belle were two of the most feared and most productive home-run hitters in the minor leagues last summer, before earning promotions to the majors. Greg led the American Association in round-trippers by a wide margin over Todd Zeile, and Joey was in a class by himself among Eastern League performers. Both earned All-Star honors and both made immediate impacts in the American League East. With few differences between them, Vaughn gets the nod because he's certain to open the 1990 season in Milwaukee, while Belle may start in Triple A.

Felix Jose has been around longer than his cohorts and has shown his outstanding offensive and defensive potential each year. Unfortunately, he plays in the Oakland system behind some of the most talented players in the game. If Ricky Henderson remains with the A's, Jose should not. He deserves a major league assignment.

Of the many remaining standouts at this position, several deserve special mention. Cameron Drew of the Astros may have topped this list two years ago. If he comes back from knee surgery with close to the same mobility he had then, Drew could make a major impact in Houston this year. Though younger and less polished than Cameron, Lee Stevens of the Angels and Rob Richie of the Tigers have the same type of star quality.

CENTER FIELDERS

1. Marquis Grissom—Montreal Expos

2. Ray Lankford—St. Louis Cardinals

3. Derek Bell—Toronto Blue Jays

Bernie Williams of the Yankees and Milt Cuyler of the Tigers may be the best pure defenders at this position and Deion Sanders may have the most speed and flair; however, for the whole package, there are none better than Grissom, Lankford and Bell. Each has the speed and power to threaten the 30-30 mark and they all should be big league regulars within two years.

Expos' prospect Marquis Grissom heads this list because of his rise through the system last summer. By late August, he was contributing in the major leagues and seems sure to remain with the club this spring. Overall, this Florida A & M graduate hit .286 and stole 41 bases in 153 games with Jacksonville, Indianapolis and Montreal.

Lankford and Bell each spent full seasons in Double A, but were no less successful than Grissom. Ray won the Texas League MVP Award on the strength of a .317 average, 12 triples, 11 home runs, 98 RBIs and 37 stolen bases. Derek bounced back from minor injuries to hit 16 round trippers and drive in 75 runs for Knoxville. Both players are slated for one full season in Class AAA this summer.

Two other players to watch for are Juan Gonzalez and Aubrey Waggoner. Gonzalez is a twenty-year-old dynamo from the Ranger organization with good power potential and excellent speed. Waggoner is an accomplished defender and base stealer in the Chisox system. While they may be a year behind the other top prospects, both could blossom in 1990.

RIGHT FIELDERS

1. Eric Anthony—Houston Astros

2. Sammy Sosa—Chicago White Sox

3. Carlos Quintana—Boston Red Sox

Right field is the domain of some of the finest all-around performers in baseball and these prospects should do nothing but add to that reputation. Eric Anthony has been the minor league home run king in each of the last two seasons and he electrified Astro fans by belting a home run off Rick Reushel in a nationally televised game less than one week after joining the big club. Power aside, however, this young man also has good instincts, excellent speed and an outstanding arm.

In terms of sheer athletic ability, Sammy Sosa is Anthony's equal. After coming to the White Sox organization in mid-August, Sosa pounded out 5 home runs, and hit .367 in 13 games at Vancouver to earn a ticket to Chicago. His late-season performance in the big leagues should make Sosa a serious candidate for a full-time job this spring.

Carlos Quintana is not the awe-inspiring talent his colleagues are. However, two seasons waiting in Pawtucket have made him a well-rounded player. Quintana makes good contact for a power hitter, he knows how to play the field and he has a strong, accurate arm. His overall production could exceed Anthony's or Sosa's in the short term.

It would be remiss not to mention two young talented athletes like Larry Walker of the Expos and Mark Whiten of the Blue Jays. They are both fine offensive players, but what may draw the most attention to these right fielders are their arms. Both rival the game's best in both strength and accuracy.

ABOUT THE AUTHOR:

Over the past five years, **Roger Landry** has been the man behind the TCMA/Collectors Marketing minor league baseball card sets. He has numerous contacts throughout the minor leagues and is constantly in touch with the progress of young prospects. In addition to his work with minor league baseball cards, Roger has produced and written copy for several other sports card sets during the past year.

Mr. Landry was born on August 3, 1961, in Rochester, New York. He earned a BA Degree in Political Science and a minor in writing from SUNY Plattsburgh in 1983 and an MBA in Marketing Management from Pace University in 1986. Roger currently lives in State College, Pennsylvania, where his wife is pursuing a PhD in Plant Physiology at Penn State University.

430